Dorothy Heathcote

Drama as a Learning Medium

Dorothy Heathcote

Drama as a Learning Medium

Betty Jane Wagner

National Education Association
Washington, D.C.

Copyright © 1976

National Education Association of the United States

NEA Stock No. 1381-6-00 (paper)

NEA Stock No. 1383-2-00 (cloth)

Library of Congress Cataloging in Publication Data

Wagner, Betty Jane.
    Dorothy Heathcote.

    Bibliography: p.
        1. Drama in education.   2. Heathcote, Dorothy.
I.   Title
PN3171.W25   371.3   76-25055
ISBN 0-8106-1383-2
ISBN 0-8106-1381-6

To my younger brother, Mason Brown,
who when I was barely literate would
do all my chores to get me to read
the funnies to him, thereby irrevocably
committing me to wordmongering.

PREFACE

Dear B. J.,

As I read your book I become increasingly aware of four debts I owe you, which I can only repay by my constant recognition of them. The first of these debts is for all the time, effort, and patience you must have spent in giving accurate written form and shape to the ideas we have shared in talk and classrooms. I find that writing about any teaching moment is an enormously complex task, for so many things occur in so many interesting dimensions, all simultaneously, and I truly respect the labor it has been for you. I also am grateful that you never in the least made *me* aware of the burden of that!

My second debt to you arises because you have received my work without either sentimentalizing it (which not only wearies me, but is unproductive) or attacking it, which is equally unproductive. Thank you for giving it attention, consideration, and analysis. Your own "cool strip" is obviously in healthy shape!

Thirdly, without spoiling your own vigorous writing style, you have paid me the compliment of preserving my own rather odd (and certainly idiosyncratic) language, which *must*, I think, have cost you much thought and labor.

Finally, I am in your debt because through your writing I can see my work now at some distance, which must help my next development and that of my future students—this development I shall continue to share with you as it emerges in my teaching and my consciousness. Thank you, B.J.

Dorothy Heathcote

ACKNOWLEDGMENTS

I want to thank a few of the many friends who helped me with this project. Two of them are Northwestern University professors: Anne Thurman, who introduced me to Dorothy and loaned me tapes of her classes she made long before I conceived of writing this book, and Wallace Douglas, who insisted that I not listen to the advice of others to make the book more "scholarly." Several teachers in England graciously invited me to watch their drama classes or talked with me about their work with Dorothy: Anthony Lintott, Chris Waddilove, Carol Northage, Tom Swann, and Cecily O'Neill, the drama warden of the Inner London Education Authority. Gavin Bolton of the Institute of Education at the University of Durham, England, and Oliver Fiala of the University of New South Wales in Australia, in long conversations analyzed Dorothy's work and their own. Elizabeth Flory Kelly, of the Martha Holden Jennings Foundation in Cleveland, shared her insights and support. Calvin Gross, President, and Dick Bagg, Chairman of the Humanities Division, at National College of Education, enthusiastically encouraged this work. My husband, Durrett, advised me to respond to the urgings of all those who said I should explain Dorothy's kind of drama, because he wisely knew this would bring me joy; our three children endured long hours of Heathcote tapes, which irritatingly drowned out their music. Finally, of course, I thank Dorothy herself, whose inspiration called forth this book.

Contents

1. WHAT DRAMA CAN DO

"I don't have a name for what I do. As a person it seems to me I simply stand midway between all that has happened before I arrived and what is now. What I do at this moment obviously shapes up some part of what is to come. Everything that has happened before me I have something in common with, and this is my secret for finding material for drama." Thus Dorothy Heathcote (pronounced "Hĕth´cut"), one of England's best-known educators, has described what she does, which she feels is not creative dramatics, role playing, psychodrama, or sociodrama, but a conscious employment of the elements of drama to educate—to literally bring out what children already know but don't yet know they know. She calls this "building volume within the student"—quality education as opposed to quantity. She doesn't deny that often it is appropriate to go for quantity, deliberately to try to cover as much ground as possible. But at other times the best thing to do is to go for quality of experience, to plummet deep into feeling and meaning; this is her goal in drama.

Behind what we see—Dorothy Heathcote's large, sturdy build, ruddy cheeks, and mesmerizing eyes—lie a keen sensitivity to the nuance of language, a profound awareness of the complexity of human interaction, and an artist's dedication to perfection in meeting the demands of her craft: drama. She works from the inside out, from a solid conviction that what she does has to feel right, and she asks children to do nothing less. She is at her most dissatisfied when she senses that her class is "doing theatrics," performing tricks, "acting" in a phony or artifical way. That is not what she's after. She's always looking for the precise dramatic pressure that will lead to a breakthrough, to a point where the students have to come at a problem in a new way, to fight for language adequate to the tension they feel.

What shaped her—hard-driving, indefatigable, and yet warmhearted and calmly patient? She grew up in the thirties, on the haunting, windswept heaths near Haworth, the Brontes' village. She remembers as "a happy family" the little village school where she went until she was 14. Still in her girlhood, she sat at a loom in the Yorkshire mills, dreaming of becoming a film actress. Then her mother, a strong, poor woman widowed at 27, took over Dorothy's looms in the mill because that was the only way she could see to it that her daughter could go to theater school in Bradford, 10 minutes from their tiny, sparsely furnished cottage. Dorothy's acting teacher was Esme Church, an actress who took a keen interest in teaching and had an understanding of educational trends—even though what she gave Dorothy Heathcote in those three years was a typical theater training to become an actress.

Dorothy Heathcote has emerged from Haworth to become what her aunts and friends proudly call "famous," a much-sought-after lecturer and teacher at conferences and workshops not only in England but in the United States, Canada, Australia, and Israel. During the academic year she is Professor of Drama at the Institute of Education at the University of Newcastle-upon-Tyne. She was appointed to this position when she was 24—two years after she finished theater school. Her typical working day is spent going from class to class in infant, primary, and secondary schools of the community, teaching them drama. She also lectures at the University to her students, all of them teachers with at least 5 years' experience. She doesn't confine her work to college and school students, however; she also does drama with mentally handicapped people or spastics in institutions, or with such occupational groups as nurses or police officers—not to produce plays, but to limber them in their approach to their duties.

Wherever Heathcote goes, she generates excitement and even adulation. She emanates power. Her power is like that of a *medium,* bringing into the present the distant in time or space, making it come alive in our consciousness through imagined group experience. This awareness stands in contrast to the effect of the mass news *media* which bring us the contemporary in time but often leave it still distant in space and remote to our sense. The plethora of stimuli that bombards us through the media deadens our responsiveness. Because there is too much coming too fast to make sense of emotionally, our feelings are seldom touched. With the artist's sensitivity, Heathcote slows the input of information, eliminates the irrelevant, and selects the single symbol that can evoke the widest range of meanings; then she lets it slowly do its work, unraveling response within each student; she never tells a student what to feel or think, never pushes for more than the student can discover independently.

This does not mean that Dorothy Heathcote doesn't press children. She does; and this is perhaps one of her most controversial techniques. Creative drama teachers in America are sometimes critical of her pressures to achieve dramatic focus, her deliberate upgrading of language, her insistence on slowing pace to allow for reflection and inner awareness. In this respect, again, she is like a medium. A spell has to be cast; rituals must be followed; conditions have to be right; the universal inherent in this moment must be realized, and she's witchlike in her control leading to this effect. She arrests attention, wins commitment, magnetizes, combining both a wildness and a control in her work. She works with children with authority, intuition, and a thorough understanding of the potential and limits of drama.

She does not use children to produce plays. Instead, she uses drama to expand their awareness, to enable them to look at reality through fantasy, to see below the surface of actions to their meaning. She is interested, not in making plays with children, but in, as she terms it, burnishing children through the play. She does this not by heaping more information on them but by enabling them to use what they already know.

This book is written to lay out before teachers some of the ways Dorothy Heathcote works, so that her techniques can be employed by any teacher who wants to help children find the feel of what they know. She is convinced that what she does with children can be learned by others and adapted to a wide variety of teaching styles and aims. She passionately wants to share her method of proceeding and insists that what she does has "no magic in it." It can be learned and employed by any teacher. Despite her obvious talent, sensitivity, and creative insight, Heathcote has no desire to deliberately make her procedures mysterious or occult. She is not a witch, but an educator, a self-conscious master teacher, who works daily to show others how to find material, select symbols, achieve dramatic focus, heighten tension, and slow pace to lead children to significant moments of insight. Her favorite way of working is to *demonstrate* with a group of children in the middle of a room while observing teachers sit around the outside of the group. From time to time she finds ways to involve these observers in the drama the children are creating with her. For example, they may become a team of reporters who ask the youngsters what they are doing or a welcoming party when a space ship has landed. In a typical class session, Heathcote first does a drama with a group of children while the adult class members watch. Then she dismisses the children and spends the rest of the session answering questions and explaining what she did and why. She wants to show teachers, who typically have had no previous experience with drama as a teaching technique, how to proceed. She is fascinated with how her own mind works, and this is the focus of a large part of her teacher-training sessions. She enjoys getting new insights from her adult students about what goes on as she leads a drama.

Heathcote feels that for too long we have been concentrating on training drama specialists, a process that has widened the gap between what these specially trained persons do with groups of children and what ordinary teachers do. The time has come to show all teachers—ordinary day-in and day-out classroom teachers—how they can use drama at times to achieve something that cannot be attained as effectively in any other way.

Heathcote reminds us that drama is not something special, but rather a technique most ordinary people regularly employ as a way of coping with new or unsettling experience. When a significant event is coming up, we frequently rehearse it beforehand in our minds. For example, if we are facing an important interview, we may try to imagine what the situation will be like. We may even project ourselves into the future event and act it out in our minds—or sometimes even talk out loud or move through the experience—to help ourselves come to terms with it. We dramatize it, in short, and this dramatic act helps us explore the feel of the experience and thus decrease our anxiety and increase our control over it.

We also use drama to learn to live with and accept an experience that has been disturbing: an operation, a driving test, a quarrel. As we relive the shock, going over and over the details, we digest the event, and it finally becomes a truth we can bear. By that time it has become a good story. Dramatic living through has done its work to crystallize an area of experience that is too unsettling or overwhelming to grasp.

Apparently all human beings except the most severely damaged or psychotic have the capacity to identify and through this process to gain new insight. To see how Dorothy Heathcote uses identification to lead toward reflective moments, those that build volume within the student, let us look at what a group of 12- and 13-year-olds do on the first day they meet with her for a class. They come together in Evanston, Illinois, to do drama as a demonstration for a Northwestern University class of adult students.

They choose to do a play about a ship at sea in 1610 and decide to begin at the point where they are putting the final touches on the ship they have built. After the children spend a few minutes carrying blankets aboard, winding the rope, caulking the deck to keep it waterproof, and so on, Heathcote calls them together to decide on a name. They name the ship *The Dreamer*. Heathcote then puts a chair on top of a table and faces it away from the group. She has a child sit up there posing pensively as the ship's figurehead. Then she turns to the rest of the students and says with authority, "Look at him carefully. He is the Dreamer; he's supposed at this moment to be in wood. Stand there till you know he's in wood."

Then she changes to a musing tone and says softly, "Nobody will ever see the front when we're aboard. It'll be a sad day if you're ever at sea and you find yourself under there, 'cause that will mean your own ship has had to be abandoned. You'll not see his face unless you're in dock. So will you now take up a position on the ship, on the deck of the ship amongst that rigging and sails, from where you can see part of the Dreamer? Find your places." She pauses while the children find a spot within the area they have decided is the deck of the ship. In response to one girl's puzzled look, she says, "Yes, the captain also will stand. Just concentrate hard on making the ship happen. We've made it look [they had earlier drawn a picture of it on the blackboard], now we have to make it happen. If there is a rope nearby, if there is a piece of timber nearby, if there's anything stashed on deck and laced down nearby—just find it and hold onto it as the ship moves out on the tide. Now you just have to do it for yourself and believe. The wood will creak, the sails will gradually fill. But for the moment she's not her own ship. She's being pulled by rowers in a small boat to get her out of the harbor." She pauses, and the children stand still. "You stand there and watch that Dreamer [the figurehead], because it's gonna' be a long time before you get back to this place." Another pause. "As you stand knowing the boat is being towed and it's not its own ship yet, note what you are thinking; out of what you're thinking might come a glimpse of what you're feeling. Now I'm going to be quiet." This is followed by a long pause.

Then she says very quietly, almost to herself, "It'll be very hard later on to try to explain to anybody what it was like before you left, at the moment of leaving, so just see if you can catch an explanation now. There's a load of people here with pens and paper." She is referring to the adult students, who are sitting at desks in a circle around the open space where the children stand on the ship's deck. "Choose one you'd like to tell what this moment is like, as you follow the Dreamer." At this point the children break the tension, sigh, and start to move and talk all at once. Dorothy Heathcote won't let that happen. "Now stop, go back into it, and when you're ready to go, go. So stand still, hold onto what you were holding onto and find again that moment of leaving." Then in a quieter voice, "Rarely in a man's life does he actually build a dream, and rarely in a man's life does anybody share in the building of such a dream. For everyone who does that, there are thousands who never know what happens beyond their village, their town—because this is not the day of airplanes. This is the day when a man travels as far as he can walk or ride a horse or take a coach or a boat." Then she stops, and the children one by one leave their places and quietly go to an adult to tell their thoughts. Heathcote then turns her attention to those who are still standing on deck. "You might choose to go in pairs if you're worried about going on your own." She directs the adults not to carry on a dialogue, as some are beginning to do: "Just act as a scribe and don't tell the children what to say." She continues to encourage those who are hesitant. "If you've any worry about going, go to somebody who's been and he'll take you to someone." Then with some gruffness she turns to the laggers and says, "But don't just stand in a limbo because nothing will happen for you. Go and get some help from each other." The remaining students begin to leave their places and approach the adult strangers. She encourages them, going from child to child asking, "Have you managed? Have you been?" She observes, "Yes, Sandra's great at taking people. . . .Did you go? . . .Have you gone? . . .Just a person to write for you; that's all. Just go sit down again now." Then to the whole group she says, "Board the ship, and we'll hear all these things that people were thinking and feeling, right?"

Many times I have seen Heathcote force children to listen to one another. She has said, "I'll not compromise on this one. Vacuums within children have to be filled, and you don't fill them easily. Unless they listen to one another, they don't have a chance to get the depth of feeling."

So when the children are settled again, sitting on the deck, she asks the adults to read what the children have told them. She tells them not to read the children's names; this is to save the children from possible embarrassment, since they are still strangers to one another and to the adults. She tells the students: "You'll always know when it's yours, but you won't know anybody else's." She pauses, then: "This ship is as strong as the people in it. This ship doesn't exist as a ship; it exists as people. Right! May we just hear what people were thinking as the ship was towed out?"

"I'm afraid I'll never get off this ship."

"It is strange to look at the figurehead up there because he seems to represent the whole crew."

"It's so great . . . .You have such pride. You're a part of all this—so proud of what you helped to create—so close to everyone. You can take part in this dream . . . . You've worked for months and months: this is the climax. You feel the movement of the ship, but mostly you feel pride, you feel power You can do anything if you set your mind to it. You're at the top of the world."

"I'm very scared. I'm not sure whether I'm ever going to see the town again. It's very exciting, and yet . . . and yet . . . I'm scared."

"I'm tired from all the work I've been doing. I'm not used to it. I'm happy we're going to leave, but I know there will be a lot more work to be done before we're finally through."

"There's a feeling of mystery, wondering what the voyage will lead to. There's sadness worrying about the bad things that could happen and thinking about the things you'll be leaving behind. And yet, there's a feeling of happiness . . . because if we find something, we'll be known and possibly put down in history."

"We all have a dream, the dream of our own. It could be dangerous, things we might encounter on the water. We're scared, but we also dream of the riches and glory that we might achieve through discovery."

"I might not ever see the place I am leaving again."

"I have a tense feeling; then I think maybe I may not come back. And I remember my friends, and I say a little prayer."

"We're leaving something of great value, and we're kind of scared that when we come back, it won't be as valuable as it was . . . *if* we come back.'

Then Heathcote, assuming her previous role as first mate, turns to the short preadolescent girl at her side and says, "Well, Captain, that's your crew."

This is a moment of reflection that plummets to universal experience—to the pulse of all those who have left behind a world that's known for the world beyond. To capture the meaning of a moment is what the play is for; no teacher lecture or summary is needed. Everything that has happened to humanity Dorothy Heathcote has something in common with; in reflective moments like the ship's setting out to sea, she helps children find that they, too, have something in common with all that has gone before. They, too, belong to humanity.

The medium has done her work. The distant in time has become the present in consciousness—not through magic, but through drama.

2. EVOKING, NOT DIRECTING

Dorothy Heathcote doesn't direct drama; she evokes it. Unlike most drama teachers, she allows the students to make as many of the decisions about what the drama is going to be about as is possible. She makes only those decisions that must be made if what they choose to do is to happen dramatically. One of the children who had been part of the ship's crew on *The Dreamer* noted, as they were leaving, "In other classes the teacher would first ask us about our character, how old we were and all that, but she talks about feelings. I like that." His friend added, "And she lets us make decisions; she doesn't tell us what to do like other teachers."

Heathcote will often let children decide what a play is to be about, when it is to take place, where the scene is to be, and in most cases, roughly what happens. What she will not let the children decide is whether to try to believe; she insists that students work at believing so they don't ruin it for others. She won't allow them to give up or laugh at the whole situation; they must try to be serious about and committed to the drama. When Heathcote finds children are making a choice that will cause them problems in their drama, she does not take the decision from them but warns them of the new difficulties this decision will cause. She will not allow them to continue the drama when she feels that they are not aware of the problems they are causing and alternate ways to deal with them. She stops the drama frequently to assess with the class how it is going. When the students disagree among themselves as to what they want to do, Heathcote lets them sort this out on their own, often physically turning away from the group to let them decide. If a minority is overruled by a majority, she says warmly to the losers something like: "Now, we'll help, 'cause we know it will be harder for you doing this since you wanted to do the other, really."

The main reason Heathcote allows the children so much freedom to decide the what, when, and where of the drama is that this helps her overcome one of the biggest problems in teaching: group inertia. She must get a group over its initial passivity and started into the drama. If they see their own ideas take shape they are more ready to participate. After they get started, there is the problem of keeping them going in a productive way; here again, a group assessment of how it is going and student decisions help stimulate interest.

Thus, the children's interests are the paste that holds the drama together. Heathcote can and frequently does guarantee to students that the drama will be interesting, because she knows that if she does what they want to do, it will be. She allows the students to make a decision; she supports that decision and then shows them some of the chinks in it, some problems they may not have been aware of. Then they make another decision; she supports that; they all act on it; and she shows some more chinks to them. She keeps asking the group for decisions, and each brings with it a commitment.

There is another reason Heathcote allows the students to make decisions. She has discovered that an essential element in her teaching is the taking of risks. She comes alive to a situation and does her best teaching when she and the students both are moving into the unknown. Too often, we American educators take a lesson-plan approach to teaching, not recognizing, as Heathcote does, the energizing effect of improvising with a class. When meeting with a group for the first time, Heathcote often begins a drama by asking the students what they want to do a play about. Typically, she does not plan beforehand beyond a moment of beginning. The outcome is unpredictable; she takes a risk. However, she knows what her own goal is and imagines beforehand what responses from the children are likely and how she can use these to work toward her end. Her aim is always to reflect on those facets of the experience that are part of the universal lot of humanity.

To illustrate, let's see how she begins the drama which was introduced in the last chapter: the sea voyage aboard *The Dreamer*. She asks questions to start the children making decisions that will lead, before the end of the first class session, to their reflections about leaving. Since this is the first time she and the class have met, and she has not been asked to relate her drama to other curricular areas, Heathcote begins by getting acquainted and soliciting ideas. "How many have never done any dramatics in school?" Two children timidly raise their hands. Then she asks the others, "Do you enjoy doing it?" Nods show they do. "What shall we do today then? I have no plan. I can't plan until I have met a class. Is there any idea you have that you'd like us to work on? (I'm asking you the widest possible questions I can think of.)" This is followed by a long thoughtful pause. A few children look at each other incredulously.

"Well, let's narrow it down a bit. Let's say there are three kinds of drama. First, there is drama that happens because things happen to people that they cannot possibly control—like the tidal wave that strikes a community or a war that begins that's none of our doing and that we could not have avoided. Another kind of drama is where some people start pushing other people around—big 'uns tellin' little 'uns what to do. And a third kind is where ordinary people find it tricky just to get on together." There is another pause. "Now we can choose any of those to start us thinking."

"I'd like a ship at sea," suggests one girl.

"A ship at sea," repeats Heathcote slowly. This is her pattern; it gives importance to what the child has said and thereby focuses the attention of the group. "Are we going to be in a situation of a disaster, which is the first type of drama? Or are we in the position of big 'uns telling little 'uns what to do, or are we going to be in the position of ordinary people who just have a bit of a problem gettin' on together—because a ship at sea is just a place to be." The children sit thoughtfully as she adds, "You need to know how you are when you're in that place to be that—

A child interrupts with, "A disaster!" and there are murmurs of agreement near him.

"You'd like a disaster," she says, magnifying the child's soft voice.

"Let's have the ship sink."

Then, from another side of the group, "When everybody disappears, then us kids, we have to know how to take care of the boat and everything."

"And we'll be way out in the ocean somewhere, and we have to—"several other voices interrupt him.

Heathcote listens, smiles enthusiastically, and says, "Yes . . . yes . . . yes," looking from child to child. After a few moments of suggestions, she summarizes, "For some reason there are no adults left in the world—in your case in this ship, if you like the idea of a ship. Can we agree for the moment that we like the idea of being in the ship? Is there anybody who says, 'Oh, no!' to a ship?" The children look at one another and smile and shrug. "I can understand somebody that thinks, 'Well, OK,' but is there anybody saying 'No'?" After a pause, "Right; it's a ship." Through this process she builds committal. The ship is their decision, and they know it.

There are times when she finds herself with a child or two who decide not to go along with what the rest want to do. She smiles at such children and tells them to watch until they see a place to come in. Then she ignores them for a while. Often she will later give such a child an important role with high status, like that of an outsider who comes into the group in some way— maybe a stranger who wanders into the colonists' village or a person with special information the group needs. Suppose this child is the one who doesn't want to go on the lion hunt the others have decided upon. She or he can then watch the hunt and, after it is over, explain to the group the horror of what they have just done, killing a creature who meant them no harm. The dissenter can choose to play a part later, after the rest of the group has begun.

After the group has agreed to a ship, Heathcote's job is to particularize it and make it come to life. Again, she does this with questions. "Now, can you please tell me how your ship is powered?"

"Sail."

"You'd like a sail ship," she repeats.

"It'd have to be a pretty big sail ship."

She nods agreement. "Well, there were sailing ships, you know, that sailed right round the world."

"It could have two sails."

"It could have even more than two."

"There were ships with hundreds."

"A lot of sailboats have motors also."

Heathcote stops them, not to add more information, but to summarize the facts they have provided. Again, she focuses with a question calling for the class to decide. "Is it a modern sail ship or an old-fashioned sail ship?"

"Old-fashioned!" chorus several children.

"It's an old-fashioned sail ship?" Watching the nods, she says, "Right!"

A child asks, "Is it in old times?"

Again Heathcote turns the decision to the class. "Well, I don't know. If it's an old-fashioned sail ship, it can be either people who are trying to sail in the old ways in our time or who are themselves sailing a new ship in the olden days. You know, it's up to you."

The students all start talking animatedly now. One says, "So it's like an old ship, and a whole mess of guys got together, and they just bought it 'cause it was cheap." They laugh.

Heathcote listens—"with her pores as well as her ears," as she describes it—smiling and saying "yes . . . yes . . . yes." When there is a pause in the suggestions, she speaks, not with authority but in a tone that leaves the decision in the hands of the class. "Now, I know of a ship in the States which is lying in want of somebody to buy it and do something with it. It's one of the last trading ships you [meaning Americans] own. And evidently the community is really annoyed about it, because outside that ship it says, 'This ship came here in good working order fully manned and with a full head of sail, and because nobody would pay the docking charge, this ship is dying here . . . .' So it's not so farfetched as it sounds."

This starts the students remembering. "It could be like the Ra Expedition where they were trying to prove that people could sail in a reed boat."

Heathcote says, "Yes . . . to prove that in the old way they could have done this."

"Like the Kon Tiki expedition that the Norwegians did."

"Right," says Heathcote. "Which is it going be, then? Did we put our money together and buy it to prove to ourselves that we could do it, or did we buy it and make it as a copy to see if people could have done it? Is it the olden days; do we genuinely live in the times when everybody used ships like this?"

"I'd kind of like to do the olden times."

"What about the rest of you?" Heathcote asks, concerned about the passive ones.

"I'd like to have made it, the ship."

"As modern men or people living in the past?"

"In the olden days," several say.

"Is there anybody who feels, 'No, that's out'?" Looking at the boy who had suggested that they buy an old ship because it was cheap, she says with a twinkle, "I know your nose was sort of going like this, which made me think, 'Ah, he's not too keen on that idea.' Will you go along with it?" He grins and nods, and she moves to the next decision: when?

"I don't know, though, what 'olden times' is to you." Laughter. "You see, olden times is different for each one of us. Now, if I go back in years, that might be just dates to you. Some people find meaning in dates, and others just hear numbers. So shall I just go backwards in time, not by dates but by what men knew at each period. You stop me when I have gone too far back, to where you don't want to *not* know about that." Laughter. Then she tells the group to come a bit closer so they can get a sense of what other people are thinking. They move nearer and sit right at her feet where she's sitting in a low chair. By this time their posture shows them to be alert and eager.

"Unless you speak, I shall just go on going back.

"On our ship we know that there is land covered in ice to the South as well as to the North, and we have instruments that will take us there.

"On our ship we have to make charts because we do not have charts for the ocean.

"On our ship we do not know the importance of fresh meat and fruit." She told her adult students later that at this point, had she been in England, she would have said, "On our ship there were men who took other men unwillingly," but since she was teaching an interracial group in America, she didn't want to land herself in the slave trade; she felt uncomfortable doing it. In order to protect herself, she did not feed in this idea.

She goes on, "On our ship we believe the world is flat; we do not know the world is round."

"I think we're too far back", said one boy, and all laugh.

"But you didn't think we were too far back over the fresh meat, and they were both about the same time."

Another child says, "I don't think he wants to be that ignorant," and they laugh again.

"Right. Let's work up forward then. On our ship we know the world is round. That's safer, isn't it?" They nod amid some giggles.

"On our ship we know all the continents that today are known."

Several children say, "No."

"Too far forward?"

"Yeah."

"Well, I'll tell you what. You tell me what you'd like to know, and I'll see if I can fix a date to it." She goes to the blackboard and writes what they agree that they know at the time of the drama. She writes, "We know the world is round." Then she says, "So that takes us to around the time Christopher Columbus because he knew. He had this idea that he could sail west and get to India in the east. So he must have thought the world was round. Actually, he found the West Indies, didn't he? But he thought they were the East Indies. So we're somewhere around the time of Christopher Columbus. I don't know the exact date . . ." she says; either as a British teacher she really doesn't know, or she is deliberately withholding her expertise to allow the class to win at this one.

"1492."

"Thank you so much," she says, as the class laughs. "Right. Not everything is discovered. Could you tell me what isn't discovered?"

"The South Pole and the North Pole." She then draws on the board a map of the world, leaving off the continents that haven't yet been discovered. "Anthing else you'd like to know?"

"I don't want North America not to be discovered, but just not explored."

Heathcote writes on the board, "We know there is land to the west." Then she asks, "Is there anything else you'd like to know?"

"We know how to store food, but we don't know what's good for us." This is greeted with loud laughter.

"Our medicine is primitive."

"Doctors are scarce."

Heathcote says, "They may not even be called doctors, of course. What were they called? You knew about Columbus; tell me." She's looking at the boy who said "1492." The children laugh and suggest "leeches" and "apothecaries." She then reads the list of what they know. They add weapons such as muskets to the list.

Then, subtly adding information, she says, "We're a pretty well-equipped ship. We probably look back on those olden sailors and say, 'How did they manage without a sextant or without a knowledge of the stars?' Now we need to know why we're on this ship and where we're heading." The class is eager to decide. They want the date to be July 26, 1610. Through Heathcote's questions the anchor of group inertia has been lifted, and the drama is ready to sail.

Heathcote works intuitively, creatively, with technique, confidence, and involvement, in a situation where students are making most of the decisions and neither she nor the class knows what will happen next. She works knowing which decisions she doesn't dare let out of her hands—such as those that could destroy the belief of the participants—and which she'll leave to the class. She takes risks, but she never plays so risky that the class doesn't sense her authority and leadership.

As she puts it, "Whatever you decide, you pay a price. You always pay in one way for what you gain in another." Heathcote knows that when she lets the class make decisions, she pays for this in that the class may make decisions that are actually uncomfortable for her. However, if she gets their decisions, she gains their committal; her discomfort is the price. "It is not something to regret; it's something to face. What you pay for, you get. You can't get everything all at once," Heathcote reminds us.

Once a group has decided what they want to do, the next problem for the teacher is how to help them believe it. Heathcote doesn't build belief by heaping information on the class, thereby reminding them of the plethora of facts they don't know. Instead, she does it by carefully selecting those few details that children might have had some experience with, and by again shifting the problem of "making it happen" from herself to the class. With the group that has decided to be a crew aboard a sailing ship in 1610, she begins by asking them what jobs they do. She lists each person's real name on the board and puts beside it the responsibility aboard ship that person volunteers to take. The class members decide to be lookouts, navigators, cooks; there are a captain, second mate, cabin boy, leech, fisherman, live-stock tender, sailmaker, tool and weapons keeper, and ship's carpenter. To the child who decides on this job, Heathcote says, "Yes, a ship's carpenter has many jobs; one of them might be to make coffins, if necessary," thus planting a clue to possible later action.

They discuss whether the captain should have another job as well, and they decide that he should not. Heathcote then reminds them, "As long as you want a captain who never does anything, you'll have to be a crew that can respect a man who gives orders but never does a hand's turn." Heathcote then decides to act as first mate of this captain, who is played by a short and shy girl. Heathcote does not interfere with how the children choose to cast themselves; whoever selects a particular role first, gets it. Her job is not to choose the best actor for captain, but to make the volunteer into a captain by setting her apart in some way. Then, what the captain says in her tiny little voice becomes important, because the rest are listening. The girl has not changed that much. She is still quiet and shy, but Heathcote has given her a platform and set up a crew to hear her soft words.

One girl can't think of a job for herself, and someone else suggests boatswain. "What's that?" asks another student. At this point Heathcote provides information to help make that role real for the boatswain. "He's the person in charge of everything to do with the ship itself, not the crew; it's pronounced 'bosun.'" She spells it and writes it on the blackboard. Again, information is provided when it is needed.

The sailors then go about their duties aboard the ship; she stops them after a few minutes and says, "If you're going to have a ship, you can't use hotel names. You don't go up to the sail; you go aloft. You don't take an elevator; you go below deck down that gangway."

She senses that they can change their vocabulary at this point in the drama without jeopardizing their belief. Except for these diction suggestions, which are to help make the particularity of the ship seem real, she lets the children work out their roles for themselves. They spend the next 15 minutes going about their duties on board that ship, getting it ready to go to sea.

At the beginning of the second session, Heathcote asks the class whether they want to just start the voyage and get the feel of the ship and, out of doing that, find out what the crisis will be, or whether they want to decide first on the crisis. They decide to just start the voyage. She notes that the group has the same inertia and willingness to let her do all the leading that they had the day before. She reminds them, "Yesterday we built a ship, and we built an enthusiasm to sail a ship. I can't make you into sailors of 1610; you have to make yourselves into sailors. If you think it matters, you'll try. And if you think it's just a game, it'll never happen. So you're at this cross-roads that every painter or sculptor or artist of any kind comes to, where you've got your material that makes it possible to go somewhere, and you don't know yet if it's going to work out. This is the hard time of creating. Do you agree with me that you would like to get the feeling of life in 1610 aboard a vessel that is someone else's dream?" They sit blankly, and a few shrug; others nod.

"I don't know what it was like, " ventures one child.

"The only way you can ever know is to try to assemble gradually all that you do know about this period." At this point, Heathcote tries to help them build belief by selecting just two particular objects that can work as symbols: a slippery, wet deck under foot—a symbol of danger; and a thick, heavy rope in the hands—a symbol of work. "I don't know what it's like to stand on a heaving deck in a storm with noisy sails, but I have enough experience and enough imagination to concentrate on it so that I begin to know what I think it would be like. I have never pulled myself across a deck that was trying to swamp me overboard, but I know what rope feels like. And I know I would want to survive, and I know what it's like to walk up a slope that's slippery. I can put all those together and find out what it's like to be on a heaving deck. But no teacher does that for me—I do it; because nobody else can live my life for me. I have to live it for myself. There's a whole host of things that have never happened to you, but you can make them happen to you. You'll never be able to prove that you were right about what actually happened. All you can prove is that you can use experience of different kinds and put them all together in a new shape and learn something new. Do you see what I mean?"

The students decide they want to start by hoisting the mainsail. She reminds them that it is heavy and that they will probably be hoisting it for quite a while. She asks if they've ever held a piece of sailcloth and tells them it is made of the heaviest linen. They decide they need a song to hoist the sail by, and they choose "Yo, Heave Ho."

"Now, get some rope," Heathcote says. "Rope has a temperature; rope has a texture; rope has a thickness. Take hold of that temperature, that texture, that thickness." Here Heathcote demonstrates again that it is not how much information you can give students that matters. What matters is how much the little information you *do* give them can do when you focus on it long enough to let it fill with power and significance.

"There is going to be a sound of stretching rope . . . . If you've got that rope now, you might feel for a moment the deck beneath your feet . . . . Get that sense of bare-to-the-knee legs, because the feet are always in salt water. That deck isn't a floor; you've got to plant your feet so they won't slip, 'cause this is a moving vessel. The pressure of these people's feet on this deck is affected by the vessel."

She turns to the adults and asks them to creak the ship. "Give us the wood." The children, still nervous and ill-at-ease, laugh. She turns on them sternly. "Why are you laughing? I'm asking them to assume the same problem I'm asking of you. It's as difficult for them to believe as it is for you." All stand quietly, holding the rope in their hands.

"Give the order," she says to the second mate. So comes the child's timid voice, "Hoist the mainsail." The song begins, "Yo, heave ho"; the children start to pull; the wood creaks as pens are pulled across the ridges of radiator vents by adults on the sidelines. The song gets louder; the children work in rhythm. Then shouts Heathcote in a booming roar of a voice—now clearly acting in role as the first mate, "Pull, men! Come on! Keep going!" Then, in a harsh, flailing tone, "Up, you lubbers! Pull! Get that sail up! You've got another fifty feet, you lubbers! Get on with it!"

At this point the children begin to look at one another in confusion. Where did this tyrant come from? Seeing this, Heathcote immediately comes out of role and says warmly, "I've taken over a rather harsh tone as first mate. See if, as I do that, something can happen between us that makes me know that you'll obey orders, but that you're *human beings,* not animals to be talked to like that. Let me know by your looks that you're warning me that I better watch it, even as I warn you that this is a working ship."

So they all go back into role, looking grimly at one another and at her as she shouts, "Come on, hoist that mainsail! Faster! Faster! Come on, you lubbers!" Then, finally, "There she goes now." By this time, the students are actually puffing; they stop and sigh. There is a long pause. The first mate says quietly, "Well, now you've got 53 other sails to get up. You five, bring out all those sails. You," looking at another group, "turn the capstan." Then she comes out of role to inform them about the shape and function of the capstan, comparing the work of the seamen to pushing a heavy turnstyle.

Before long, there are three working groups: one turning the capstan, the others hoisting sails. She asks each group to develop its own rhythm and chant and repeat it over and over. Soon, while she is shouting as before, "Come on, you lubbers!" one group is saying in a low tone, "Pushshsh . . . Pushshsh . . . Pushshsh," as they turn the capstan round; another is slowly calling out, "Hoist the sail! Harder! Harder!" and the third, "Kill the mate! Kill the captain!" The shouting gets louder under the cover of simultaneous noise, and in the shouts is buried the seed of the later action. For on this second day of the drama, the shy girl who chose the captain's part the day before has not come to class. They have decided not to replace her, but to go on with the first mate in charge. The mystery of a ship setting out to sea without its captain at the helm haunts the crew. Before the end of the hour—an hour in which one group have been loudly shouting, "Kill the mate! Kill the captain!"—they decide that the captain has been murdered: that's why he doesn't come out of his cabin.

Belief has been built by focus on the particular, on a few specific tasks aboard ship and a few physical objects on the ship's deck. There is nothing vague about the drama that has now begun. It is precise and real for the students, and they know it is their work, their implicit ideas made explicit in a shape they can sense. They are no longer embarrassed children standing weakly, laughing nervously, or feeling foolish. They are laboring seamen.

They get the sails up; they swab the decks; they take shifts on the lookout and at the ship's wheel, in the tiny hammocks of the crowded sleeping quarters and in the steam and noise of the galley. They fish and mend sails.

Heathcote stops the drama to have each child report on what she or he does during free time aboard ship. She introduces and defines the word "scrimshaw" to the sailor who has been carving. When one girl says she's been writing in her diary, Heathcote says, "You'll have to ask yourself how a man who is sailing with no officer's rank came to be able to write in 1610. There may well be a reason, but it was not common for a man in those days to be able to write and be in such a low position." This starts a lively discussion of the diary writer's past. Again the information is introduced at the point where the children need it and not before. Heathcote is a master at withholding her factual expertise, at building a need for information before she loads it on the child, and in some cases, of simply leaving the implications unstated, the ends untied, so the class goes on wondering. She resists the teacher's continual temptation—to tell all she knows.

For example, at the end of this second hour of drama, the ship's crew have found their captain, the dreamer, dead. Dorothy Heathcote has them lay the body out on the deck for all to see. Then she stops the drama and recites Whitman's poem "O Captain! My Captain!" which she learned as a child.

> O Captain! my Captain! our fearful trip is done,
> The ship has weathered every rack, the prize we sought is won,
> The port is near, the bells I hear, the people all exulting,
> While follow eyes the steady keel, the vessel grim and daring;
>> But O heart! heart! heart!
>> O the bleeding drops of red,
>>> Where on the deck my Captain lies,
>>> Fallen cold and dead.

O Captain! my Captain! rise up and hear the bells;
Rise up—for you the flag is flung—for you the bugle trills,
For you bouquets and ribboned wreaths—for you the shores a-crowding,
For you they call, the swaying mass, their eager faces turning;
    Here Captain! dear father!
      This arm beneath your head!
        It is some dream that on the deck
          You've fallen cold and dead.

My Captain does not answer, his lips are pale and still,
My father does not feel my arm, he has no pulse nor will,
The ship is anchored safe and sound, its voyage closed and done,
From fearful trip the victor ship comes in with object won;
    Exult O shores, and ring O bells!
      But I with mournful tread,
        Walk the deck my Captain lies,
          Fallen cold and dead.

The class is hushed. She says softly, "I didn't realize Walt Whitman was writing about Abraham Lincoln when I first learned it. I always thought it was about a captain like Nelson dying in the middle of a battle."

"I don't understand how it's Abe Lincoln," puzzles a student.

"Well," suggests Heathcote, "perhaps it's something you have to think about a little."

"When you're in bed," says one boy.

"Yes," agrees Heathcote, "when you're in bed it will come clear. You know, some things you can't understand by asking; you have to just sit and think 'em out."

"But he got killed in a theater."

"That doesn't mean he wasn't a captain," says another child.

"He was the captain of the country," came a boy's strong voice.

"Oh, yeah? How is the country a ship?"

Heathcote muses, "And he died when the ship was safe home . . . . Hmmm . . . . I don't know what the difficulty was that the country had just overcome."

"The war; I think that was the difficulty."

"Um humm," says Heathcote, "and slavery."

One child says decisively, "I think what Whitman meant was that the war was over now and everything was done. Abraham Lincoln had done what he'd dreamed about doing and everything was safe then, but he died just after it was over."

"What about Martin Luther King? Was he a captain?" asks Heathcote. "I've heard he had a dream." The students nod. "How far had his ship gone when he died?"

"Half way."

"I don't think it had even gone half way!" says one tall, black girl. "He'd just got started."

Heathcote adds, "He'd started his voyage. Was the ship sound?"

"Yes!"

"Is it still sailing, or is it resting in a harbor somewhere waiting?" she asks.

"It's resting."

"No, I think it's still going."

"It's still where he left it," comes a strong, cynical voice.

"It's like a captain trying to get a crew for a ship. Every once in a while he gets someone—one man after one man until . . . ."

Then Heathcote, sensing that the time for this session is nearly over, stops them abruptly: "And you are in the same position in America with Martin Luther King as you are on this ship with our dead captain. You're spending time finding who's at fault when you could be going on with his dream. I don't know whether that's true in America, but it does happen in England."

This brings the group right back to their problem in the drama—whether to try to find out who murdered the captain or to go on following his dream. Although Heathcote very much wants to have the class follow the dream, she doesn't load the question. The class is free to choose, and they choose to find the murderer. So the next and final day's session focuses on finding out who has killed the captain.

At the class's suggestion, Heathcote starts the session by handing out a slip of paper to each student. As in the old parlor game "Murder," one slip has the word "murderer" on it; the others are blank. For the rest of the period, the child who picked the marked paper has the burden of not letting others know that she or he killed the captain and of deciding why she or he did it. The rest of the class has the problem of finding out who did it and what they are going to do with the murderer when they do find out.

As first mate, Heathcote says she'll leave the body of the dead captain stretched out on the deck while they go about finding the murderer: "I'm not coverin' this body even though I respect it, 'cause whoever killed 'im is gonna' look in his dead eyes whenever he passes on this deck. And everybody's gonna' take a stint at sittin' by 'im."

So the crew takes turns sitting by the body of the captain, one of the adult viewers who has volunteered to lie stretched out there. The girl who had volunteered to be captain on the first day has not returned. The seamen go about their jobs quietly, eyeing one another suspiciously as they turn things over in their minds. The tension mounts. They accuse one another. They devise tests to find the murderer. One by one they put their right hands on the Bible and say, "I swear on this Bible that I did not kill the captain." They decide to work in teams of two to keep an eye on one another and note anything suspicious. Dorothy Heathcote is as much in the dark as the rest as to who did the deed. They read the captain's diary; they look at his charts, which map a voyage into unmapped seas.

When, a few minutes before the end of the hour, none of the tests has yet

revealed the true murderer, Heathcote asks the class whether they would like
to go to bed, close their eyes, and have the actual murderer get up and sit by
the captain in the night. They agree and all sit or lie with their eyes closed.
One quiet girl steps forward from her bunk and sits beside the captain's head.
Heathcote rings the bell softly for dawn, and all the seamen open their eyes.
They look. There is a long pause.

"So that's who did it!"

"No wonder she said she didn't want to kill any more."

"She's the one—"

"She never said anything during the conversations about—"

"Get rid of her!"

"Throw her in the sea!" They're shouting now.

"Killing her won't do any good, 'cause that makes us all murderers, 'cause
we will have killed somebody."

"Why did you do it?"

"Yeah, why?"

The comes the murder's voice—quiet, steady, thoughtful: "He never had a
dream. He *told* me he never had a dream. Those charts—they led to nowhere.
He never had a dream."

"Then what was the purpose of the charts?"

"Then why did you come?"

"I didn't know it 'till I got on board; then he told me. And I killed him."

"Why did he tell you?"

The first mate asks, "What did he tell you?"

"He told me he never had a dream. He just wanted to sail away."

"Where?"

"He didn't know. He just wanted to sail away."

"What would happen when we ran out of supplies?"

"Have you proof?"

"Did he say whether he cared about what happened to us?"

"Why would he tell you and not anybody else?"

"I don't believe her!"

"I believe what she says," says Heathcote solemnly as first mate.

"So do I!"

"That doesn't make her any less of a murderer."

"I believe it."

"What I want to know is why he told her."

The first mate says, "It was in his diary."

"Throw her overboard!"

"Forget it!"

"All we can do if another murder happens on this ship is blame it on her."

"What? So we leave her on board to kill another one of us?"

Here Heathcote stops the drama, and they talk about what has happened.

She congratulates the murderer: "You handled that explanation very well."

"It was a super reason for killing," says one girl.

They ask the murderer how she held it so long without telling. They ask her how she felt when she had to swear on the Bible. She says, "What I said was, 'I did not kill *a* captain,' not '*the* captain,' because by that time he was not a captain to me."

"Here we all believed he had that dream, and the ship was labeled *The Dreamer.*"

"But if somebody had said he knew about the dream, you know, then she would have had to change her reason."

Heathcote agrees. "Then she couldn't have used that. She was so clever. She used the one reason we couldn't possibly go against. It was a reason I felt that somebody would kill, didn't you? Could you believe that somebody might kill because they found that the person they had thought was all big inside had suddenly become small, had no stature at all, because although he was a captain and had status, he hadn't the stature inside to be a captain."

"Wouldn't any explorer in the olden times have risked the lives of all the crew?"

"Any man with a dream might take you where you're in danger. You might want to kill him to save yourself."

Then Heathcote comes back in a clearly rougher voice as first mate, "It's made me realize that I'll never sign aboard a ship again without a memory that makes me look at the captain very, very closely. It'll affect me every time I go aboard."

The children through their own choices have become seamen facing a murder. Drama happens not because they go through motions or follow techniques but because they, like all other human beings, have a fantastic capacity—the ability to identify. No human being, even a murderer, is so berefit that we can't find a way to get inside him. Heathcote uses drama to help children understand human experience from the inside out. On this ship's deck she has stood solidly between all that has happened before and what is now. She has evoked at a gut level the drama of our humanness.

3. EDGING IN

If you have never used drama as a teaching tool, there is no clear, clean beginning point; there is only what Dorothy Heathcote calls "edging in." You have to start from where you are, and she frequently reassures teachers that "wherever you are is all right." You begin by figuring out what minimum conditions you need to feel successful as a teacher. As in any teaching, your own condition is the first and most important element you begin with. There are two other realities that teachers must take account of: the condition of the class and the nature of the material or subject matter.

Heathcote suggests that you begin by examining very honestly your own condition as a teacher. There are at least six areas in which she feels each teacher must determine her or his own threshold of tolerance:
1. Decision taking
2. Noise
3. Distance
4. Size of Groups
5. Teaching Registers
6. Status as a Teacher

When a threshold has been crossed, a teacher loses poise, control, and satisfaction. Therefore, it is up to each teacher to know just what her or his own security requires, so as to keep from crossing a crucial threshold.

One threshold is the proportion and kind of *decisions* you can comfortably let students take. As we noted in the last chapter, Heathcote finds taking risks a bracing challenge and typically works in such a way that the students themselves make most of the decisions about what the drama is to be about and its time, place, and plot. She wants them to learn to make decisions and to understand the rewards and demands that come from them. Her planning prior to the drama is supplemented by fast thinking on the spot as she examines the implications for the drama of the decisions the students have taken. Thus, she rises to the tension of improvising and solves the problem of group inertia at the same time.

However, Heathcote knows that other teachers may well need more specific plans and may need to keep a higher proportion of the decisions in their own hands. She never says to teachers, "Do it my way"; rather, she says, "Do it my way if it doesn't matter to you which way it goes. What you need to know is what decisions you don't dare let out of your hands. Don't give away decisions that will land you where you don't want to be, and don't play so risky that the class doesn't sense your authority." Thus, if you need to know your material before you start a drama, you would be ill-advised not to keep in your own hands the decision of what the drama is to be about. You should not feel guilty about what you can or cannot do; it's not a question of what you should do but where you stand and what your thresholds are. If you know that solidly, you will know the conditions for your security and effectiveness as a teacher. Without this, you lose your belief in what you are doing and you cannot be successful. The important thing is to determine for yourself how many decisions you are willing to risk entrusting to the class.

The *noise* threshold is the point at which we feel the students are making too much noise or the wrong kind of noise. Heathcote's panic button on noise is the point at which it is changing the children's goal. Although she knows that noise often suits the dramatic situation, she wants only noise that fits the purpose. She knows that you get more and better tension if you don't have uncontrolled noise; often she will stop a boisterous scene to reflect on the feelings it evoked. She never deliberately works toward noise, and when it occurs, she examines its effect and permits only that noise that can be justified dramatically. She is also honest in admitting that if you have a noisy class, you lose status as a teacher in England. You would in many American schools as well. Heathcote engineers a quiet handling of drama partly to give drama a good image.

To determine your *distance* threshold, ask yourself as a teacher how physically and emotionally close you want to be to your students. Some teachers feel the most comfortable when telling students what to do, when setting tasks for them in a formal way. This traditional teacher stance builds distance between the teacher and student, which is an important source of confidence for many teachers. Again, you need to decide for yourself what your threshold is.

Heathcote prefers to reduce as much as possible the distance between herself and the students; she likes to become involved with them, to pick up signals from them and to get into their minds as much as possible. She wants to sit close to and look right at students, touching them when the drama calls for it. She does much of her teaching "in role," as one of the characters in the drama, imposing on herself the same problems of believing and improvising that she asks of the children.* She is as much a receiver as a giver of signals when working with a class. Her distance threshold is very close to her. The

---

*See Chapter 11, "Using Role in Teaching."

advantage of this intimacy is that students continually feed her, and she is close to where they are and what they are thinking and feeling. She can quickly assess their social health by watching to see whether they can look the teacher in the eye, share space graciously, and forget themselves long enough to give themselves to a group task. This closeness has disadvantages: there is no escape from involvement, nor is there the built-in authority that a more distant stance brings.

For some dramas, distance is precisely what you want, of course. If you want individual differences to emerge and do not want the class to have a sense of the group, then a good way to get this is to seat them in desks that isolate individuals. Some roles that you assume as teacher—the foreman at the other end of the walkie talkie, the governor of the colony, the supervisor on the telephone—demand that you be physically distant from the group. If you are used to a typical, distant teacher stance, this kind of role might well be what you choose as you ease yourself into drama.

You may ask, aren't teachers too caught in a traditional telling role or too committed to formal teaching and maintaining distance to ever begin to use drama? Heathcote would say no, that any teacher can employ dramatic techniques even if she or he just sets tasks from a position of authority. The important thing is that each teacher know what she or he is ready to try. She even recommends that you begin by starting drama the last 5 minutes of a class period if you are worried! That way, you won't have to go on with it if it isn't working. This is what Dorothy Heathcote means by "edging in."

Similarly, you should work with a *size of group* that is comfortable for you. Some teachers start by breaking the class into small groups; others keep the whole class together at first. Heathcote prefers this latter because it helps coagulate the group. Then, too, she can get basic signals from the class of their interests and the level at which material can be pursued. She wants to find out quickly which students are timid about their opinions; who, if any, are the scapegoats; how children respect one another's ideas; and how they function with her.

However, her main reason for keeping a class together is that she's committed to helping students get the idea that drama is about what's underneath the action. She knows most of them won't get to that point—to the universal inherent in the particular—without her leadership. On the other hand, once they have had that experience, they'll know it forever.

Heathcote feels very safe working with large groups at the beginning, and she feels other teachers would find they, too, feel safe if they tried it. Nevertheless, she won't push them until they feel ready. Again, she tells teachers, "Be very honest about what size group works best for you. Don't say that just because I work best with large groups, you should too. You'll just plan rather differently if you feel more secure with small group work at first."

If you work by dividing the class into small groups, you pay, in that you won't be able to signal the quality that is within you simultaneously to everybody in the class. You will have the problem of spreading that quality around, and that is hard to do. Once you have the class broken into small groups, one group might make a decision that the rest are not ready for—a decision that you might regret but have to deal with because you chose to let it happen. You cannot back down after you have told the group they can develop their own drama.

Heathcote had this problem once when she was leading a group in a Stone Age wedding. The girls were giggly, and a top priority for her became getting those girls to stop giggling. To work with them, she separated them from the boys and started wedding preparations. The boys were at a different believing level and did not need her help at this point. So she deliberately cut herself off from half of the class in order to deal with the giggling. The price she paid for this decision was that the boys took a direction she had not predicted. It was a decision which she knew was absolutely right for them, but which completely changed what the entire group was doing. So, of course, she had to accept that change.

They were planning a wedding, but the boys from the start didn't want a wedding. The bride was the oldest, most sophisticated-looking girl in the class, but the bridegroom was the littlest boy. So Heathcote went away with the girls to get ready for the wedding, which they agreed should be in white bearskin. She worked on the giggling, getting them to stop laughing at what they were doing and to start believing in the bearskin they were sewing. After a little while, the boy who was to be the bridegroom came over to her and tapped her timidly on the shoulder. He whispered, "You know, I'd rather be dead than married." She said to him—doing a quick double-think, but knowing she had no right to deny him this decision—"Well, it seems to me that if you're hunting a bear, you stand a good chance."

When she said that, she knew the wedding was over. He went away and was instantly mauled by a bear and killed. That was the price she paid for dividing the group. So she turned to the girls, who were in the midst of their wedding preparations, and said somberly: "I'm sorry, but that which was to be a happy event is now a tragic one." She did not laugh, nor did the girls. If you break the class into groups, some of which are working without you, you must be prepared to deal with the decisions they make.

By *teaching registers*, Heathcote means the attitudes you employ in putting yourself at the service of the class. Her definition is not the more common definition of "register": "social variation in language use." It's not that she doesn't employ this kind of register. She does, mainly when she teaches in role as one of the characters in the drama. It is then that she uses one of the widest ranges of register as commonly defined that I've ever seen a teacher use.* In role she assumes an appropriate socioeconomic class dialect,

---

*See Chapter 11 for more on teaching in role.

providing a model for the pupils to follow in extending their own range of language registers. She can move up and down the socioeconomic scale—from humble to powerful and back—varying her dialect and posture as the role demands.

When she is talking about register as a threshold, however, she means something more inclusive than the range of language registers or social variations in dialect that a teacher uses. She means the attitude implied in the way the teacher relates to the class. This attitude can be exhibited whether or not the teacher is in role as a character in the drama and, if in role, in any dialect, tone, or social variation in language appropriate to the dramatic situation. Here are some of the teaching registers Heathcote uses:

The *one-who-knows* register is a register Heathcote uses very seldom. It says to the class, "Now, you listen, because I know this." She saves this register for those times when students are destroying the work of the drama and she knows that they can't go on that way and have anything at all to show for it. She'll say: "You're laughing at it; I'm sorry, it can't go on like that." She stops the drama because she knows that the class has torn up their work. She uses the one-who-knows register primarily to preserve the quality of the drama. I have seen her use it at many such times as the beginning of a video-taping or filming session. She says to the children, "Don't look at that camera after we start, 'cause if you do, I will not allow this work to be shown, and that's a promise." Then she lets them have a last look at the camera and introduces the camera crew, who tell a bit about what they will be doing. After that she tells the class that from now on, neither those cameras nor those camera operators exist.

The *would-you-like-to-know* register is a gentler one-who-knows register, in which she invites the class to request information. She seldom provides historical facts unless the students ask for it, the drama itself demands it, or she is absolutely certain that it will not jeopardize their belief. If the students indicate that they do want to know what actually occurred historically or would occur in the present in a certain circumstance, she gives them the facts if she knows them. If she doesn't, she tells the class that there are records they can look at that will give them answers to their questions. She frequently does historical research on a question right along with the students.

The *I-have-no-idea* register is a favorite register of Heathcote's for evoking responses from students. She thereby plucks the class out of the familiar stance of trying to guess what's in the teacher's mind and frees them to explore an idea with her. For example, she does not ask a class in a one-who-knows register, "What is sand?" If she did, many children could not answer, because they do not know its constituents and they assume the teacher does. To this question a child might respond, "I can't begin to deal with all that; the teacher knows too much, so I'll just keep still." So instead of asking,

Heathcote assumes the I-have-no-idea register and slowly picks up an imagined handful of sand. She lets it sift little by little through her fingers, saying, "I've never been able to understand how sand came to be." Now the child's mind can work. Heathcote's I-have-no-idea register has left the pupil room to wonder with the teacher.

In the *suggester-of-implications* register, Heathcote wonders with the class in a musing tone, presenting alternatives of action in a nondirective and open-ended way. She'll say something like: "I don't know how you're going to settle. You don't have any credentials as you enter the country. How do people introduce themselves to other people who didn't ask them to come?" In this register the teacher becomes a restless spirit recognizing where a class is and seeking where they can go, now that they have arrived here. The teacher provides a balance between what has just happened and what might happen next.

In the *interested-listener* register, Heathcote listens with her whole presence. She clearly signals to the children that she is taking in whatever they have to say and is pondering, not pouncing, on it. This register is another rare one for teachers. Usually they listen just long enough to pick up clues for more direction giving, saying, "Yes, well, the thing you should do about that . . ."—which isn't really listening at all. We need to respond by taking in or repeating whatever a child says, letting her or him know that we're thinking about the words.

In the *I'll-get-what-you-need* register, the teacher puts herself at the service of the class, making sure that their ideas get implemented. A teacher of younger children may actually become the carrier of things the students in role need. For example, she or he might find them a blanket, or might say, "I know where you can buy some food for the Queen's baby." Teachers of older students tend to carry ideas and information when they are in this register. "We shall have to go to the County Clerk's office to look at the deed."

Heathcote sometimes assumes the *it's-no-use-asking-me* register. She will deliberately withdraw from involvement when she knows the drama is going well without her or when she feels the class can function better without depending so heavily on her. She frequently uses this register, like the others, when in role, turning the responsibility for what happens in the drama back on the class.

Heathcote uses the *devil's-advocate* register only when she is clearly signaling to the class that she is not speaking for herself, but is in role. She finds this register hard because it sounds as if you are speaking for yourself, and if the students think you are, it's harder for you to put the good cards in their hands so they will win. She wants to engineer an interaction with students whereby they are dealt the good cards. If she thinks the children are getting confused as to whether she really holds the position she is advocating, she immediately comes out of role to reassure them.

Once Heathcote was doing a play with five-year-olds who had begun their drama by finding a baby left on a doorstep. The group was going from house to house knocking on the door. Each time Heathcote would answer and be a different woman, saying, "No, it's not mine"; "What a terrible thing!"; "No, I'm sorry, I didn't lose one." Finally, when they came knocking on a door, plaintively asking, "Have you lost a baby?" Heathcote said in a fierce, witch-like voice, "No, but I've always wanted one!" She grabbed the doll-baby out of the arms of a startled child. Then she came out of role and asked the children whether they wanted her to be a witch who gets the baby. "Yes!" they shouted eagerly. Then she asked whether they wanted to win the baby back in the end. Another enthusiastic "Yes!" At that point in the play, she didn't want to worry the children too much, so she held the baby as anyone would, only a bit harder. Later in the drama she could hold it up by one foot, because by that time they were really winning against the witch and were more certain that they'd get the baby back. She prepared them for winning by suggesting that to get the baby back, they'd have to have stronger magic than she. Then she went about her work in her house talking loudly to herself about how her magic rules were in her book here. She later asked them, "Where's *your* magic?" This is an example of feeding good cards to the children. Once the children had an idea how they would get the baby back, Heathcote started treating the doll roughly. "Hey, look at her! Look at what she's doing to that baby!" Right away they started saying magic spells. She bolted the door against them; they hurled stones at the door. She started looking through her book. "I want a piece of magic that shows me how to turn babies into witches." The five-year-olds said, "She's trying to turn it into a witch!"

"We ought to stop her!"

"Let's freeze her hands."

After a bit of this, they couldn't come up with anything more on their own. Heathcote came out of role and asked, "Do you want to get my magic book?" They did. "You're going to have to be cleverer than I am to get my book." Then she went back into role, still playing the devil's advocate. "I think I'll take my book outside today and read in the shade." So again the children had been dealt a good card. They could win. The devil's-advocate register was a pretense; the children knew it, and they felt free to fight against her in role.

Heathcote uses the devil's-advocate register whenever she wants to get a group united against her. When she succeeds, she can come out of role to congratulate them on their effective expression of feelings. She once had a group of fourth graders who wouldn't let anything happen to them. So she came in as the mineowner and said, "You're in my mine cottages. Come tomorrow morning at six, all your children over eight years old are going to be down my mine." After a few thoughtful moments, one boy said, "I'll send mine down if you'll send yours," and the drama had begun.

Using the *going-along* register is what Heathcote calls "letting the class go past." In this register the teacher appears to be agreeing to whatever the group has decided. It is in this register that Heathcote often assesses the dramatic potential of a class's decision and decides what her next register will be.

There are other registers, of course. The important thing for you to know is what your most comfortable registers are, which register is the most appropriate for what you want to happen, which register you are in at any moment, and how to signal to the class that you are in that register. When you switch registers, you need to know that you can't expect the same response of the class. Each teacher will have an individual set of teaching registers. Your register threshold separates you from the type of register you dare not move into because you feel uncomfortable with it.

You have to determine what *status as a teacher* you must preserve in order to want to return to teaching the next day. What do you have to get out of an experience in order to want to continue? For Heathcote, the status she has to carry home is the conviction that people found it interesting working with her. When she gets a rejection on this one, she goes out on all fours, metaphorically speaking, even though she may look the same. What you need to know is the minimum response you must get from a class to maintain the status you require. If you let things happen in the classroom that cross your status threshold, you are in the worst position possible—for you and the class.

When your status has been shattered, you need to talk with someone about it. Very seldom are teachers encouraged to talk about their problems. In many schools it's considered bad manners to share, in such a place as the teacher's lunchroom, a feeling that you've just made a fool of yourself. Heathcote firmly believes that the first job of a principal is to make sure a climate is created in which teaching problems don't get shoved under a rug. Otherwise a teacher may get the idea that she or he has problems, but nobody else does. What actually happens, in many schools, is that principals create a climate where the real concerns of teachers don't get aired. Instead of concentrating on how to change teaching patterns and thus solve problems, teachers too often fall into the easy trap of not looking at their own methods, but blaming the learners: "That Karen Jones is impossible!" One of the most valuable safeguards Heathcote knows is to have a co-teacher watch and take notes on everything you do while you're teaching. Then you do the same in return. This opens an area of self-perception and communication; it frees both of you to share problems.

Many teachers have no one outside the school they can share their problems with; lacking this, they often come into school with broken wings the next morning. If they have someone who shares their concerns, they can assess what went wrong, decide how to avoid it, and stop feeling guilty. They then can get to the point where they can shrug and say, not "I'm a failure as a teacher" but "That was that; now I'm going to try it this way and see what happens!"

It's not enough to know where you stand and where your own thresholds for security lie; you must also get to know the class. Each class has a different condition and potential. It's no good wishing you always had good classes. Some groups are simply more difficult to manage than others. Heathcote has observed that American children have less of a "herd-like" quality as a group than English children do. American children have more initiative. They also have an "I, I, I" approach that poses the problem of leading them to balance their personal desires with those of others so that they'll end up with a "we" experience. This is not to say that American classes are more difficult than English ones. It is simply that each presents a different kind of problem. Both the "herd-like" quality and the "I, I, I" quality are problems—are conditions of the class that have to be recognized and overcome if drama is to move.

Through the first questions she poses to a class, Heathcote tries to assess what she calls the "content level" at which they can best work, the level of complexity of experience with which they are capable of dealing. For example, when one group of children decided to do a play about stealing the *Mona Lisa*, she asked whether it would be easier to get into the Louvre at night or in the daytime. She was really asking, Wouldn't it be more fun to get in at night? When the children eagerly said, "Let's do it at night! Oh, yeess!" she knew they were answering on the feeling level. If the group had had more experience, she would have asked instead: "At what hour of the day or night would the *Mona Lisa* be least likely to be best guarded?" Then the students would have had to base their answer on calculation—for example, knowledge of guards, or of the floor plan of the Louvre—rather than just on feeling. She assesses what the condition of the class is and what facts they are going to be able to use as she asks the questions that focus the drama.

Dorothy Heathcote has worked with classes in every conceivable condition—not only with so-called "normal" children in the Newcastle schools, but with inmates in reform schools, prisons, mental hospitals, and wards for the handicapped. Where the group is and what it needs determines what she decides to do.

One time she was working with five mentally handicapped children who posed a problem that might daunt any ordinary teacher. They ran away whenever they became anxious, which was most of the time. They were used to living in isolation; escape into quiet corners was the only way of coping that they regularly tried. Heathcote wanted to trap them into new experience, so what she did was to literally tie them to her, with pieces of elastic tape. They couldn't escape then into their abyss of nothing; they had to stop and bump into her and each other. They couldn't ignore that strip of ɪelastic. With every group Heathcote is looking for an elastic of some kind that will trap them into facing something they've not faced before.

With another group of severely retarded children, she tried bringing in an adult man who was dressed as a derelict, unkempt and wild-looking. The presence of this hopeless character evoked sympathy and helping behavior from children who had only been the recipients of help before.

With another group of children who had been cared for all their lives—this time spastics—she brought in an adult all tied in a box. He was cramped up, rolled in a ball inside a box barely large enough to hold him. The class awkwardly started to help him get out. Then they painstakingly showed him how to sit on a chair and how to wash and groom himself. They were trapped into the new experience of sharing with a helpless adult many of the skills they had painfully learned despite the frustrations of an undependable nervous system. His need of their help evoked responsible behavior.

She takes any class from where they are. One day she found herself with a class that, by reputation, was one of the hardest to teach. She went in knowing this and found on the blackboard these words: *gangsters, gambling den, robbery.* She assumed this was what the class had been doing with the previous teacher. That teacher had left the class so upset that he decided not to teach any more. He simply didn't want to spend the rest of his life bawling kids out like that.

Heathcote girded up her loins and decided she was not going to be undone by this antisocial group. She got to the classroom 10 minutes early and decided to arrange the desks so that no child could push or shove another— this was one of their problems. She knew that if she arranged the children in this way she would lose the chance to get at the dynamics of the group (which she usually wants to find out first), but she decided this was a fair price to pay for the advantage of ensuring that they wouldn't just come in and fight, as was their custom.

After she got all the desks arranged, she thought, "Humm. . . if I put just one desk in the middle, that's a tension." She didn't know exactly why she put it there, except that when those kids came in, one of them was bound to ask, "Hey, Miss, what's that for?" Then she would answer, "It's for you." This would, of course, be a risk, and she had no idea at that point what would happen beyond that. As it turned out, the boy who first asked the question was not one of the tough ones; he was a rather quiet boy. She made him sit in the middle. She had thought she would ask the class to tell her what they thought might have happened to make one person have to sit by himself like that, but she didn't because as the rest of the class came in, they asked, "What's up, Miss?" "What's goin' on here?" At that point Heathcote looked up at the phrase *gambling den* and thought, "Great!"—she was ready to begin.

Assuming the role of one of a group of men, she looked squarely at the one in the middle and said, "You have played cards with every one of us this night." She had asked herself, "Why is this bloke isolated in this gambling den?" She knew that his isolation was a symbol of something. She went on, "You've lost money to every one of us, and you're not leaving until you pay up." Then, after a pause and in a less threatening tone: "He's lost twenty quid to me." She turned to another class member: "How much does he owe you?" This one was too good to miss. The kids who wanted to be tough guys were plunged into a drama where they could be just that.

It was not long before this antisocial group began to work on the problem of how to get what they wanted. One said, "Look, you, we don't mean you any harm, but you're not leaving until you pay."

He said, "Well, I have a Ford Torino I could sell."

"Where is it now?"

"It's parked down in front."

"Give us the keys."

Heathcote asked, in role, "Are you sure he owns it?"

"Hey, where's your insurance?"

"I haven't got it on me."

"Guys like him never have it on them."

"Well, how are we gonna' prove it's his own car?"

"We'll have to go to his house."

"And what's the missus gonna' say?"

"She'll just have to face it. He's not comin' back till he pays."

Heathcote, wanting to heighten the tension by seeing to it that their problem isn't solved easily, said, "Well, you can't believe wives. You never know if they'll tell the truth or not."

"We'll get one of his kids. Kids tell the truth."

"She'll never let one of the kids out at one in the morning."

At this point, then, this tough class is focusing on the problem of how to pursuade a mother to trust them with her little boy to go down and tell the truth for his Dad. They've been trapped into a new experience, just as surely as the mentally handicapped children were trapped by the yards of elastic that tied them to Heathcote. The class with a reputation for a total inability to cope with one another had been led to figure out how to deal with the problem of trust. Heathcote didn't have to worry now about how to end the drama. As long as the students were interested in it, they wouldn't let the boy in the middle go home. This drama went on and on, staying in the same area, exploring the relationships among this group of men. Because it stayed in one spot, there was time for the relationships to be explored. The boys needed the adult, not to "direct" the play, but to engineer it so it stayed long enough in one place to build toward something.

Without an adult, children's dramas tend to be episodic, a set of adventures with no time for the build-up of tension or the exploring of what lies between people, of that aura that can be felt in a human situation. When children produce fast-paced plays (Scene 1, The Battleship; Scene 2, The Dungeon; Scene 3, The Pub; Scene 22. . .), all you get are four lines and Bam! the climax. This is what children see in television cartoons; it's also what they think they're seeing in the theatre, and all too often, they're right.

As you have seen in the previous chapters, it's only when you deliberately plan to have the drama stay in the same place that the children have to pull out new information, are trapped into new experience. This is when they plumb to what they didn't know they knew. It's only when children have to fight for answers that they find their own resources. If they don't want the drama there, they stop struggling and get edgy. Then you know you must move on, because they're at the end of the resources and you mustn't let them spiral into failure. The trick is to know the condition of the class. Then you can push them into an area where they discover resources they have not yet touched, and can avoid moving them to where they are adrift because they have lost their moorings. You must work with an awareness of the thresholds of both the teacher and the class.

You also need to take account of the nature of the material. In many American classrooms, particularly in the junior and senior high schools, what you do with classroom role playing is expected to fit into a specific area of the curriculum. As a teacher, you may decide that you want to use drama as a way into an area of history or a particular piece of literature. If this is the case, obviously you don't begin by asking the students what they want to do a play about. If your goal is to relate the drama to specific subject matter, you take that limitation as a starting point.

Not only your starting point is different; the direction of the drama is limited by the fact that if you are relating it to specific written material, it must not contradict that material. You have to realize that if, for example, you want the facts in an historical sense, you'll have to give up some emotional depth in the drama. There's no way to get both a large number of accurate facts and deep feelings at the same time. When you move, as Dorothy Heathcote does, into a humanities side of experience, you work on what a specific object or event symbolized. You use whatever information the children have—no matter how inaccurate or anachronistic—as the grist to get into what the event feels like to the people who live through it. If your goal is to recreate an historical event or period with authenticity, you do it at the expense of depth of feeling. Again, this is not something to regret but something to face. What are your priorities, and are you willing to pay the price of getting what you are going after? This is the question you must ask.

Obviously, if you give top priority to historical accuracy, you put yourself into the one-who-knows register more often than you would otherwise. An example of this can be seen in a five-day drama that Heathcote did with a group of English nine-year-old students who "covered" 1,200 years of history. Her goal was to help the class understand this historical concept: It is by chance that things survive, but when they do, we want them to continue to survive. She began by having the children laboriously create a medieval document to use in the play; they decided it would be a Bible. Each child took a Biblical passage to copy, using pens with nibs like quills, and to illuminate ornately on a page of the manuscript. In order to do this, the children had to scrutinize carefully copies of actual medieval documents. Heathcote assembled a classroom library which included a copy of the *Lindisfarne Gospel* and the *Book of Hours* of the Duc de Berry. She also showed slides of illuminated pages of *The Book of Kells.* In the one-who-knows register, Heathcote introduced a great deal of information about Anglo-Saxon manuscripts. By the time the drama began, the children had invested a great deal of energy in the book they had created, so it was easy for them to accord it importance. The drama then centered around tracing the losing and finding of this book through 1,200 years of history, ending with the present time.

Early in the drama, the class decided that the person instrumental in the saving of the book would be the bastard son of a feudal lord. (They wanted this partly because it sounded very grown-up, of course.) The boy was to have found the book just after the Battle of Hastings, in a place where it had been hidden from the Danes two centuries earlier. They had no idea where an outcast child would have grown up in the eleventh century, and in their sympathy for him they put him in an orphanage. It was at this point that Heathcote broke into the drama in the one-who-knows register and said, "Listen, in those days children were not thought of as they are today. There were no orphanages, though there were always kind people who would watch a child. Many children just fell down holes between people because nobody would take responsibility for them. So it's no good you making up something that couldn't have happened at that time. If you want this play to be true to the historical sense"—and this was her top priority, since she'd been asked to do this as a history project—"you'll have to do it this way." After the drama was over, the class asked: "What happened to all those children nobody wanted?"

"I don't know," she confessed, "but I do know that all through time in England there have been records of children and what happened to them. I know where I can lay my hands on some." This became her next material, and the children began a new research, this time not to find out how pages of medieval manuscripts looked, but to see what had been written about unwanted children.

After they had examined historical records, the next question was: "How far have we come today in our caring for children?" After they discussed that a bit, Heathcote pointed out, "Somebody built this school. It is evidence of their caring. This building epitomizes some of the values they held when they built it." That led to a close examination of what the school symbolized, what its structure and decoration told them about the values of the builders.

The children began saying, "You know, I've never seen my school before. I've never looked at it properly." Then came a tour of the school, so they could actually look at what it symbolized—the ideas of their parents and educators as to what learning was about. They began to look at the library books, saying, "You know, these cost money. And somebody chose these because they wanted children to know about this, or they thought we'd be interested in it. They cared what happened to children." So although some of the depth of feeling for the bastard son back in the eleventh century was lost by Heathcote's interpolation of historically accurate material, the children were given a touchstone for experiencing the present differently.*

Sometimes the nature of the material establishes parameters for dramatic activity. You must know these limits before you begin. Armed with this knowledge and a clear recognition of the limits imposed by your own condition and that of the class, you are ready to "edge in" to using drama.

---

*For more on this use of drama see Chapter 17, "Code Cracking: Other Areas."

4. FINDING MATERIAL THROUGH BROTHERHOODS

Dorothy Heathcote laments that teachers waste so much energy worrying about where to get material for drama. She has discovered an efficient way of finding it through a deft bit of lateral thinking—she jumps sideways through time and across social strata, hanging all the while onto one constant or element in a situation. She calls this system for finding material the *Brotherhoods Code*. No matter what she or a class is doing, she can say, "We are in the brotherhood of all those who . . . ." For example, if she is carrying in her daughter's breakfast, she says to herself, "I am in the brotherhood of all those who serve another's needs," and immediately she has dozens of images at her fingertips—from a waitress at a drive-in to the servant of the king.

By keeping only the inner experience itself constant, a person can span all time and circumstances, all social strata and age groupings. Instantly into a teacher's hands come dozens of situations in which the inner experience of the participants is the same.

	SOCIAL STRATA			
HISTORICAL PERIODS	Lower Class	Middle Class	Upper Class	Royalty and Other National Leaders
Modern Times				
Middle Ages				
Classical Age				
Preclassical Age				
Primitive Times				

For example, if you gasp, "I've cut my hair off, and it looks terrible!" you are in the brotherhood of all those who find themselves with exactly what they asked for: the robber with the stolen jewels, the bridegroom at the altar, young Arthur with the sword Excalibur freshly wrenched from the stone, Salome with the head of John the Baptist. No matter what you are doing, you can say to yourself, "At this moment I am in the brotherhood of all those who . . . ." and find yourself leaping to events that might look radically different on the outside, but on the inside, feel the same. We can identify with all those, all through time, who have been in this brotherhood. The external events may differ, but the underlying significance for people is similar.

Wherever you are, you can limber up on this Brotherhoods Code. For example, if you are wearing a necklace, you are of the brotherhood of all those who choose to adorn themselves. How many different people adorn themselves, and for how many different reasons? You are in the same brotherhood as tribal warriors ritualistically dressing for the battle, or actors preparing for a play, or Cleopatra getting ready for her journey down the Nile.

Thus, a teacher can look at a class and very quickly get an idea for a drama that suits their behavior and interests. For example, if she or he meets a group of boys who are all sitting around in a disgruntled mood, the teacher may think: they are in the same brotherhood as men with a problem sitting in a pub, a group of miners facing a shutdown, or a motorcycle gang finding out that the race they just finished was rigged.

One value of the Brotherhoods Code is that it enables you to transcend quickly the notion that drama is acting out stories. Because any story is about relationships among people, you will find dozens of different dramas underneath the top layer of any story, underneath the story line. Each separate drama is the link between the story and the brotherhood of all those who have been in that same situation.

Heathcote illustrates this with the story of Cinderella.* The story line or surface tale begins with a little girl who finds herself with a dad and two stepsisters and an ugly stepmother who does not love her. Then, in story terms, she finds the sisters going to a ball that she can't go to. Then her fairy godmother comes, and Cinderella finds that she can go after all, but when she gets there, she isn't too good at watching the clock. So she runs away and in the process loses her glass slipper. Then she discovers that the prince's men are looking for the lady who wore the shoe, and she tries it on. Of course, it all ends happily ever after.

To be sure, the story of Cinderella has those events in it, but that doesn't make drama. You don't need a story to get drama. A story may help you if

---

*See the film *Dorothy Heathcote Talks to Teachers,* Part 2 (listed in bibliography, p. 236).

you need that feeling that you know where you're going. But where you are going in teaching is not to the end of a story, but through the story to an experience that modifies the children. Heathcote is not saying that stories aren't good for children, but that drama is not trying to get through a series of events.

How does the story of Cinderella become drama so that the children learn anything? To get at this, we can look at how many things *Cinderella* is really about. I find myself with two sisters who are mean to me. It's about that. I find myself having to come into a house that suddenly doesn't belong to my own mother any more. A strange lady is washing up the dishes. It's about that. Heathcote once asked a group of boys, "Hey, what's *Cinderella* about?"

They said, "*Cinderella* is about a man daft enough to marry a woman who only likes her own kids, Miss!" So it's about that as well. A group of 17-year-olds said it was about a fairy godmother who set things up but was never around when you needed her. When they did their drama, they explored how a fairy godmother ever knows the results of her actions, and whether or not a fairy godmother might be more useful just as a person who listens. To a group of police cadets, *Cinderella* was the story of the guards of the prince and their attempts to persuade their charge to have another look around. This is why playwrights can use the same material and find a million plays; they don't deal with the story line. Instead, they ask, "What is implicit in the relationships of the people in this situation?" In classroom drama, too, this is what we have to get at when we try to use *Cinderella* as a starting point for learning.

Heathcote once met with a group of young women, all unmarried and all pregnant. What is *Cinderella* about for a group like this? It's about a girl who hasn't any stockings to wear and two girls who have stockings and are not going to lend them to her. So Heathcote has a girl get down on her knees and start scrubbing the floor while the others jeer and chide. *Cinderella* is about what she does when that happens, and how she feels. If you care about that—and those girls who are pregnant *do* care about that—then you don't want to move on to the next part of the story too fast; it is staying here that makes something matter. It's staying here that helps the class to reflect.* Staying in one place may sound very dreary, but Heathcote knows it is not. It simply means the group takes the drama at their own pace, not the teacher's. If they want to stand and swear at one another for a while, the teacher has to allow it. As Heathcote puts it, "I can't make a lot of 18-year-old, pregnant, unmarried women do what *I* want. All I can do is help *Cinderella* modify where they're at. It may help them to dream about wearing pretty clothes again. This might move very quickly into another area that begins with "If I could ask the fairy godmother for anything, it would be . . . ." Thus the

---

*See Chapter 8, "Dropping to the Universal," for more on reflection.

drama moves into what we call "the left hand of knowing."*

As a teacher, Heathcote knows *Cinderella* is not merely a story line to be followed, but a safe way to give those girls a chance to get rid of anger at being pregnant. When the story has used itself up for that need, Heathcote will know because the class will lose interest. Then she might have a chance to drop to a universal human understanding and say, "Do you think Cinderella had anything to be angry about?" Then she could use the Brotherhoods Code to find her next material. Who else had a good reason to be angry like Cinderella? She and the students might then explore the implications of the idea that Cinderella is in the brotherhood of all those who have suffered at the hands of their siblings. So their next drama might well be like the one in Lillian Hellman's *The Little Foxes* or in the story of Esau or of Joseph.

The potential for finding material through the Brotherhoods Code is multiplied a hundredfold by the fact that in any given moment you are in touch with not just one, but many different brotherhoods. For example, when you are washing dishes, you are in the brotherhood of all those who cleanse, which puts you in touch with a primitive Maori washing gourds, a soldier cleaning his gun, or a priest performing a ritual baptism. A dishwasher is also of the brotherhood of all those who work with their hands and their utensils, so he is one with a goldsmith making jewelry, a chemist mixing solutions, a surgeon wielding a scalpel, a witch mixing potions. As you sit on a bus you can say to yourself, "I am in the brotherhood of all those who find themselves in transit; of all those who must be prepared to wait; of all those who must make a journey; of all those who can fold themselves up; of all those who will possibly meet strangers; of all those who are going into the unknown; of all those who are prepared to see what the outcome will be."

When the Apollo astronauts sit in their small traveling world ready to blast off for outer space, they, too, belong to many different brotherhoods. They are of the brotherhood of all those who *will go*, will be responsible. They are of the brotherhood of all those who cannot get out until the time comes—just like the chicken in the egg. They are of the brotherhood of all those who must trust other people to have built well, and of all those who can hear voices from the air—and that puts them in touch with Joan of Arc. They are of the brotherhood of all those who have the courage, of all those who fear, of all those who must not turn back, of all those who may not return, of all those who understand tools—which takes us through all time since the Stone Age. They are of the brotherhood of all those who will venture, of all those who carry their houses with them—be they modern-day campers, homesteaders in covered wagons, or Moses and the Israelites. Each situation is pregnant with hundreds of brotherhoods, each of which leads you to more material for drama.

---

*See Chapter 14, "The Left Hand of Knowing."

The great value of this Brotherhoods Code is that it enables a teacher quickly to find a common ground between two seemingly different acts. Thus, a group of men working with crude tools to hew a cross and a group of men in leather jackets with stockings over their faces putting bullets into a gun are in the same brotherhood—the brotherhood of all those who are preparing for another's death within a convention appropriate for their time. As a child sees the relationship between one experience and others which are like it in some important respect, the experience is illuminated by the light of that comparison and a way into a new situation is provided. This new situation might on the outside look far removed from the child's own experience, in either time or circumstance. Yet, because the people in that situation are in the same brotherhood as those who are familiar, the child can focus on the common element long enough to identify.

In any drama, the isolation of one factor that a student can relate to makes focus possible. Without this focus a situation is less significant, less dramatic, less tense. Because each of the brotherhoods focuses on the inner significance of the outer act, each contains within it a potential tension.*

After a drama is over, Heathcote and the class can use the Brotherhoods Code to isolate a significant element in that drama and use it as a link to the next one. After a drama of Galileo, for example, Heathcote may say, "This man was in the brotherhood of all those who deliberately set themselves apart by what they believe." Thus she is able to help the students think of many other circumstances in which this element is a significant one and choose one of these for another drama. By using the Brotherhoods Code, she can change the outer circumstances and make the next drama seem different because externally it is about something else; still, internally, it can be about the same thing. The class can stay in the same place at their deepest level of identification and yet not feel they are circling around the same material. By coming at the problem in a new way with new material, they can gain a fresh perspective on it.

The Brotherhoods Code is Heathcote's way of getting out of the trap of story line and into the rich fullness of all of human experience. She no longer needs to wonder about where to get material for drama.

---

*See the next chapter and Chapter 12, "Theater Elements as Tools," for more on how to build in and develop tension, one of the essentials of drama.

5. FROM SEGMENTING TO DRAMATIC FOCUS

Either the curriculum prescribes or the class members provide a general subject for a drama: the Middle Ages, an airplane crash, monsters, hospitals, pirates, pioneer days, King Arthur, witches, the Civil War, China, Indians, mountaineering, being rich, a space trip, the Olympic Games. How does Dorothy Heathcote make a broad, general topic like this work for the class as a drama?

She begins with a two-step process. First, she very quickly thinks of all the various aspects of the chosen subject that she can. This she typically does in her head, not with the class. She calls this process "segmenting" and diagrams it like this:

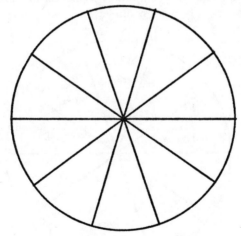

Each segment is an aspect of the lives of the participants in a drama about the general subject the class has agreed upon.

Heathcote's second step is to take one of the segments and, through questions, to arrive at a particular moment when the essence of that experience is likely to be the most fully recognized. The questions she poses lead the class to the moment of beginning.

Let us go back now to segmenting and see how it operates. Heathcote urges her adult students to practice throwing up segments, thinking of a general subject and then listing all the common experiences they might expect within that way of life. Segmenting is something that can be learned slowly, anytime and anywhere, without the pressure of the presence of a class. However, segmenting with a class in front of you needs to be done very quickly. Heathcote warns her teachers not to worry if in some cases only one segment comes to mind. That is enough for a start; if that's all you've got, you simply have to take it and make it work dramatically. However, the more you can imagine, the less you care about the one you have taken, the less you are married to your own idea, and the more open you are to considering which segment will work best for this *particular* class.

Heathcote has found it helpful, as she is bubbling up the segments of a subject, to think of those areas into which any culture may be divided. Often each area will suggest a segment of a certain general idea. Here are the areas Heathcote has found useful (for these she acknowledges the influence of Edward T. Hall's classification*): commerce, communication, clothing, education, family, food, health, law, leisure, shelter, travel, war, work, and worship. All material for drama embraces some of these, so with a little practice a teacher can learn to segment general ideas into usable parts very quickly.

Let's look at a couple of examples of segmenting. If the general subject is King Arthur, the segments might be these:

---

*Hall, Edward T. *The Silent Language.* Garden City, N.Y.: Doubleday & Co., 1959. Chapter 3, "The Vocabulary of Culture." Here Hall distinguishes 10 primary message systems.

The teacher chooses the one segment that best suits the maturity, behavior, and interests of the class. For example, a teacher who decides her first graders are ready to enter the segment of training is going into that aspect of all culture we call education. What does a knight in King Arthur's time need to know? How to clean his armor and don it, how to sheath his sword and wield it, how to ride a horse and hunt game, how to kneel before and address the king, how to conduct himself at the Round Table, how to worship at the cathedral, how to make the castle safe during a siege, how to live under Arthur's law. The teacher will start with the more concrete aspects of training and progress to an ever more subtle understanding of the Middle Ages—all through dramatizing the training of a knight. The daily tournaments and banquets (at milk-and-cracker time) might well go on for weeks, with a new event each day to give them a new face. Queen Guinevere has lost the child; there is a new knight to be initiated; the crops have failed in the drought; they prepare for Whitsunday mass; the scop has a new song about the King; a servant is accused of stealing bread.

If a class wants to do a play about killing the President,* as a group of delinquent boys in prison once did, Heathcote quickly segments this idea into everything she can think of that has to do with assassination. She does not reject their original idea—after all, she asked them for it—although she knows that it is an antisocial act they want to perform. What she wants most is to harness the class's energy and drive; obviously they have chosen killing the President because it has in it some "kick" for them. These teenagers in the first crush of being men want to be known as "tough guys," and killing the President sounds like a brave thing to do. By letting this group do what they want, Heathcote is at first actually reinforcing their antisocial desires, but she knows that she can work through these to expand the range of their present understanding of what the act means. She can get to the point where she can say: "Now let's look at what you've done. The President is dead. What do you suppose is happening inside you, and what happens to the people immediately concerned?" They will be trapped into facing living with a murder on their conscience, the problem of succession of power, and the feelings of a family bereaved. This in turn can lead them to examine their own values.

As soon as Heathcote gets the boys' suggestion for a drama, she segments that general idea into all the aspects of it she can think of. The pie diagram at the top of the next page represents the sum total of what she's capable of imagining at that moment about killing the President.

---

*See the film *Improvised Drama, Part I*
(listed in bibliography, p. 237).

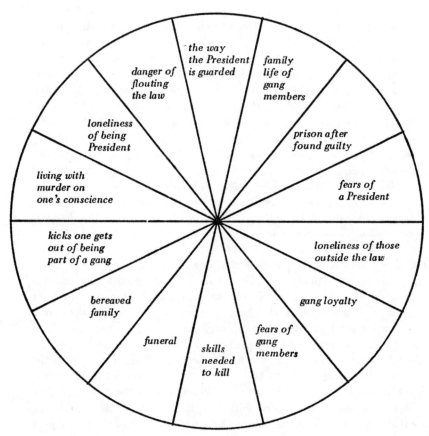

After segmenting, a teacher is ready for the next step, which is to choose one of these segments and ask the class enough questions about it that they can all arrive at a specific, particular moment—one with a pressure or tension of some kind in it—for the beginning of the drama. This is a process of funneling:

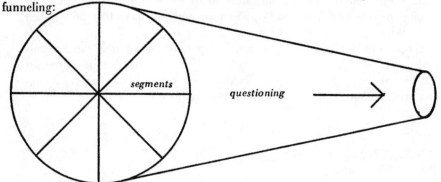

The more segments a teacher has thrown up, the more flexibility is possible in the selection of one that best suits the needs of the particular class. Some segments will obviously be more suitable for a class with poor social health, or for students new to drama. Others will demand a more subtle and complex involvement and thus be appropriate for a more mature or experienced class. To find the segment that most interests and suits the class, a teacher asks questions. If the class have decided they want to do a play about pirates, the teacher can ask them what a pirate looks like. If their idea of a pirate is a fellow with one eye, one leg, and a hook for a hand, then the teacher knows that the segment of being pirates to zero in on will be the *danger*.

A teacher can also size up other clues to help determine which segment to use. For example, he or she might look at the physical arrangement of the human bodies in the room. Are they close to one another, touching each other comfortably, expectantly looking to the teacher for leadership? Or are they isolated in desks or chairs, sitting apart from one another, awaiting information or direction? Are they clustered in little groups, indicating the closeness of subgroups within the class? Are the boys sitting separately from the girls? Then the teacher can take in their postures, facial expressions, willingness to allow and respond to eye contact. All of this information helps him or her decide which segment to use and what limits will be imposed on the beginning moment of the drama. The condition of the class determines to a large extent the shape of the beginning moment.* For example, if the children are separated from one another in the classroom, and if their skill in using language is not very developed, it is no use finding a focus for the beginning of the drama that demands that they crowd together and talk. Instead you win them to closeness and talking by letting them stand apart and be quiet first. So you choose a segment that can begin with pantomined movement to build up experience from the inside, hoping this will lead to a moment when talking comes.

If a class is hyperactive and a bit antisocial, then you're going to have to put them in a situation where they have to work together and cooperate and listen to orders. Thus if they choose to do a drama about pirates, you don't begin with the segment of a raid of another ship at sea (though the children might like to start there), because you know all you'll get is a lot of fighting and punching. Instead you start by having the crew work together to prepare for the voyage, battening down the cargo and storing the provisions. Then they all have to work together to get the sails up. These activities use their hyperactivity but begin to modify their antisocial behavior. Before the end of the drama, you hope to give them their kicks for long enough to win them to listening to one another, to cooperating on tasks rather than shoving one another about. You lose the class if you let them fight first—although there's

---

*See Chapter 3, "Edging In."

no denying that they may be saying by their behavior, "We're good at fighting." Instead, you promise them the fight they are seeking, but you tell them they will need to wait a bit first. The fight will come when you can trust the class to carry on that fight with control, with an awareness of its context, with a discipline to keep it believable, and with a restraint appropriate to the situation.

In the "Killing the President" drama, Heathcote does not choose to dramatize the life of the President. She feels this group of delinquent boys is not ready to identify with a President or his complex political world. Instead, she chooses the segment of gang loyalty, and out of that she moves to the focus for the opening moment. She asks the boys where their gang headquarters is and how they can keep themselves unknown to the police. After they decide on all the particulars, Heathcote asks, "How do you get past Charlie the doorkeeper and into the gang's hideout in the warehouse?" The boys choose a password, and the drama begins. Each boy in turn comes to the doorkeeper and is let in. This beginning has enough of the elements of mystery and toughness to appeal to the class. Out of this beginning, Heathcote is able to move to another segment, that of skills needed to kill, and asks: "Who's clever enough to fire that gun?" and "Will you have the patience to wait?" So now she has moved from the general idea of killing the President to its segments, has chosen one of these segments that suits the condition of the class, and has used questions to get them to decide on a particular moment for this segment to be realized and symbolized. This moment is the beginning. When Heathcote needs to move the drama on, she has at her fingertips all the segments of the subject she has thought of. She can select one of these and from it develop a new dramatic focus.

Getting the drama going and keeping it alive is not Heathcote's goal, however. She wants to use the drama to develop the boys. So the instant she can, she tries to drop the level to get at what is fundamental and human in this situation, not to make the outside of the drama or the development of the story better. Since drama is a means of using our experience to understand the experience of other people, Heathcote often stops the drama or enters it in role and drops its level, demanding reflection on what is happening. If the class can't at their present stage of development handle this reflection, Heathcote moves back into the events of the drama and looks for her next chance to drop the level. Perhaps she'll ask students to take turns telling each other how they feel about what's happening, or to think about the implications of what they've chosen to do. This deepening of the level of the drama is the one thing classes cannot manage without a teacher, and the one thing Heathcote is committed to effecting. Without this dropping to universal human experience, Heathcote sees no point in drama in education.

Let's see how this might work in the drama about pirates. The segmenting of the general subject might look like the one on the next page.

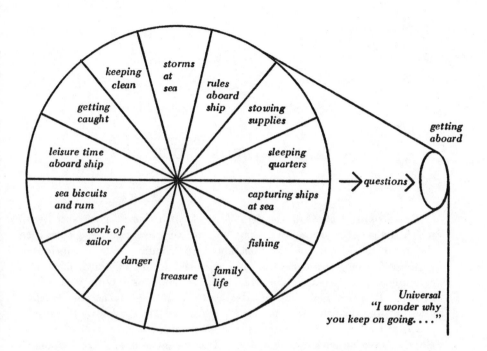

If the aspect of danger is chosen, then Heathcote, in the role of the sea captain, might begin the drama: "All right, you lubbers, if you can show me you·can get aboard my ship and hoist those sails without the usual complement of arms and legs, then you're OK as far as I'm concerned." And of course they can, because that's what they were asking for to begin with. Then, the first opportunity she gets, Heathcote will drop to the universal with a musing reflection, such as: "I wonder why you keep on going to sea when you know it's so dangerous?" With this, reflection and with it volume development have a chance to begin.*

In a theater performance, getting to the particular, the sharp dramatic focus, the small end of the funnel, is the end of the process. It is assumed that the audience can do the reflection for themselves. In a classroom drama, the end point is the discovery of universal human experience, the reaching of a deeper insight about the significance of the act or situation in the drama. In most cases classes cannot reach this endpoint without concentrated teacher guidance. The teacher can show them the significance of things that might otherwise seem insignificant. The teacher can move the class from a general idea to a dramatic focus and then to a universal.

---

*See Chapter 8, "Dropping to the Universal" for more on this.

6. LEADING THROUGH QUESTIONS

One striking feature of Heathcote's work with classes is the speed with which she gets the group drive going. Within a very few minutes, she has even the most recalcitrant or inert members contributing to a discussion or participating in group decisions. How does she do this? Through the use of carefully honed questions that are honest solicitations for the ideas of the group. I have never heard Heathcote ask a characteristic teacher-question—one loaded with the heavy implication that she knows the answer and is just asking to see whether the student knows it as well. Nor does she ask those phony questions that begin "Don't you think . . .?" or "Wouldn't you like to . . . ?" Heathcote's questions are real, and she does not reject the responses she gets. Whenever she asks a question, she is prepared to take in and deal with whatever comes.

Questioning is her most important tool. This doesn't mean she does not have other ways of getting the group drive going; she uses a wide range of nonverbal signals, symbols, and her own contributions of specific information or ideas. In using all of these stimuli, however, her goal is the same: to get the class involved in, committed to, and finally reflective about a drama that explores significant human experience.

Heathcote is sensitive to the difference between a threatening question and a freeing one. A threatening one is like the kind of question illustrated in John Holt's *How Children Fail.** The child tries to deal with this kind by guessing at the answer the teacher wants, the only *right* answer—which, of course, the child may not know. At this point, the pupil is too anxious about failing to think creatively about the range of responses that are possible. A freeing question, on the other hand, is one to which the teacher clearly signals there is no one right answer. He or she poses as a person curious and wondering and asks the class for help. In this way the teacher takes rank and status out of the question and frees the child to wonder, too: "I just can't

---

*Holt, John. *How Children Fail.* New York: Pitman, 1964. 181 pp.

imagine . . ."; "I've often wondered . . ."; "You know, it seems to me . . ."; or "I have never understood why . . ."

Since Heathcote uses statements as well as questions to evoke class response, for the purpose of this chapter I am defining a *question* the same way she does, as any verbal utterance that signals that a response is wanted. I have known Heathcote to use at least seven varieties of such utterances:

Questions that seek information or assess student interest, including

Those that define the moment

Those that stimulate research in books or other documents or call for asking adults for information

Questions that supply information

Branching questions, which call for a group decision between alternative courses of action

Questions that control the class

Questions that establish mood and feeling

Questions that establish belief

Questions that deepen insight.

The last three kinds of question will be discussed and illustrated in the next two chapters. Let's look now at the first four kinds, with examples of each that I have seen Heathcote use.

The first kind of questions seek information or assess student interest:

- What shall we do a play about?
- What must you take with you?
- What are we going to do about it?
- Where is the door to the rocket?
- What things shall we take with us from the wreck of the plane?
- How many horses do we need?
- What kind of food do you want to take with us?
- Where would you like the magic carpet to take us?
- What jewels do you want to steal?
- How should we plan the robbery?
- What part of that story is the most interesting?
- Where did the assassin come from?
- Do you remember the way we finally got our water problem solved, when we organized it?
- Do you remember what it was like the first day we arrived in this land?
- By that suggestion, are you asking to be scared?

In asking a question to assess student interest, keep the wording as bland and broad as possible without overstepping the boundary into vagueness. You will know if you have crossed this line because the class will be bewildered as to how to respond.

Heathcote typically begins a drama session by asking the class for as much information as is consistent with her teaching goal. Once, for example, she set about to help a group of nine- and ten-year-olds understand the meaning of the words: "A nation is as strong as the spirit of the people who make it." She wrote the words on the blackboard and began by asking what they meant. Then she asked the children to help her decide how they could make those words come alive in a drama.

All through a drama Heathcote asks questions which are requests for information. In this way she gets an idea of what the children are believing. If a girl is obviously cradling something in her arms, Heathcote will not ask, "Is your baby well?" but rather, "May I help you with that burden?" Thus she lets the child tell her what she is carrying as she responds to her offer. When you're seeking information, the goal is to keep from giving any clue as to what response you expect and to genuinely accept and act on whatever information you get.

A subgroup of the information-seeking questions defines the moment:

- Where might we all be together in this village?
- What time of day is it?
- Are we carrying anything?
- What will we all be doing?
- What is the weather like?
- Where do you think we should place the stove?
- How are we dressed?
- What do you suppose it is like on Mount Everest in a snowstorm?
- What problem is uppermost in our minds?
- Do you want to pack up your supplies in your rucksacks now?

The particulars of the moment must be precisely pinpointed at the beginning of the drama. It's no good if all the participants are not in the exact spot, at the same time of day, and under the same circumstances. If the class feels that a drama calls for half of them to be cowboys and the other half Indians, Heathcote pushes them to decide in which camp they want to be at first. If they decide to be in several different places at once, Heathcote immediately moves into a role that unites them. She might become a captain of a disabled space ship, radioing each of the places to see whether they could help her land. Heathcote's instinct is to ask questions that unite the group in time and problem, even though she grants their right to choose to be separated in place.

A second subgroup of information-seeking questions are those that stimulate research in books or other documents or call for asking adults for information. A class is encouraged to find the answer to this type of question either before or after the drama:

- What did coaches look like in those days?
- Where does Chicago get its water supply?
- I wonder what sort of reins a horse might have had in the French cavalry at that time?

- Do you have to pay for water in the United States?
- How did a Roman housewife dress?
- Exactly how big *is* a bed?
- Where does a Navajo woman do her baking?

When her goal is to stimulate a need for facts and an interest in texts, Heathcote deliberately sets up a situation in which the class needs to know more.* Although she doesn't start with a plethora of facts as a basis for drama, she will frequently let the emotion generated by the drama lead directly to research. At these times, her goal is to use the drama as a stimulus for fact gathering.

A second major category of questions is those that supply information:

- When you have collected and sterilized the medical supplies you need, may I please inspect them at this table?
- How many gallons of water should we take on the journey?
- If we do decide to use TNT here in this mine shaft, we'll have the problem of getting the men to safety, won't we?
- Does anyone know if we still have the canary we used to use to test for gas in the mine?
- Do you want to use my kiln when you're ready to fire your pot?
- Do we need a lookout?
- Have you found any of that manna God promised us?
- Would they have had a ceremony for something like this in those days?
- Have you heard the order to fire the retro-rockets yet?
- You're actually going to ride that tall horse?
- Well, why are you carrying your gun if you do not intend to move in anger against these people?
- Are we well supplied with blood plasma?

Instead of directly giving the class facts they need, Heathcote will focus clearly on the immediate problem or task they face and word her questions so that the decisions she poses have embedded in them a great deal of specific information. This makes the class feel as if they know without being told. She will call unfamiliar tools by name and pantomine their use. If Heathcote tells a girl who is a seaman on board to wash the sextant and the child starts to scrub something that is flat on the floor, she clearly has no idea what a sextant looks like. Then Heathcote hands her one, pantomiming its telescope shape with her hands and saying, "Leave the rest of the deck cleaning to the others, lad; can't you see this lens and these numbers are all dusty?" As she asks her question, she is supplying information by outlining the arc of a sixth of a circle mounted on the telescope.

A third kind of questions, called branching questions, call for a group decision between alternative courses of action:

---

*See Chapters 16 and 17, "Code Cracking: Literature and Language" and "Code-Cracking: Other Areas," for more on this.

- Shall we be in the past, present, or future?
- Shall we be all men or a group of both men and women?
- Do you want to be scared by the new world we'll find, or by the fact that we'll never get back home?
- Should we do a play about people in trouble or about helping people in trouble?
- Should we stay by the wreck and build a fire or go out and look for help?
- Are we in trouble because we are in danger or hungry?
- Do you want to be in the war or negotiating the peace?
- Do you want to be fighting with despair or hope?
- Should we look for food or clear the land of rocks first?
- Do you two want to decide this or should we call all the householders together for a vote?
- Are we going to camp here and risk an attack by a grizzly bear, or should we hike on even though we're exhausted?
- Would you like to plan a bit or trust me to start it?
- Would you like to be powerful and superior or friendly and sympathetic?

A large proportion of Heathcote's questions are branching ones: The drama cannot go in two directions, so which will it take? Of course, in any situation there are more than two possible courses of action; by limiting her branching question to two clear choices, however, Heathcote simplifies the decision for the class. Branching questions are particularly appropriate for groups that are socially immature and have difficulty answering more open-ended questions. The class's response determines what Heathcote calls the area of strike—the scope within which the drama can take place. Just as the knight in chess can guard only territory in a prescribed pattern of spaces defined by its position, so a drama can move only in a prescribed pattern defined by the answers to branching questions. Suppose Heathcote asks, "Should we begin before the christening ceremony or at the ceremony itself?" and the class answers, "Let's be dressing for the celebration." The area of strike will then be the dressing room; whatever interaction takes place will have to go on while the class is preparing for a ceremony.

The answers the class give to branching questions indicate what "kicks" they want. They will choose the area they want to "get on with," and a wise teacher will stay in that area as long as the student drive is strong.

A fourth kind of question is the ones that control the class:

- How can we keep the king from hearing us as we sneak past?
- How are we going to make ourselves look like soldiers?
- How could we set it up so I wouldn't have to scream at the orphans, "Get your room clean"?
- Are we too tired to start on the hunt today? Had we better rest first?

- Do you want to stop this drama now or go on with it?
- Stand up if you're ready to go with me single file into the submarine.
- Can you all hear what this person just suggested?
- Are you good at working together in pairs to saw down the trees?
- Will you help me write this on a scroll?
- Are you good workers?
- Can you manage to believe in that fishing line for a bit?
- Should there be any system for organizing this expedition?

Questions that control the class are the hardest to learn and the most important for teachers to know. The teacher must not use a controlling tone, of course. Instead, he or she should appear to be wondering aloud in a musing way or to be eager to get on with the action. This disguises the real motive, to get the class to exercise more self-discipline. Of course, branching questions, too, impose limits and thereby help control the class. The class's behavior—whatever it is—simply must be harnessed, put at the service of the drama. What this means is that you take the present condition of the class and figure out a way to channel their attitudes into a dramatic situation.

If Heathcote meets with a group of students who are obviously disgruntled and miffed about something, she knows it's no good to start with the implication that they should not feel that way. Instead, she acknowledges their feeling with a supportive question: "Have you just had a bad half hour?" Then, after they tell her what has upset them, she can suggest that they do a drama in which they are a group of people who are all upset about something. With a series of branching questions and controlling questions she can lead them to channel their negative attitudes into a cooperative venture, a drama in which the participants also have good reason to be angry.

Sometimes a controlling question can be in the form of a warning: "Are you sure you're ready to sign up for this mission? It won't be an easy one, you know!" "Do you think you can stay at a boring job all day long without stopping? What will you do with your mind while your hands are at work?" or "This won't be easy. We may not make it through the enemy line." This warning serves both to unite the group in their commitment and to give them a chance to fail without losing face.

In leading a class with questions, you are seldom in the characteristic teacher stance of the one-who-knows. Instead, you are candidly asking the child's viewpoint and interpretation of ideas, because this, and not your ideas, is what is significant for improvised drama. This is not to say that you don't also offer a viewpoint and interpretation, but yours is just another one. No view is judged right or wrong; each differs, however, just because any two people differ. You, the teacher, have more experience to draw upon, having lived longer and having a more-often-tested set of values. However, this does not give you the right to be anything more than the questioner and responder. You are not the determiner of what happens in the drama. It isn't that you don't lead, but simply that you lead by acting as guide, questioner, participant, and onlooker.

These roles take some getting used to for some teachers. Pedestals are comfortably distant places to stand on. But once you step down, you can discover the power of a new relationship. Heathcote likens it to that of the Renaissance painter with his school of students or of the sculptor Ivan Mestrovic working together with his students on one monument. The children offer the teacher their fresh way of looking at things, and the teacher offers the children the extra life experience of the adult. This is of great advantage to both. It frees children to bring their real selves to the situation. In so doing, it releases the energy they all too often channel into trying to hide their true feelings and give the teacher what they have learned is expected. It frees the teacher to be natural and relaxed, unencumbered by the unrealistic and impossible burden of being "all-knowing." Each recognizes the strength of the other in the relationship. Controls come out of mutual respect and the class's willingness to respond responsibly to controlling questions, because they are committed to a work which they see is clearly theirs and which matters to both them and the teacher.

7. BUILDING BELIEF

The first thing Dorothy Heathcote goes for in getting a drama started is belief—her own as well as that of the class.* Everyone involved must at least try to accept "the one Big Lie": that we are at this moment living at life rate in an agreed-upon place, time, and circumstance and are together facing the same problem. She doesn't say, "Pretend with me. . .," "Let's fantasize. . .," or "Can you imagine. . .?" Instead, she says something like, "I can believe in this knife and this carrot. Can you?" Heathcote admits this kind of believing is not easy to jump into, but it is crucial to the success of the drama. She sympathizes with those who find a situation preposterous, who reveal their nervousness by giggling and casting helpless glances at one another. "I know this is not easy for you, but try not to spoil it for the rest of us. It may be too soon for you to believe, but watch a while and see if you can find your own way into the life of this village later."

Whenever Heathcote finds the class is distracted by one person's disbelief, she stops the drama and works on that one person's problem. For example, in one group of six-year-olds there was a boy who kept giving the rest of the class signals of his own disbelief, largely with glances which were skeptical and scoffing. Heathcote concentrated on him. "I'm going to bring out a big horse now; do you think you'll be able to believe it?"

She went out of the room and came back with her hands on reins that came from a horse's head as far above hers as an ordinary horse's head would be above the heads of those six-year-olds. The right proportion was what she wanted to make real, not the actual size. No good, though. The boy said scornfully, "There's no horse there." Then she appealed to the group to help him see it as she held firmly onto the reins and reached up to pat the horse's neck.

"What a pity we can't get on with the play because you don't see my horse," she shrugged. His classmates started describing the horse that they by

---

*See Chapter 19, "Teacher Training," for ways she helps adults develop their own belief.

this time could see. "Let's have another go, eh?" coaxed Heathcote. "He's black and white with hooves as black as ink." The boy could feel the class's pressure on him. "We can't get this saddle on. Can you help us?" Finally the boy was convinced he had more to lose by not accepting that horse than by at least trying to see it. Then Heathcote suggested to the class that he be the one to lead the horse, since the drama was harder for him; this he gladly did. As she carefully handed him the reins, one at a time, drawing her hand down the long length of each, he got the recognition he was seeking, and the drama was no longer destroyed by his problem of disbelief.

The one Big Lie is like the well mixed paints in an art class. Without it, there is no suitable material from which to form the drama. Instead, there is a silliness and self-consciousness that comes from the two big problems class-room drama poses: the students themselves and the belief they bring to the situation are the essential material, and the rules of making a drama work are very difficult to perceive. When paint runs, it's clear the mixture is not right. When a drama falls apart, the class's mix of belief, commitment, awareness of each other in space, and focus on task is harder to look at, but it is just as fundamental for the success of the work as paint.

To get belief, Heathcote simplifies a situation to the attitude a person in it might hold. She might ask a class, "Do you have any idea how this bloke might be feeling as he steps up to knock on that door? Who can help us?" Suppose a little girl volunteers. Heathcote asks her not to assume an elaborate character, but merely to be willing to stand there on those steps just for the present. This way the brave volunteer doesn't have to commit herself beyond that initial stance. In most cases her belief will expand as she stands there; before she knows it, she'll be choosing to go on and enter the door when it is opened. However, Heathcote has left her a way out, and she knows it. After all, she only volunteered to knock on the door. This concentration on one thing—attitude—is not in the same tradition as most creative dramatics work in the United States. Teachers here tend to start by developing a character as fully as possible, elaborating a setting, and often deciding on the outline of a plot as well—all before the drama begins.

Except when she has chosen to work in a curriculum area that implies a more explicit direction, Heathcote starts with identification only. Because her focus is on the inner experience, the feeling, she feels no urgency to get into action. Identification can take place as effectively in a discussion as in an improvisation.

Sometimes she will begin with a few simple actions, like donning helmets or sitting astride motorcycles with feet wide apart and a firm grip on the handlebars. Class members need only to know how they are going to get that motorcycle started, which way it is leaning when stopped, where the accelerator is, where the brake is. Whether they end up with an image that accurately reflects a real motorcycle is not important; what is, is that each person believes in the machine, gets the feel of its weight and power. After this brief, kinesthetic identification, the motorcycle gang might sit on their machines and carry on the drama solely at the discussion level for a long time before they are ready to balance the standing cycles, rev up the engines, and take off.

All a classroom drama normally has to work with are space and bodies—albeit living, moving, breathing, feeling bodies. Belief has to do the rest. If students are to be a motorcycle gang traveling together, it will probably help their belief if they position themselves in relation to one another in such a way that they are headed in the same direction, two abreast. The teacher will probably need to help the students deal with the limitations of the class space (no classroom is without some limitation) so that it can most effectively lend itself to the drama.

On many occasions I have seen Heathcote spend a full half hour asking questions of a class to examine the life of a particular group before they together assume the attitude of these people at a specific moment in time. This discussion is not just a lead-in to the important thing, the drama; it is a significant part of the whole experience. It is where identification begins. Of course, Heathcote also stops the drama frequently to get to reflection and a discussion of implications.* It is these moments of reflection that most mark-edly set her work off from that of most American creative dramatics teachers.

Why doesn't Heathcote discuss or develop an idea of who each character is before the drama begins? She explains it this way. To develop a character first is to begin from outside a person. She starts from within, trying to get every child to put something directly personal into the role from the very beginning and gradually to realize and to reflect on the attitude the role is eliciting. She lets each one bring as much of the purely personal into the situation as is consistent with the attitude being projected. She goes on to suggest that we are known to one another only by the attitudes we reveal. She affirms that she will never thoroughly know her character; she only slowly learns about it by looking at the attitudes that come naturally to her, or that she has to fight to get. So when she begins a drama, she is solely concerned that people try to assume a single attitude. At first this may be a very crude, a simple attitude, but as people mature, they win more and more subtle attitudes and become more aware of the effects of these on others.

Whatever the top layer of the drama might be, Heathcote is always tunneling beneath the surface to get the belief going and the attitude right. In the last chapter we showed how she sought information from the class through questions. By taking the students' answers seriously, she shows respect for whatever they can at the moment contribute. Anything they try is better than not trying, so Heathcote takes whatever suggestions come and upgrades them by repeating them, commenting upon them, acting on them.

*See the next chapter for more on this.

Whatever students suggest brings with it their involvement, feeling, and eventually commitment as well. By acting on this, Heathcote makes sure she captures the heart of the matter, the feeling, which is what makes the drama vital. Out of this the children can spin threads into an intricate net of elaboration, a web of their own making in which they can catch new experience and relate it to the center. All good teachers of young children instinctively stimulate the child's elaboration of experience in art, language, movement, drama. Far too often, teachers of older students irrelevantly paste extrapolations of experience onto the outside of their students. The students could discover these extrapolations for themselves, making them their own, if only they were allowed ample time to spin out their own elaborations. Heathcote feels that the technique of elaborating probably contributes more than anything else to the process of the student's becoming a mature person.

With the assumption of attitude and belief comes identification. Once a class identifies with the people in a drama, their drive is released, and the situation becomes what Heathcote terms "educationally explosive." The subjective world of the students becomes sufficiently a part of the class task that the drama can be extended and exploited. The learners can then "fare forward" into new insights and fresh soundings of the situation in which they find themselves.

Questions that help students identify may be those that particularize their task, such as: "Which is your stall in the marketplace?" They may be branching questions that demand a decision involving identification, such as: "Do you want to be the skipper or one of the crew?" The main thing is to be sure the situation the child is trying to enter has something in it that latches onto something in the child. The child who perceives an entire scene to be strange and outside all previous experience will not be able to get inside it and make sense of it. For example, a child who is told to be a blacksmith in a medieval market may well be overwhelmed by the complexity of a task that seems impossible to visualize. On the other hand, a child who volunteers to sell eggs and milk can bring to the job what he or she knows about those products and how they have to be stored and handled. If the child starts by having them refrigerated, the teacher doesn't interfere as long as it doesn't bother another class member. There's time after the drama is over to discuss any anachronism. The child's believing in the eggs and milk and identifying with their vendor is what matters first. Nor does it matter if half the class volunteers to sell milk and eggs the first day. Once they believe, they will be more likely to be able to make their market more authentic and to assume other roles that call for more understanding.

Another way to internalize belief in the Big Lie is through movement, miming the actions of the participants. A shy child can go through the motions of selling two eggs without having to come forth with much language just yet. In one drama a class decided on a banquet, but at first they had real trouble believing. Heathcote moved very slowly to establish belief, bringing in platters of food one by one until all the children were won over to seeing each entree as it came in. As they passed the turkey, poured the wine, buttered their rolls, or asked for salt, they began to forget themselves in the drama. Before the end of the period, they were so well into that banquet that they could accept as real the problem of a starving Italian farmer who lived on only four olives and a quarter of a pound of bread a day. At this point, they had transcended their need for movement and for imagined concrete objects. They were now able to believe that which they learned about only through their ears.

In another drama the class decided they were stranded in a boat without sails. Heathcote in role asked them, "Have you any means at all of getting somewhere?"

"We could paddle with our shoes," they said. This suggestion, Heathcote saw, would lend itself to unison movement that would help crystalize belief.

"Are you sure that that will work?" she asked. "Show me how you do it, and I will fit in, using my shoes." So they began to paddle. She asked if someone could supply a rhythm, and a child eagerly did. As they paddled to his chant, they began to genuinely believe in that boat and in those shoes.

Sometimes Heathcote begins a drama with concrete objects—a wedding ring, an old musket, a rare coin, a medal, a pair of tiny glass slippers, a letter yellowed with age, a skull—to arrest the attention of the group and help their belief. For example, she once used two Viking chess pieces, carved in the twelfth century—a king and a queen sitting on handsome, ornate thrones. She showed them to a group of 5- to 7-year-olds, saying, "I don't seem to be able to stop the Queen from crying." Because the queen's face was sad, the children soon accepted her as real. They decided she was sad because she had lost her baby, and they set out to find it for her.

For another group of children, getting dressed in paper, plastic, or cloth costumes might be just the concrete experience they need to get their belief going. When three boys who were to travel as the Magi decided they needed camels, Heathcote helped them use what was at hand to make the animals. They put chairs on tables and covered them with blankets and P.E. mats to make appropriate humps. They painted cardboard cartons for heads. Heathcote reminded them that "a man who journeys takes those things with him that he dare not leave behind," so they collected lots of paper towel packets—the only handy item they could find to suit the purpose—and labeled them "food for the journey," "water for the journey," "tent," "instruments," "gold for Jesus," "frankincense," "myrrh." These they roped in large clusters onto their camels, and their journey could begin.

At other times Heathcote uses photographs, paintings, or art objects. To help children understand the meaning of the words, "A nation is as strong as the spirit of the people who make it," she stapled onto sheets of typing paper about fifty portraits from *The Family of Man*.* When the group of about twenty-five children arrived, she asked each of them to select one of the pictures and become that person in the drama.

In some classrooms Heathcote uses paper and paint, or if not that, just a blackboard to help the class visualize the drama. For example, a group of elementary children who are dramatizing the story of Demeter and Persephone may have trouble visualizing the retinue of Pluto. Heathcote will have them spend a class period or two creating a great mural of what they think the underworld is like. In the process the slime on the wall, the black marble throne, the 12 black horses in their stalls of coal all help make Pluto grow.

If a group of children are going to the moon, they draw a picture of the rocket, labeling the various compartments. If they're on a sailing ship, they draw a model of it on the board. If they are turning themselves into a settlement of colonists, they draw a diagram of their village. One by one, a representative of each household goes to the board and draws in that family's farm, labeling it with the initials of the children who live there. Heathcote asks where they get water, and they decide they have a well. This is shown by the picture of a pail in the center of the village. Then the children draw in their own paths. Heathcote is pleased when all of them lead to the well, because this makes the water important and provides a central place to unite the colonists. Then the villagers put their jobs beside their initials, strengthening their identification as colonists. Through their jobs, they each now have their own way into the drama.

Then Heathcote asks the children to go into their houses, look out the window, and tell what is out there, as far as the eye can see. They tell her about the trees and fields, valleys and hills. These she draws, so they end up with a map like this, but with initials and jobs listed beside each house:

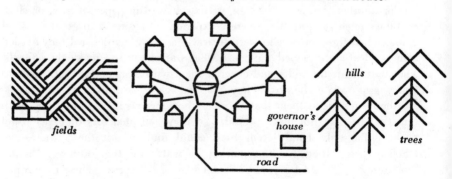

---

*Steichen, Edward. *The Family of Man.* New York: Museum of Modern Art, 1955. 207 pp.

Then Heathcote puts in the road which goes past the door of the governor and tax collector, a role she has assumed for herself. Not only has the drawing on the board helped the class's belief; it has planted the seeds of tension as well.

In another drama Heathcote has trouble getting three groups of 10- and 11-year-olds to believe in the countries they have chosen to be in. She asks each group to list on the board three things their nation needs to survive. She gets these lists:

Africa	Germany	The Bahamas
shelter	food	fishing
land	money	fruit
food	health	tourists

She reads the lists aloud, upgrading each contribution by her serious and uncritical tone. Then she asks, "What three things does your nation prize above money?" They write:

Africa	Germany	The Bahamas
people	people	people
animals	oil	animals
oil	water	trees

Then comes a third question: "What three things will you try to do for your people this year?" The responses are:

Africa	Germany	The Bahamas
transportation	winning	keep peace
homes	land	get back tourists
(they cannot think	entertainment	fight sickness in
of a third)		people

Then she asks whether a flag tells something of what a nation stands for. The children nod. "Could you design a flag that would help me recognize some of what your nation stands for?" She then gives them white and colored paper, scissors, paste, and magic markers, and they go to work, spending most of the hour painstakingly putting together elaborate flags of their countries. The girls, who comprise the group from the Bahamas, cut out paper flowers; the black boys, who have chosen to make up the African nation, draw animals onto their white flag; and the white boys, who are Germans, draw cars and factories. They begin to believe in their countries through a concrete task that is not drama but contributes to the heart of it—the identification. The flag is a concrete symbol for what they are.

After a class does a drawing, Heathcote might get at implications by asking them what the drawing says to them. A rocket might say power; a sailing ship, loneliness; a colonial settlement, neighbors. Thus the drawing becomes a symbol of the life even if, unlike the flag, it is not explicitly called a symbol.

Because it is with the energy of feelings that belief is fashioned, Heathcote often begins with what she calls a pudding of feelings. "A drama is a pudding of three types of feelings; some are positive; some negative; and some in-between, neither good nor bad but giving rise to action. These last are the states of being that cause us to do certain things." Then she puts on the board in three columns all the feelings the children can think of that illustrate each of the three types. One group of fourth and fifth graders came up with the following list:

Good feelings	Upsetting feelings	States of being
happiness	anger	concern
anticipation	worry	responsibility
excitement	hatred	interest
job	sorrow	
	being scared	
	being afraid	

The words the children used were not always nouns, but Heathcote translated what they told her as she listed them on the board. For example, when a boy volunteered that "fooling around" was a good feeling, Heathcote suggested that this might be happiness. The boy agreed. Another suggested that one upsetting feeling was "being yelled at;" she pushed for what the feeling would be called. Another child volunteered "angry." After someone had suggested "scared," one girl added "afraid." Her neighbor corrected her, "That's the same thing as 'scared.' " In a typical move to upgrade every contribution, Heathcote said, " 'Afraid' may be the same thing but it may be a bit more. 'Scared' may lead you to being afraid, really frightened." She put up both words.

Then she asked the class to choose one feeling from each list for the drama. They chose concern, anger, and happiness and decided to show these feelings in that order. She asked them who they were and what they were concerned about. They decided to be Americans concerned about an epidemic in Russia. Before long, they had turned themselves into a medical team that was not only concerned about that epidemic, but also determined to get to Russia with their medical supplies to help. Heatcote stopped the drama from time to time to ask them whether they were keeping the concern going. As the team packed their bags, each member told her what special equipment or supplies she or he was taking and how these would help in an epidemic. The feeling of concern led the children to assume an appropriate attitude for members of a medical team on an important mission. When this team got to Russia, Heathcote pressed to keep the concern going. She did not worry about facts of Russian culture, for that was external to the heart of the drama—the belief of the class.

8. DROPPING TO THE UNIVERSAL

In previous chapters I have often referred to a process Heathcote calls "dropping to the universal" in human experience. Everything she does has this as its goal; she uses what is happening in the drama as an occasion to remind the group that all through time people have found themselves in the position they are in at that moment, that there is an underlying significance to this event which can be recognized by examining its implications. In a sense, dropping to the universal is like using the Brotherhoods Code. Reflecting on the universal, however, is something Heathcote gets a class to do for themselves, to help them identify with a wider range of other human beings throughout time, whereas using the Brotherhoods Code is her own way of finding material for her next drama.*

As noted in the last chapter, Heathcote begins by building belief; once that is firmly established, she moves towards depth of insight about the experience. Whenever possible, she tries to move the class to a moment of awe—or if not that, a moment of new awareness. True gut-level drama has to do with what you at your deepest level want to know about what it is to be human. How would you act under pressure? Do you change in an extremity? What can you discover about yourself as you respond to a threatening difficulty? What do you find you must have, you cannot live without? In what way are you like all people who have faced this situation? Your response to this last question is a plumb line from the drama to the universal.

The universal is the wellspring, the source of human understanding. Instead of starting with this source, however, drama, like all art, starts with a very carefully selected, precise and particular, unrepeatable instance—one that then acquires significance as it reverberates in the chambers of the universal. For most classes, the teacher needs to sensitize students to feeling this resonance, which takes them not out of themselves, but rather more fully into themselves, and into the experiences of the real world as well as those of

---

*See Chapter 4, "Finding Material Through Brotherhoods."

the drama. In our real lives, we seldom stop for this kind of pondering; in drama Heathcote deliberately makes time for it. Such reflection is the only thing that makes drama worth the doing. If you cannot increase reflective power in people, you might as well not teach, because reflection is the only thing that in the long run changes anybody.

With great conviction Heathcote urges teachers to train themselves to look for the implications that lie beyond the actual work of the drama—or beyond real life situations, for that matter. For example, every artifact implies a maker; every tool, a task; every gesture, a feeling; every action, a goal; every word, an experience; every decision, a value. As you learn to see in this reflective way, you find you have in any environment, no matter how barren, a starting point for drama. Any artifact, then, can be a point of beginning. The drama that grows is always a group examination of what that beginning implies.

In order to attend to the implications of what a class begins with or chooses to do, you must learn to phase out of your own consciousness any evaluation of the students' behavior or values. No students, no matter how poor their social health, should be rejected in your mind. Instead, you must watch keenly and respond to them as they are at the moment, even as you work to find a new way to extend the range of their behavior. Any idea they give you can be viewed as a rough stone which, through the drama, you can facet and polish as a gem so that it can reflect the universal.

Thus, even the shallowest beginning can give rise to deeper thinking. Whatever the class chooses can serve for reflection. For example, if a group of children decide to have a wizard with three legs and six ears, because it's fun to imagine such a creature, Heathcote will see to it that he is still motivated by human goals and values that the children will recognize as believable and true. Unless that wizard operates in a way that can evoke at least a temporary identification, the children cannot be stretched to expand their understanding of human experience.

Although you plan to deepen the level whenever possible, you can never predict when that will happen. Often the class is not ready to pick up on your probes to a deeper level, but you keep trying. Not to interfere with the class's drama, not to try to deepen the level when you sense a way to do so, is to deny the class the power of your adulthood. Although you are open to accepting the class's ideas and to making them work, in so doing you by no means abdicate your responsibility to lead them into deeper reflection whenever possible.

In this chapter we shall consider six ploys Heathcote uses to deepen the level: stopping the drama to reflect; slowing the pace within the drama; imposing rituals; classifying responses of the class and giving them back to the class in categories that reveal their implications; interjecting probes and presses; and using symbols.

Heathcote often stops the drama for reflection. You have seen how she did this in the drama of *The Dreamer* at the moment of the ship's leaving the harbor. Admittedly, drama is more difficult than the other arts to reflect upon or contemplate in the classroom because the product—the drama itself—cannot be held up and looked at as can a painting, sculpture, or poem. By the time the participants are reflecting on it, the drama has vanished into air.

When Heathcote stops the drama, she'll ask a question like, "How are you feeling now?" She often goes around from person to person asking what each has been feeling. As these inner responses are shared, new depths are sounded. For example, one time when a group was doing a drama about a voyage into outer space, a girl who was in role as one of the astronauts' wives told the group that she had trouble getting through her usual morning routines. "I forgot to put butter on the twins' sandwiches because I was thinking about my husband and was feeling all upset."

Heathcote echoed her attitude: "Our feelings do seem to interfere with our actions sometimes." Then she pressed for more depth. "Can you find language or words to tell us what you were feeling?"

"I'm not sure. I was mixed up, sort of. I felt proud he was going, and thought how the twins would see their Daddy kind of like a hero. I thought I'd better tell them, like Mama tells me, not to brag out loud, but just be glad inside that he's their Daddy. Then, suddenly, I felt sad and thought, what if he doesn't come back? How awful it would be if they didn't have a big, wonderful Daddy at all. We'd miss him terrible. Our space here would be awful—like that out there. I can't really say what I felt. It was hollow and sort of achey. Then I wished the children would come home, and I went to the window to look out for them."

As participants look at what they've lived through and felt on the inside, they gain the double effect of knowing internally and reflecting on the product of their knowing. Learning to distance oneself from the emotion of the moment without denying the fullness of the feeling is a sound mental health strategy. Reflection is what makes the knowing something that can be touched and assimilated for later use. What the right hemisphere of the brain has pulled together, the left hemisphere analyzes and codifies and stores.[*] This process is the education of feeling. Feeling without reflection may simply be experienced and forgotten; with reflection it can become an insight, an understanding, that makes possible later modification of behavior in the real world. One has learned something of the nature of feelings and the now predictable consequences of expressing these feelings. One has also learned how to transcend the personal *feeling* of, say, fear, and think about fear itself. Stopping to reflect at the height of the action is possible in drama, but very difficult in real life.

---

*See Chapter 14, "The Left Hand of Knowing."

Heathcote's tendency is to stop the drama not when it's faltering, but when it is going well. This is because there is no risk that the dramatic focus cannot be readily refound after a pause to look at it, enthuse about it, challenge it, deepen it, and upgrade it. At these pauses, Heathcote usually uplifts the language, summarizing in classic rather than domestic language to give significance to her words.*

Heathcote's reason for stopping the drama is never to preach or moralize to the class. This does not mean that she does not frequently introduce a moral element (no human being can ever quite give up moralizing), but she does it in a musing and not a didactic tone, so that the class often picks this up and responds with affirmations of their own values. Here are some of her characteristic musings:

"I wonder why anyone would want to kill a baby?"

"Why do you suppose people decide to set up schools?"

"A scaler of mountains is a little like a fly, isn't he?"

"I wonder why we need leaders of tribes and nations, why throughout history people have accorded some persons power?"

"I wonder what makes a man want to go to the moon?"

"How does an astronaut feel, I wonder? Is he thinking about where he is, or is he too busy monitoring all his equipment to worry about that?"

"Isn't it interesting that the thing we hold in common is that we all have money to get things that are not money?"

"It seems that there are some things we simply cannot explain; their mystery defies our attempts to understand, doesn't it?"

"How many women in childbirth must have wished for the old gods, knowing it was forbidden and yet saying, 'Just now it's too important to worry about that.' "

"It seems there are some things we simply have to submit to because the time has come."

"A village isn't just a place; it's a symbol of the lives of people, isn't it?"

A second strategy for getting deeper, one Heathcote uses in every drama she leads, is to slow the pace to provide a pressure for a long enough time that a transformation within the children can take place. Just as it takes pressure and time for coal within the earth to shine forth as diamond, so it is with human insight. It never comes lightly or quickly, although we may see it in a flash. When a drama stays in the same place long enough and under enough pressure, experience can be explored. To slow pace, you have to face the fact that you must move against the class's natural impulse, which is usually towards action, not reflection. This does not mean you relax the tension. Just the opposite; as the pace slows, the tension increases. The action the class seeks is held off while they sense more and more fully what it is to anticipate it. If the bear is killed, the wall scaled, the journey completed, the witches'

---

*See Chapter 15, "Classifying Drama," for more illustrations of this.

brew concocted, or the great chief buried too quickly, the significance of the act is lost. One of the hallmarks of Heathcote's teaching is her patient, deliberate, solid holding-back of action. She is unconcerned if there are long, quiet pauses. In fact, she builds towards these; she never rushes for the sake of her adult observers. Her pace is unhurried and child centered.

When a group of adventurers are climbing high in the Andes, Heathcote slows them to the pace of the actual act they are dramatizing with words like these: "Go slowly now, hand over hand; your breath comes in deep, slow pants, your legs are weary. You are very high on a steep and dangerous ledge. See if you can get the great size of the mountain and the littleness of men as you let this mountain slowly take you higher and higher, up away from the world you know. You sense you are in a place that is different. Give yourself time to feel it."

Often she will ask travelers to stop for the night, to keep on with their concern or goal, but to rest just for now. As they stretch out and pause, watching the flames of their campfire, she asks them to reflect on their mission, to think or dream about what they are experiencing. This is an effective means of slowing pace and cutting out the chatter that precludes individual pondering.

Before a moon rocket blasts off, the astronauts rest in their cramped space capsules and wait for the countdown. Heathcote says in a low, solemn tone, "Some people are chosen to be very special. They train themselves to do difficult work that has never been done before. All through time people have stretched themselves to do new things, to achieve something that no one else has yet mastered."

Whenever a significant event happens in a drama, Heathcote, often in role as one of the participants, will slow the pace and reflect aloud. When a group of nine- and ten-year-olds finally succeed in killing a mountain lion that has been threatening their village, Heathcote won't let them stop with a feeling of relief. She has them carry the lion to the top of the cliff and all stand and look at him. After a pause she muses, "I have never looked at a lion like this before. He's dead now, strong and powerful, but dead. Look at his paws. Are his claws out or sheathed in death?" Their answers tell her what they see. "Is there anything about this lion that you can see only in death?" By now they believe enough to see new dimensions. The dead lion begins to work symbolically in this moment of reflection that is within, not outside of, the drama.

I have watched Heathcote dramatize two different burials—one at the pace the children chose, and the other at a much slower rate which she imposed. The former was simply a perfunctory going through the motions of digging a hole and carrying one of the girls to it. She had been killed by a British soldier who was guarding the flag in the Boston riots. Before the entire village had time to respond to the horror of the murder of one of their children, the gravediggers were at work. Heathcote chose not to stop this, so there was no reflection, no plumb line to the universal. Most groups of children need a teacher to slow the pace if they are to get to the reflection.

The second burial took a full 30 minutes. In a branching question, Heathcote warned the class (the same group that later killed the mountain lion): "Do you want to do the funeral now or do you want to have it be after this man, Walt Buckeye, is buried?" They chose to do the funeral. The dead man's mother wept softly into her hands as the villagers stood beside the body. When the children tried to rush Heathcote to the cemetery, she refused to go along. She chose to sit beside the body and invited the others to join her. When they resisted, she came out of role: "Stop! This man won't be buried until we give him a life." Then, less harshly, "It's very hard to invent a life for a man, but let's see what we can remember about Walt Buckeye." Then she went back into role as a member of the community, musing, "I wonder why he was off on his own when that mountain lion mauled him? He always was a bit of a dreamer, wasn't he?"

The class followed her lead. His mother said, "I remember when I told him to get something for me, he'd always forget what it was."

"I remember his smile."

"He was always nice."

"He always acted like a gentleman."

"And he always helped people; he did what he could. I wonder why he was on his own up there on the mountain today?"

"Probably he didn't feel he wanted to bother anyone else with his problems."

"Probably he was thinking his own thoughts."

Heathcote said with the smile of a sudden memory, "Do you remember the time he went to market and lost your money on the way?"

His mother said quickly, "I scolded him when he did that."

"I know. We all went looking for it then." Thus, Walt Buckeye's life took shape; the children were ready to slowly dig the grave and gather the flowers for the funeral.

Heathcote came out of role to ask the dead man if he could trust his friends to carry him. Then six of them bent over to take up the body and start the long journey down the mountain to the burial ground. Heathcote urged them not to start walking with him until they were sure they had him securely and could walk with a kind of dignity. She asked his mother, who had not left her place beside the body, to come to the edge of the grave and wait for the men to bring his body the long way down the mountain.

Pallbearing was too much for the boys. They felt foolish and showed it. They kept letting the body slip and leaning over to recover it. Immediately, Heathcote came out of role: "Hold it a minute. I don't believe you care about this, so unless you can prove you care, I'm going to stop it. Either it is a funeral or it isn't a funeral. If you want a funeral, you'll have to do it right; it's no good just playacting! You're going to have to stop fiddling and get down that valley so that everyone can see you believe it. The instant it isn't real, it stops." In a softer tone, she added, "I can believe in it; I can believe in the flowers and in that cross you have made to mark the grave." Looking from child to child, "Can you? Can you? Can you?" She looked at the men carrying the body, and they nodded. "This time, see if you can sustain it longer," she told them. Then, musingly, "Everybody wonders about dying. Do you ever wonder about it?"

Amid the nods and uh-huh's came a hesitant voice, "I—I don't know how it feels."

"I don't know how it feels either; nobody knows. And some of the greatest plays in the world have been done about dying. It makes you wonder why people are always making plays about dying. There must be some reason for it, mustn't there?" Then, bringing them back to their challenge, Heathcote went on, "If we're going to be in this tradition, we will do it right. Otherwise, we're not doing it." Then she looked right at the pallbearers and repeated, "See if you can sustain it this time." They started again the long way down the mountain; now every back was erect and every eye straight ahead. This had become a funeral procession inside those boys' minds.

So far we have seen how Heathcote stops the drama and how she slows the pace. Now let's look at a third strategy for dropping the level of the drama: the use of rituals. This ploy serves to slow the pace and at the same time demand a response of each participant. It constitutes a pressure to reaffirm individual commitment to the drama.

Heathcote employs two types of rituals in drama: the nonverbal acts in which everyone usually participates simultaneously, and the verbal rituals which call for a response from each person in turn. These verbal rituals may have a nonverbal component, of course, but they differ from the nonverbal ceremonies in which all act together.

An example of a ceremony is the planting of the United States flag on the moon. Beside the flag a group of six-year-olds solemnly buried a message they had written for the next visitors. Each child took a turn shoveling dirt over the message. Then they stood back and sang "My Country, 'Tis of Thee" as they looked at the flag. When their moon rocket finally arrived back on earth, the adult observers acted as a welcoming party. Forming a receiving line, they shook the hand of each of the brave adventurers and congratulated each in turn on the successful mission. The event became significant through a ceremonial ritual

Nonverbal rituals need not be ceremonies, of course. Sometimes Heathcote will work towards depth by having the entire group move together in a ritualistic way to internalize the rhythm of experience. To help a group of mentally handicapped children understand the cycle of the seasons and the rhythm of growth, she had them plow the soil together while she supplied the words for what they were doing. At first, she signalled to them nonverbally while they slowly walked around in a circle, holding their hand plows. Then they listened to her words as they sowed the seed, taking it from sacks on their backs and flinging it out, continuing to walk in a wide circle. They reaped the grain, using long-handled scythes; they gathered it up and carried it on their backs; they winnowed it and stored it away in bins. All the while Heathcote provided the language for what they were beginning to understand with their bodies. The cycle of the seasons slowly became implanted in the right hemispheres of their brains.*

Whenever possible, Heathcote employs rituals in which she calls each person by name. For this reason, she likes a class which she doesn't know to wear name tags. When she faced the problem of getting a group of un-committed, educationally subnormal teenagers involved in a drama about Stone Age people, she began by asking, "Could you catch a fish if I gave you a line?" They assured her they could, so she went to each student and formally called him or her by name as she handed over a length of fishing line. This slow ritual gave her a chance to look each person firmly in the eye, to touch each person's hand, and to signal her seriousness about the belief as she did so. Another time she used ritual with the group of six-year-olds on the moon trip. As they arrived for the second session of the drama, she handed each of them a card like this:

```
┌─────────────────────────┐
│  The Child's Name       │
│  ASTRONAUT              │
└─────────────────────────┘
```

Then , when they were all assembled, she began the drama: "Do you have your credentials? Is there a card that says you have been through the training and are now an astronaut?" The ritual of card-giving had upgraded each child's status and helped belief.

Let's look now at the rituals that evoke words. After Heathcote asks a group to go off and find jobs for themselves—aboard the space ship, in the factory, in the mine—she will stop in a few minutes to ask each person in turn, "What are you responsible for?" She treats each contribution with respect, often repeating what the child has said to give it volume and importance. She never denigrates any statement, even the one that is simply a lame repetition of what another child has already said. This way she avoids building competitiveness in children. Every person has an equal chance to impress her; she is clearly not comparing one with the other. If a significant proportion of the class members don't know what their jobs are or have trouble describing them, Heathcote has them all go back to their tasks. Then

---

*See Chapters 13 and 14, "Movement" and "The Left Hand of Knowing."

she goes around and helps each one get on with it, largely with movement, not words. When she is sure each person has a feel for the job, she will stop again for another ritual, this time asking perhaps, "How is your work going?" She may change the face of the ritual by assuming the role of a roving reporter and coming in with her microphone. "Ladies and gentlemen, it is difficult for those of you in your homes and your cars to realize how demanding these jobs are. In just a few moments I shall be allowed to ask these people to tell you what they do." This kind of ritual is never boring, for each child feels the tension of knowing that his or her turn will come to be under pressure to verbalize.

One of the tensest rituals I've watched Heathcote lead was in a drama of the American Revolution. Heathcote in role as the governor of the colony calls the colonists one by one to pay their taxes. Each householder must decide whether the family has enough money for the tax, and if not, why not. So the children come one by one. The first girl says plaintively, "I had to buy bread for the children."

The governor is harsh. "You give your children far too much food. That's your trouble. You must be wasting bread."

"Maybe a child wants to eat more than one piece?" the mother asks in a pleading tone.

"I'll put you down as owing three pieces of silver. You owe one for last month and two more now. Is that understood?" The child shrinks away. Heathcote makes sure all the rest of the class can see what is going on; she asks them to keep quiet and keep thinking, as a rebel would have to do, storing evidence as they watch these people come one by one to pay their tax.

The next two colonists pay in full; then comes a tall, proud black girl. Heathcote senses her strong spirit and so presses her, "You! Have you the five crowns?"

"No!" she says defiantly.

"You are taking a very high tone. Why have you not the five crowns?"

"Because I need them for other things besides King George," she says with a sneer.

"My dear woman, there is nothing more important than His Majesty! I will ask you to remember that. What do you mean there are more important things?" The woman stands tall and silent. "Come on, tell me! What have you spent the money on?"

"More important things," she says truculently, throwing her chin high.

"Such as, madame? Tell me!"

"I spent them on bread."

The governor responds sarcastically, "Oh, really! No doubt the finest white bread, the most expensive bread. You now owe five crowns, madame."

The defiance mounts after this brave child's confrontation. The governor concludes, "It is my misfortune to rule a colony that is lazy." One of the colonists reminds her that he has to arise at four and work until well after dark to feed his family and still pay the tax. She responds, "Getting up at four o'clock in the morning is only the proper and religious thing to do. You must rise with the sun, of course. Your first duty is to His Majesty, King George, then to your family." She won't let them off easily.

One man can pay only part of the tax because he hasn't enough time to keep up with the farm work. The governor challenges, "Really? Did it ever occur to you that some of your family could be out working?" The colonist reminds her they are too young. "They are four years old so they could be out helping you! I remind you a child of four is perfectly capable of doing work. Do you not realize that in England they work in the mines when they are six? I would advise you, sir, to have your family start helping you; see to it that they get put to work so you can pay this tax."

The next person who pays in full gets a congratulation, "Ah, this is a change. Lay it on the table. You see, citizens of New Bristol, some of your neighbors are capable of proper work. Thank you, madame. What a relief it is to find someone who places pride ahead of greed." Finally Ken, a somewhat flippant class leader, comes to the governor's table. "Your taxes, please."

"No!"

"You mean you cannot or you will not?"

"I will not!"

"You will not, sir? Do you realize what this means?"

"Yep!"

"Very well, you will be detained at His Majesty's pleasure," she says, elevating the language. "Stay here!" She seats him with his back to the group, explaining that it is a sort of prison room. She makes sure, however, that he can hear the rest of the ritual so his rebellious spirit continues to be fed by the plight of his fellow colonists.

She has to remind the next taxpayer of who he is when he asks petulantly, "Why should I pay you anything to keep you and your British guards around here?"

"You cannot talk that way. You are addressing the representative of the king, your own king."

"My own king?" he asks, taken aback by a fact he had never before assimilated.

"Your own king!"

"I'd rather have Samuel Adams as my king!"

"I've heard of this Samuel Adams. You are setting up this Samuel Adams against the royal blood of King George III? Enough of this! Follow me."

"Where are you going?"

"Here," says the Governor firmly. "You wait until all these people have paid their taxes."

"What is this?"

"This is a prison! I trust you will find this accommodation comfortable." Then Heathcote goes back to the ritual of collecting the tax, a ritual that by now is coagulating the group against her and implanting the seeds of the rebellion that is to come. Heathcote the teacher has made it work by insisting that the colonists wait their turns in silence and listen to what the others are saying.*

Rituals like these help make the experience feel right, generate energy and drive, and at the same time, hold the potential for dropping the level to universal human experience.

A fourth strategy Heathcote consciously employs to drop the level of a drama is to quickly classify in her head the responses a class gives her and feed them back in categories that illuminate their implications. This process is a way of not denying any of the material a class gives, yet funneling it all into something so simple that they can manage to respond to it and gain insight about the meaning of what they have just said. Of course, if you accept only what you expect to hear, you have no need to classify it all; you have only to accept what fits into the framework you bring into the situation in the first place. However, if you are committed, as Heathcote is, to soliciting honest responses from the group and to dealing with everything they give you, then you have to learn to classify in order to pull it into a meaningful order.

The simplest type of classification is of objects. A question that leads to this might be, "Well, now, when we build this palace, what are we going to need?" The children are likely to give back what Heathcote calls a "shopping list," a set of unrelated items, their implications unrecognized. She might categorize these and feed back to them, "So we'll need things to make the palace strong and safe, things to make the palace beautiful, and things to represent the power of the king and queen. Right?" Not only has she shown them implications, but she has provided a way to divide the group into three discrete task forces to build the palace.

Another question that calls for classification of objects might be, "We're going to have to leave in a hurry; what must we not leave behind?" The answers to this question will be largely objects that are necessary for survival. If, on the other hand, you want answers that are more likely to be related to the heart, you ask, "What can't we leave behind? What things are personally of great value?" Thus, a single word in the phrasing of the question provides a totally different focus. If the group is an army, the question may well be, "What dare we not leave behind for the enemy to find?"

If the class has decided to be Separatists boarding the *Mayflower*, you might ask them to each bring along what they cannot leave behind. Suppose

---

*See page 201 in Chapter 17, "Code Cracking: Other Areas," for another verbal ritual of this group, in which each tells what freedoms they have won.

that in a ritual they tell you that they have brought their mother's picture, the family Bible, a glass jug of water, a prayer book, medicine, bandages, clothes, blankets, flour, a handbag, a sister's picture, and a little dog. You might quickly classify all this into private things and community ones, perhaps in role as a person of authority on the ship: "Where should we put the things that everybody can use? Will you bring over here those things you brought for the benefit of the community?" . . ."Now where will we put the private things?"

If you are facing the problem of abandoning a ship which has been locked in ice on a polar expedition, you may have to limit each survivor to one pound of personal items. When Sir Ernest Henry Shackleton faced this limitation, he tore the flyleaf from the Bible Queen Alexandra had given him and left the rest behind on his ice-locked ship. The items your explorers choose to take may well be classified into those that will help them keep from freezing, will help them find their way, will add to their personal comfort, or will nourish them. If one of the children insists on bringing the dogs, you can press, "Are you prepared to be responsible to feed something in addition to yourself?" Such a question provides tension and a clue to later action.

To help us adults learn to classify quickly in class, Heathcote gave us lists of typical responses a group might give to our questions. She pressed us to categorize them in ways that would exploit the dramatic potential of the material and show its implications so that greater depth could be sounded. For example, suppose you ask a high school group how they'd spend $5 million if they had it. You might get responses like these—an ox farm, the pill for India, grain for hungry people, books, a jet-set trip around the world, beautiful homes in the world's best resorts, houses for poor people with big families, the world's finest race horses, gifts to my friends, schools, publicity on the need for conservation. How would you classify them? One teacher in our class admitted that her first classification seemed pedantic and dull: "Personal, local, national, and international." Heathcote's response was that her idea was fine; it was only her vocabulary that was at fault. She suggested that she feed in a bit more information and show implications in her classification: "Some of us think of charity beginning at home; others think it means giving to other people." Another student suggested, "Health, living conditions, and leisure." Heathcote proposed an alternative, "Some think money should be spent to make life more healthful; others, to enhance the quality of leisure time." Heathcote's classifications categorize without putting separate items into vague or highly abstract classes. The language she uses provides a handle for subsequent dramatic action.

After the teenagers in the Stone Age drama caught their fish with the lines that were ritualistically distributed to them, they gathered around the fire and cooked them. Heathcote suggested, "When you have eaten your fish, you may have a use for what is left over. *Is* anything of use?"

Their responses were: "Bones make hooks to catch more fish." "The eyes, because they once were beautiful." "The skin to make a bag, a purse, any container, or more fishing lines." "The liver for medicine." "Their bones make pins to join things together." "The guts, because people think they're magic."

Heathcote quickly classified to feed back implications: "So we have four kinds of uses for things—for tools and useful articles, for enjoyment for their own sake, for making us well and keeping us healthy, and for making us strong and powerful."

Sometimes Heathcote determines the implications of the class's responses, not so she can feed them back to the class, but rather so she can decide on an appropriate content level for this particular class. For example, when the junior high seamen were telling how they felt at the moment of leaving the harbor, Heathcote classified what they were saying into these categories:

1. Feelings
    a. Looking back
    b. Looking forward
2. The physical sensations of the ship
3. How other people would view their voyage

This showed her what they were ready for, what held dramatic interest for them.*

Now we shall consider a fifth strategy for getting deeper: the use of probes and presses. A probe is an attempt at depth or reflection which the teacher throws out in the heat of the drama, hoping the class will pick it up. It is called a probe because it is exploratory; the teacher can only follow a hunch that the timing is right, that the class is ready for it. If they reject it, the teacher forgets it for the time being and inserts it in another form later in the drama, again hoping for a response. Sometimes the first attempt at a ritual is essentially a probe, in that it is a test to see whether the time is right for evoking individual contributions. If it is not, the ritual comes later. After an unsuccessful probe, the teacher goes back to the story the class is dramatizing; for example, the class may want to get on with building a rocket and forget thinking about its significance. If the probe is successful, it may be a good time to stop the drama or slow its pace to examine implications. Sometimes a first probe will be ignored, and yet a second one, later in the drama, with a different symbol for the same insight, will work.

Here are some of the probes I've seen Heathcote use: She'll hold up a dead animal the hunters have just killed and say, "This had to die so I can live." She will stand at the ship's rail and reflect, "This water looks so gentle and

*See Chapter 15, "Classifying Drama," for other ways she classifies to help her analyze what's happening.

innocent and yet it is so strange. I cannot understand it." She hopes the class will reflect with her about the power of this gentle-seeming water, but, of course, the musing is so worded that they feel no responsibility or guilt if they are not ready to take it up. When a group of six-year-olds are exploring the terrain on the moon, they find a rock made of gold that they decide can make their heads disappear. She feeds back as a probe an implication that might lead to mystery: "So when you hold this rock, you lose your thinking power." The children are not ready for this, so when they write their message to leave buried on the moon for the next adventurers, they go back to their own interpretation: "Be careful of this rock. It is a gold one. If you touch it, your head will disappear." When another group of six-year-olds are meeting the ghost of George Washington, she asks them what is happening in the White House today. They tell her about Watergate and say that Nixon has been doing a lot of bad things. Had this group been high school students, Heathcote told us later, she in role as George Washington's ghost would have inserted the probe, "Oh, I am so sorry to hear about that, because what the President does today determines how I shall be interpreted." It's a probe to the universal, but she avoided it with the six-year-olds because they were not yet ready to think about how history gets written. When the eight- and nine-year-olds were dramatizing the American Revolution, the rebel leader, Ken, reminded Heathcote of the medieval martyr, Wat Tyler, who led the Peasants Revolt of 1381 against Edward III. When Ken said, "We're going to have a meeting about this," he was in the same position as Tyler, a villager who said, "I'll go this far and no further." Wat Tyler roused a whole country. He died for his revolt; but the country was never the same again, because his demands for reform were taken up all over the land. Heathcote wanted to share this reflection with Ken to provide a probe into what for him was probably a hitherto inaccessible period of English history.

Probes for depth are diagnostic; they are used to assess a class's ability to respond. The class can either take them or leave them. Presses, however, are deliberate reinforcements of probes. They do not let the class off the hook, but demand a response. Most of the verbal rituals described above were presses, because all the participants felt their contributions were clearly expected.

Naturally, Heathcote uses presses only when she senses the group is strong enough to deal with them. Thus, in a drama when she asks a farmer how he or she feels about the work, the response might be, "I feel good; I brought in two bags of corn today." Then instead of offering congratulations, Heathcote in role as overseer might provide a press, "All right, but what is the quality of this corn? It is not enough to just bring in two bags, you know."

Many times Heathcote begins with a probe and finds the class is ready to pick it up. Then she presses; because the class has not dismissed her idea, she takes their first slight response as a clue that she dare push them to respond at greater depth. Her press then provides a tension and a challenge. She keeps the dynamic of that pressure alive in the situation until the class has had a chance to make new discoveries about themselves as they stretch themselves to endure it.*

The purpose of a press, as Heathcote puts it, is to advance a group "into a less well-known and understood territory and a deeper consideration of a situation." She introduces a press as often as possible. This doesn't mean she hurries a class through a drama that still holds challenge for them, nor does it mean she denies them a recognition of having achieved something. What it does mean is that once one problem is solved, the students realize a more mature perspective—a resource which Heathcote exploits as she works toward her next press, which will be deeper and more significant. In this way the achievements in drama, like those in real life, become platforms for facing the next challenge.

At the same time as Heathcote is pressing for greater depth, she is choosing each press on the basis of the feedback she is getting from the class. A press has to be in an area the class is interested in and must provide the experiences they seem to be seeking. For example, if it's clear the class really wants to be angry—righteously angry, of course—she will press them very harshly and unfairly in role to give them a reason to join in anger against her. Then her next press will be to understand the implications of that anger at greater depth. Suppose they decide to express their wrath by killing off the governor of their colony? What then? Heathcote will not deny them this decision, but will warn them of the likely consequences of such an act. Her next press will be to keep them onto the challenge of dealing with those consequences: the trial and punishment of the instigators, the bereavement of the governor's family, the coming of a new governor. Through all of these there will be a press for greater depth.

Without presses, nothing significant happens. When the class has to submit to your press, when you won't let them out the easy way, modification of the class has a chance to happen. If you let them solve every problem easily, there is no drama, only a set of happenings.

The final strategy for getting deeper which we shall consider in this chapter is the use of symbol. Like the other strategies discussed here, the use of symbols can have other purposes than getting at depth and implications. One of the most common is to provide a focus for a drama. Any drama has to begin with a decision to limit the beginning moment to a particular time, a distinct place in space, and a specific set of circumstances.** In other words, to have a play at all, each of the participants must zero in on one center and agree to make the drama happen from there. If each of the arrows is a

---

*For use of presses to raise the level of language, see Chapter 16, "Code Cracking: Literature and Language."

**See Chapter 12, "Theater Elements as Tools."

participant and the center is the Big Lie, we might diagram it like this:

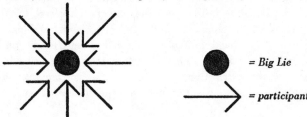

= Big Lie

= participant

At the same time, classroom drama has the potential for reflection, either within the play itself or outside it when the teacher deliberately stops the drama to reflect. This makes possible a divergent process which can be diagrammed like this:

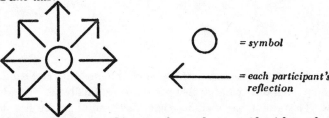

= symbol

= each participant's reflection

A real or imagined concrete object can be used to provide either a focus, as the first diagram illustrates, or a symbol for reflection. Whenever such an object is used to begin a drama, it is important that the class agree on which, out of the many things it might symbolize, the object will in fact symbolize. If this is not done, the drama is likely to go in dozens of directions instead of just one.

Heathcote often starts a drama with an actual concrete object. One time a girl in a group of 17- and 18-year-olds hands her a copper bracelet to use for a drama. Because the bracelet has an Aztec design on it, the group decides to make it an Indian bracelet. They choose to do a drama about an encounter between Indians and whites. Heathcote asks the branching question: "Would you rather be a tribe of Indians or a group of white settlers?" Still sitting rather apathetically on the floor, they choose to be Indians. "Do you want to invade my territory, or do you want me to invade yours?" Not surprisingly, they decide she should be the white person who comes into their camp. At this stage in the drama, their main reason for choosing to be Indians may well be their reluctance to move off their bottoms, which are firmly planted on that floor. Heathcote sees that her challenge is to find a compelling reason for them to leave their comfortable spot and come with her. She also has to figure out why a solitary white woman would approach their camp. So she goes away and comes back carrying the bracelet ahead of her in her hands; she says, "The fact that I bring your chief's bracelet is proof to you of my truthfulness. Your chief lies sick at my house." These carefully chosen words limit the bracelet to a symbol of just one thing, not many. It stands for something this tribe dare not ignore, the power of their chief. Making this bracelet a symbol of the chief sets up the one Big Lie out of which the whole drama develops. It is what Heathcote often calls "the true pin on which the whole cathedral can be built." When she chooses that the bracelet symbolize a chief's power, any other things it might symbolize are set aside for the moment. Heathcote's own reflection becomes the dramatic focus.

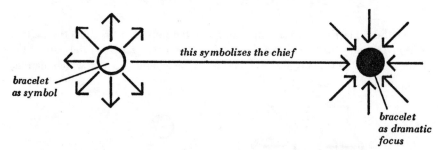

This bracelet, as a symbol of the chief, is a lure powerful enough to get the group up from their comfortable positions and finally into the white woman's house. The group has a choice, but they cannot ignore her, because they cannot ignore their chief. They have to go and investigate, and in so doing, they have to relate to her. In choosing to go, they find she is in a sense in their power: they can decide what they will find when they get to her house. She has not said whether or not they will find the chief dead, for example. She only says, "Your chief lies sick in my house, as he has for three days, refusing food; he will not drink broth at the hands of a white woman."

Later in this drama Heathcote uses another item of adornment, this time not to start the drama, but to symbolize the difference between a chief and other people. She focuses on this by asking: "Why is he wearing clothes that are so very beautiful when you are all dressed only in one feather."

"Because he is more powerful than we are."

"Why does one man have such power?" she asks.

"He was born to it, and he has achieved great things. The gods know he is greater than we are; he knows more than we do."

"My God believes all people are equal," she says calmly. "Where does your chief go after death?"

"He goes to a rich hunting ground."   .

"Will you go where he goes after you die?"

"No, because we are of a different station; we have not won this stage." In this case the symbol of clothing has led to an examination of two contrasting ways of life. A whole culture is growing from the clothing of a dying king. It is a symbol that leads not to a focus for the Big Lie as the bracelet did, but rather out into reflection. Look at the diagram on the following page.

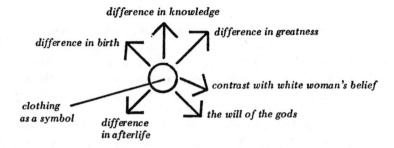

The white woman's house also becomes a symbol, a focus for reflection about her way of life as seen from the "outside"—that is, from *inside* the Indian way of seeing. So they ask, "Why do you shut the light out and cut out the trees? Why do you build this dark building around you?" One girl takes up a book and thoughtfully turns a page or two as if she has never seen one of these before. "Why do you keep these things with marks on them in your house?" Because Heathcote has trapped them into coming to her house to find their chief (who they have now decided is dead), these Indians can examine a white home—something they might not otherwise have a chance to do. In such moments of reflection, a class can speculate on all the various symbolic meanings that shine forth from an object.

In another drama in which the class has turned itself into a tribe of early Britons, each individual chooses a particular job within that primitive community. One boy decides to be an arrowmaker. Heathcote stops the drama a little later and in a ritual asks the community members, one by one, what their occupations might symbolize. The arrowmaker discovers his occupation might symbolize any of these things: the skill of the tribe, the level at which the tribe understands metal, the power of the Britons, or war. Because Heathcote treats an occupation as a symbol, its implications are exposed. The class is ready then to use the Brotherhoods Code to find another particular situation, perhaps in a vastly different time or place, where an occupation can be found that symbolizes one or more of these same things.

In a lifeboat drama, Heathcote asks that each person say what personal meaning the word "boat" conveys. Their answers punctuate the rhythm of their paddling. Many hold symbolic potential: "alone"; "father"; "fighting"; "despair"; "going back"; "self-sufficient"; "we survive"; "discovering about ourselves"; "tension"; "conflicts"; "facing death"; "finding another island"; "discovery of a new, strange place." They reflect on these symbols a bit, then choose one to explore as the focus of the drama. Later Heathcote stops again to reflect, "Does what happened in this boat happen to every group that is thrown together in this way?" Their response is a sounding to the universal.

Often when a class comes up with something that holds the potential for functioning as a symbol, Heathcote picks it up and helps them see its significance. For example, in one drama she starts in role as a guide who takes the children on a journey over the mountains. At the journey's end, she stands with them as they look down over the valley below. She says, "This valley is yours. As your leader I can only take you to this spot. You'll have to do the rest yourselves." The group lies down and rests. She lets them relax for a while, then presses, "The minute you step down that mountain, you are beginning to possess the valley. That will be the start of your living under your own laws." They aren't yet ready to take up the challenge, so they eat and drink and sing songs. They begin to assume responsibility very tenuously by deciding to have a special song as a symbol of their new nation. They spend some time trying to find one, discarding several in turn. Finally, they settle on "Edelweiss," which they sing as they build their homes. Then they go on into house play, which is a very appropriate way for them to get the feel of being a nation. This goes on for quite a while; finally, they decide that it would be nice to have a child born and that it would be good if they had to wait for it and if everything were against its being born. So they wait and plan how this baby's birth will be celebrated in the community. They make laws about who shall be allowed to eat how much of the scarce food supply and come up with a law that strictly limits food consumption to the capacity to work for the community. Then they discover that the future baby's mother cannot do her share of the work. Thus, a gentler law comes into being. The new baby becomes a symbol of a community where people matter.

Sometimes mere physical position has symbolic value. When one person is set apart, physical location may be symbolic of psychological position. Once Heathcote was doing a drama to illustrate the kinds of trials that test the strength of a community. She asked for a volunteer, then sent the rest of the class out for a recess. When they came back in, they found this one boy sitting apart at the far end of the room. She had given him no instructions but to stay there. She told the class, "Mannie wants to leave us." His physical distance had become a symbol for his apartness.

Mannie had no words yet; he just stood stubbornly apart. Before long, under the pressure of his classmates' pleading, he came up with a reason for his decision to leave—a decision born in the implication of his position in relation to the group. "There's too much freedom here; no one has a fixed job. I want a place where there's a schedule for everyone."

Heathcote does not limit her press for symbolic meaning to classes of normal children. She often asks severely retarded or mentally disturbed patients what a particular thing stands for, or what its purpose is. When she once asked a group of mental patients what fire was for, their answers were the universally shared ones: "For burning," "For warming," "For keeping fear away," "For keeping safe by," and "For telling stories by."

Some things have a significance that is widely shared among all people in our culture and, to some extent, throughout all human communities; they function as symbols. Bread is a symbol of survival, humility, poverty, the seasonal cycle, sharing, work, and reward, to name just a few of its meanings. The possible meanings are limited by the situation, however: to function as a symbol of poverty, bread must be the only food a people have, and there should be not quite enough to go around. Once Heathcote was hoping to make the first fish caught by a Stone Age tribe a symbol of survival. She wanted to pose the tension of dividing a single fish so small that they would all be left hungry after it was shared. "Although at one level this is just something to eat," she pointed out, "at another it is more than that. It stands for all the problems our tribe faces in this harsh land by the sea." Just when she was getting the whole group's attention focused on that one little fish, however, someone caught a bigger one, then another, and her chance to make the first one a symbol of survival was washed back into the sea.

Here are some symbols Heathcote has found useful and some of the more widely shared meanings associated with them:

Bowl	Need, receiving, home
Candle	Security, calm, light, solemnity, faith, loneliness, knowledge, shelter, fragility, time
Chest	Wealth, travel, secrecy, security, mystery, inheritance, burden, ownership
Cloak	Authority, travel, comfort, power, strangeness
Coffin	Loss, protection, faith, mystery, journey, destiny, ritual, vanity, preservation, eternity, death, no return
Cup	Group agreement, alignment, intrigue, sharing, hospitality, healing, ritual, heritage
Fire	Sun, destruction, life, cleansing, eternity, faith, hope, consuming, magic, protection, superstition, passion, radiance, eternity, comfort, anger, warmth
Flower	Life, growth, innocence, beauty, death in life, ritual, promise, cycle of maturation, fragility
Key	Security, limitation, freedom, cordiality, opportunity, intrigue, maturation, punishment, discovery, power, privacy
Ring	Union, power, circle from the moon, feminine, womb, crown, eternity, power of another, magic
Sheath	Trust, vigilance
Staff	Authority, control, wisdom, defense, ritual, magic, guidance, age, dependence, tree, growth, male
Star	Remoteness, mystery, guidance, steadfastness, enchantment, humility, aspiration, infinity
Sword	Self-preservation, power, authority, conquest, ritual, honor, justice, retribution
Water	Cleansing, baptism, change, life.

Because responses to these symbols are widely shared, they can be used very effectively in classroom drama. They provide a concrete way of experiencing an event even when feelings about the event have not yet been aroused or, if aroused, are not yet expressible in words. The symbol itself can help give rise to the feeling or, if the feeling is there, provide a group the means of expressing it. When a feeling is expressed through symbol, a wider range of meanings can be discovered than when it is expressed only in a cognitive mode.

As we noted early in this chapter, everything implies something beyond it. In this sense, we can look below the surface of any moment to its meaning; any event can become a symbol of something that transcends it. What transcends it are the universals, the ultimate meanings that seem to matter to human beings, without which a person is barren of satisfaction and of growing points.

Heathcote does not invent ultimate meanings, but she facilitates their discovery. Reflection makes possible the distilling of experience to its essence. You cannot get classes to this kind of reflection without expecting a response from them, without probing and pressing for it, without demanding that they try to get deeper. By insisting that they try to reflect, Heathcote earns the respect of her classes and deepens her respect for them.

9. WITHHOLDING EXPERTISE

Dorothy Heathcote often deliberately puts herself into a situation in which she clearly signals to the class that they know more than she does and have information she needs. She quickly and deftly communicates that it is their ideas, not hers, that will make the drama work, and she asks questions she knows they and they alone can answer. Their answers are the material she dare not ignore, for they show her the children's interests and desires, and carry with them the children's commitment. She does not correct their misperceptions or misinformation at the moment she receives them—she lets her own expertise dribble out little by little as the drama proceeds. For example, if the group decide to be pirates in the olden days, she may ask them what they will do as pirates, and they may answer, "Bury treasure." Then she will ask them what they need for this job. If they say, as one group did, "old rusty shovels" (since that was their perception of "olden times"), she lets this muddled understanding stand for the time being. She might try to correct it later by suggesting that they build a new treasure chest or buy new sails. In any drama she begins by taking the information the class gives her just as it is—with three exceptions. She corrects misinformation if it will interfere with the belief of the others; if it cannot be included without blurring the dramatic focus; or if it interferes with her goal of presenting the historical period accurately.

Thus Heathcote withholds her own information but does not deny the class her feelings, her response, her presence, her power. She is wholly there at every moment; her expertise is at the service of the class, but she shows it in her questioning, not in her telling. She wants the children to discover as much as possible through the drama itself.

Often with American children she uses what many of us might consider a disadvantage—namely, the fact that she herself is British—to advantage, turning a limitation into a strength, as she so often advocates. She will say to American youngsters, "I don't know how you go about this in America. Do you. . .?" Her warm smile and soft-spoken bewilderment are lures too good to miss. The class jumps at the chance to help her understand.

Here's how the first half hour with a group of eight- and nine-year-old Americans goes on a July third. Heathcote begins by asking forthrightly, "I don't really know why everybody's on holiday tomorrow. I know it's a thing called the Fourth of July. What is that about?"

"Independence."

"The Declaration of Independence was signed."

"By Americans?" she asks.

"Yes."

"Is there a piece of paper somewhere? You know, in a museum or some-place?"

"Uh-huh."

"In Washington."

"Is it?"

"That's where most stuff like that is kept."

"Can you sort of go round and look at it? Is it in a glass case? Does anybody know?"

"Yes. Probably."

"Ordinary people can walk in. I'm very pleased to hear that," she says with a smile. Then she leans forward and asks earnestly, "What were you wanting to be independent about?"

"Freedom. Religious freedom."

"Religious freedom? I see. Well, who had been telling you you couldn't have it?" she says, beginning the subtle process of turning the class into colonists.

"Britain."

"*We* have said to you that you can't worship whom you like?"

"Right!" one boy says with determination as others nod.

"That's terrible. I feel embarrassed about that. . . .Why didn't we let you worship whom you like?"

Ken, the slight boy who has answered most of the questions, says eagerly, "Oh, I think I know. It's because Britain—well, we had to pay taxes to Britain. . . .Britain made the colonies pay taxes for things they didn't even buy, and they made them pay taxes without being represented in Parliament. Something like that."

Several other children are nodding and saying, "Yes!"

"You mean we were sort of holding you almost as subjects"—and, noting the puzzled looks at the word, Heathcote adds—"and slaves to do what we wanted?"

"Yes! Yes—and pay taxes!" The children were almost shouting now.

"That small country over there tried to tell this big country. . . ."

"It wasn't as big as it is now," Ken interrupts. "It was only thirteen Eastern states."

"Only part of the country," adds another child.

Heathcote, unlike many other teachers I have seen, does not congratulate the class on their information, nor does she encourage competitiveness by rewarding Ken with a special praise. Instead, she focuses on her own learning; she lets the children teach her. "Oh, I see. Yes. Yes." Then she pauses, stands and summarizes, "It's very easy, isn't it? To write in a book. . . ." and as she writes large on the blackboard she says, " 'And on July fourth'. . .What year was it? Do you know?"

"1776!" shouts Ken.

"1776? Is he right?" she asks the others.

"Yes."

So she finishes the sentence on the board, "On July fourth, 1776, the American Declaration of Independence was signed." By using their information and either feigning or exposing her ignorance, she harnesses the children's energy; they are ready to decide for themselves whether or not to make a drama about the War of Independence. "You know, I wonder what it was like really? Are you interested in going back in time? Suppose we said we are going to make a TV program for the people of America so that they will understand something about the War of Independence. Would you be interested in doing the TV program?" Some say yes; others nod uncommittedly; some shrug their shoulders; but all decide to go along. To win the interest of the others, she asks more questions: "Let's begin by deciding what we want to tell people about the War of Independence. How many things happened that you know about that must have been very exciting? Were men ever in danger?"

"Yes, yes!" say the children. Heathcote hands out several pieces of chalk to the group and asks them to write down anything they can think of that has to do with people in the war. Most are hesitant; they pass the chalk from one to another and stand uncertainly. After a few moments, a few children have put onto the board:

> Boston Tea Party
> Tensions
> Battles of Lexington and Concord
> Declaration of Independence
> War

Not much, but a beginning, and it is this tentative list that Heathcote must start with. She reads each word carefully, upgrading it by the seriousness of her tone. Her primary goal at this point is to get the children's belief going. She knows she can do this only by building on the scraps of information the children have given her. More information is not what they need first; what they need is confidence in the information they have and a willingness to try to identify with those early colonists. By withholding her own factual expertise, Heathcote gives the children a chance to use their own experience, to act on what they know. If they start to worry about too many details, belief is lost, and there is no drama. Heathcote knows that working this way means inevitably wading into a woolly mess of misinformation. She trusts this process of wading long enough to get what she's after—belief and commitment. Misperceptions can be corrected later in the drama or after the drama itself is over.

On her first meeting with a group of six- and seven-year-olds, Heathcote shows a picture of a group of children of about the same age. She explains, "I have a group of English orphans; here they are. I need a place for them to stay, but I don't know how you go about getting houses in Evanston. Can you help me? How do I find out if one's for sale?" At first the children grin and look at one another in disbelief, but then the answers start coming. By the time she asks, "How will I know if it's a good place for children to live?" the children are ready to start talking about yards and beds and places to eat.

She thanks them for their suggestions and then asks, "Are you good at giving advice?"

Of course they are, and they nod and say "Yeah."

"Oh, I would appreciate it very much," Heathcote smiles. "The advice I want is this: I've been told there is a house in Evanston, but I need to know if it's big enough." She shows them a picture of the orphans again; they examine it quietly; then they all count slowly in unison until they reach 19. "Nineteen orphans; could I get a house in Evanston big enough for nineteen?" She turns to the board and draws a house, asking the group whether it seems big enough. The children suggest she put a door in the middle and a room on this side and a room on that. She has a few volunteers join her at the board, and they draw American houses that would be better suited than hers for 19 orphans. They suggest that the orphans need a back door and a door mat.

"You could put 'Hello' on it," suggests one child.

"Yes, to welcome them," adds Heathcote.

"Do they speak American?"

"I don't know," says Heathcote, leaving the problem of a "Hello" that orphans cannot read for later follow-up if the children choose. The four volunteers at the blackboard are busy drawing elaborate houses. All watch for a moment, and then Heathcote turns to the others and focuses on how much such a large house would cost. The answers range from $20 to $1,000. Noting the disparity in their guesses, she suggests they go home and ask their parents. Then she softly muses, "So you really know about American children. I wonder, will these orphans be all right here in America?"

"Pretty much," says one girl tentatively.

"Lots of times they'll take dope," says a short six-year-old with long blond braids.

"Oh, I couldn't have them do that!"

"Well, that's what they do," affirms a boy seriously, "so my sister says."

"Would I be able to prevent it?" The children shrug. "Do all American children take dope?"

"Only in the last grades."

"Well, none of these are in the last grades yet. But what if they do when they get to the last grades? You'll have to advise me about this." The children are silent. She prods, "Is this something you can advise me on?"

"Not so easily. You can't just tell them to stop it."

"Can't you? Do you think if I started them young enough?"

"No, they'll just stay out of school, playing hooky." All the children are talking at once now, most agreeing with the last speaker.

"Oh, you do fill me with a lot of worries," Heathcote says, reflecting their concern about the difficulty of this problem without inserting any glib moralisms or solutions. She asks a child to make a note on the board to remind her that she has to stop the orphans from taking dope. She tells the class again that this is one of the things they will have to advise her on.

Perhaps to cheer her up, one boy suggests, "Well, people from other countries, I don't think they take dope."

Other children agree, "No."

"Well, I'll just hope, then," says Heathcote, not removing from the children their responsibility to help her solve the problem.

"There are some schools where they don't take dope," says one girl.

"That's only grade schools," a boy reminds her.

"If you watch, my sister says, she knows when they take dope."

Heathcote says, "I think I ought to meet your sister, really. Perhaps you could find out more things from her."

Then she turns and looks carefully at the houses the children have drawn on the blackboard. She notes aloud *for herself* the features she needs to remember: at least three floors, windows, lots of rooms. Again she is not praising the children for exhibiting their knowledge, but simply thanking them for helping her with her problem.

The class is now ready to go to that house that's for sale and look it over. She directs them to stand up, and they all take her to the bus stop, showing her how to pay her fare in America. When they arrive at the house, she asks them to look it over and tell her whether it's suitable for 19 orphans. Again she has dealt a hand of good cards to the children, giving them the one task they can do better than any adult in the room—to look at an imaginary house from the point of view of a child who would live there.

"I'll stay in the hall here," she says, standing beside the blackboard in the room where her adult students are gathered. "Every time you find something I should know about—that's something about being an orphanage—come and tell me." The children scatter, looking into all the classrooms that open onto the hot, close hallway of the church building where this Northwestern University summer school class is being held. Before long, a residence takes shape in the children's minds. They find a TV set, four floors, a piano, a whole room that is empty, pretty big windows. Then one boy gives Heathcote a gift she hasn't expected—what she tells the adult class later is a great godsend—something that provides the focus of the next day's drama:

"We looked down in the basement, and it was a never-ending hall."

"A never-ending hall?" Heathcote repeats slowly. "That sounds marvelous for an orphanage." Then, musingly, she upgrades the language: "Hmmm, a never-ending corridor." Then children stop shouting out what they have found long enough to muse a moment with her. Heathcote senses that this hall might be used to keep open the fantasy world, to serve when the children want a story.

George, the boy who discovered the hall, adds, "I found there's a window at the end. It looks like you can see a coastal line; I think it goes to China. In China they see it from down below, but you see it from up above."

Heathcote later tells her adult students that this information is something she hasn't time to sort out or use, so it becomes one of those fragments that lie about, the pieces the teacher chooses not to pick up, which might serve as material for later drama. George may have been giving Heathcote his understanding of the mystery that the world is round. He may have been told that down below our feet is China; his conception may be that this is a coastal line that can be seen from a basement window at the end of a never-ending hall. For Heathcote to stop to sort out concepts and provide expertise at this point would be to move out of the drama and into a teacher-giving-information role. Instead, although at this point not too many of the children have even picked up the never-ending hallway, Heathcote chooses to make this one thing come alive to as many of them as possible. This way she provides a point of entry for the next day. The coastal line has to be dropped for the time being.

The children keep finding things orphans would like and shouting eagerly: a fireplace, two couches, a table, an elevator, a chair, an exit sign, a fire escape, a fire extinguisher.

Heathcote repeats, "A fire extinguisher and fire escape," writing it on the board. "Do you think those are important for children?"

"Yes."

"They won't have had them in the houses they've been living in, but you think in America they ought to be sure they have one?"

"Yes, because if they live in a big house, how are they going to get down the stairs if they're on fire?"

"Yes, I see," Heathcote warmly encourages them to care for the welfare of these orphans. "Do you find there are many fires in America?" They go on to tell her about the Chicago fire "in the eighteenth century."

She looks over the list on the board and asks which things are necessary and which would merely be nice to have, stretching the children to classify the information. She asks, "Do we need an elevator? How will they get strong legs?" Instead of judging their contribution, she uses a question to help them see its limitations. She leads by withholding not only her expertise but her judgment as well. After some discussion, the children finally hold that an elevator is *necessary*, not merely nice; strong legs will be developed by bikes.

It's as if Heathcote says to herself, "I'll ask the children to tell me what this house is like, and anything they say I shall accept and make use of, unless it is patently absurd"—as it is when one boy says he found 2,038 windows. At that point she puts him to work writing what the others find. Every other suggestion she takes very seriously. When someone finds a mirror, she puts her hand to her chin and muses, "I don't know if we need a mirror for children. Why would they need one?"

"For making funny faces in." This answer she accepts and repeats. She lets the children tell her that they need to play, and thus plants a seed for action. The next day, she appears as a ghost who doesn't know how to play, and the children show her how.

When the children find a music room, she doesn't say in a teacher tone, "Oh, how nice! We can teach the children music." Instead, she asks, "Do we need a music room for an orphanage? Is music necessary for children?"

Their eager "yes, yes!" commits them to a value they are openly acknowledging is theirs, not just the teacher's. They decide together that music should go on the list of things that would be nice to have; TV is on the list of necessities. Again Heathcote makes no judgment.

The next day they furnish the rooms of the orphanage, drawing plans for each part of the house. Again Heathcote relies on their information. For example, when they are trying to decide whether a certain room is large enough for a bedroom with 19 beds, they decide they need to know how big each bed would be. When Heathcote asks how long one might be, a boy suggests that it should be about the size Heathcote is tall. "Oh," nods Heathcote, "he means if I lie down, the bed would be as big as I am tall." So she lies down on the floor while the group measures with a string. "Should beds be the size of a person or larger?" she asks.

"Larger."

"I wonder why we need the extra length in a bed?"

"No one wants to bump their head."

"No."

"Or fall out."

"I quite see that. Right! Well, get to measuring."

"How will we measure in feet?" one boy asks.

"See if the lady of the house has a yardstick. I can't just order a bed from here to here." They make guesses and try to figure out how long a foot is without a yardstick. She lies there, not solving but magnifying the difficulty. "It's such a problem; I'm five feet six inches; does that help?" They finally agree on beds six feet long. Again by withholding her expertise, she transfers the tension of problem solving to the children.

Heathcote sits up and asks, "What makes you happy in your bedroom?" They start talking animatedly with each other. "I like it 'cause I can jump up and down on the beds."

"Lots of stuffed animals."

Heathcote smiles. "I'd like for these orphans to be happy."

Before they leave the bedroom, she asks whether it needs to be kept tidy. They agree that it does, so that people can walk around. One child suggests that she'll have to scream out, "Get your room clean!"

"How could we do it so I don't have to shout like that?" she asks. This question stumps the class. They think for a few minutes. "You could make a rule: put away what you use."

"How do we get people to do that?" They talk about this for a while and finally decide that her job would be to clean the bathrooms and dust, and each of the orphans would clean up his or her own things and vacuum. So a social order begins to take shape—one based on their own understandings of how a household should operate. She asks them what else the orphans would need from her.

"Protection."

"If they fight."

"Protect younger ones from older ones."

"Make sure the house is safe."

"Protect you from robbers." It is obvious that the children are interested in helping her figure out her role.

"Anything else but fighting and robbers?"

"Cooking."

"Lock the door."

"They'll get in anyway."

Heathcote asks, "Nothing else I can do?"

"Look after first aid."

"I was hoping I could do things that are more important than that."

"Washing kids up."

"Help with reading if they have a problem."

"Answer questions."

Heathcote nods, "A big responsibility—to be able to answer all the questions. I'll bet you've got some interesting questions—real hard ones. Come tomorrow with real hard questions for me to answer, ones you'd really like to be answered, and tomorrow you be the orphans to try it out." So the session ends, and the children walk out talking to each other about what they'll ask her the next day. What they choose are the kind of questions children are experts at—riddles.

No matter what the subject matter of the drama, Heathcote manages to feel her way into a situation where the children provide the know-how. For a final example of this, here is what she does the following day with this same group of six- and seven-year-olds. They meet in the large social hall of the church for this class. It becomes the orphanage where the orphans eat their evening meal of macaroni and cheese together and then go to sleep. In the middle of the night their fairy godmother wakes them to take them down the never-ending corridor, where they have agreed they want to meet a ghost. Sure enough, a ghost is there. She is standing with her hands over her face, moaning a high-pitched cry. As the children approach, she looks tentatively out at them and asks, "Who are you?"

"The orphans!" they tell her eagerly.

Then Heathcote as the sad ghost asks, "Can you help me?" They all say yes. "I've lost my mother and father, and I don't know where they are. Have you lost your parents?" They all nod and say yes. "But how can you be happy? Did you manage it better than me?" Choosing to be in role as a ghost who is an orphan, she probes to see how much orphanness has become a part of the children. She asks, "Where did your parents go to?"

"We don't know," answers one girl plaintively.

"I don't know where mine went either," says the ghost, starting to weep again. Then she looks up. "Do you suppose you could teach me to be happy?"

"One boy suggests, "All you can do is make friends and then you'll be happier."

"But I have no friends. I don't know how to make friends," she moans, covering her face again.

"We'll be your friends."

"I don't know what this word means," she says, pressing them to examine their experience.

"It means to play with each other."

"To share." Several talk at once now.

"You like each other."

"I think I could like you," Heathcote says tentatively, "But I haven't anything I could share with you."

"That's all right."

"Could I share my corridor?"

"Yes!" the children chorus.

"Will you come see me sometimes?"

"Yes. We just came."

"I know, but it was an accident this time. I've been here such a long time. And nobody ever came. I thought nobody cared." The children assure her they care, and they agree to come again to teach her how to play. Heathcote comes out of role and asks them what the ghost should be doing while they are away from her. They suggest that since she's a sad ghost she probably cries all the time. One child suggests that she might do something else.

"But there isn't anything to do," presses Heathcote, still out of role.

"We can put a swing up and you can swing on it," a boy suggests, looking up at the vaulted roof of the church hall.

"Hey, you know, you could put a swing up here all right. Those rafters are like Westminster Hall!" another boy shouts.

"And it would be a looooong swing!"

"Is swinging a good way to play?"

"The children chorus, "Yes!"

"Do you use it to go backwards and forwards?" Heathcote gestures her puzzlement.

Again the children shout, "Yes!"

Still in her own person and not in role as ghost, Heathcote asks, "What will you do if I'm afraid of swings? Is anybody ever afraid of swings?"

Some children shout, "Yes!"; others, a scornful "No!" "You might have a problem, a little," acknowledges one girl.

Heathcote warns them, "I think *you* may have a problem, because I don't know how to play. Would you like to try and teach me?" The children say they would. "There are more things than swings, aren't there, to play with?" They nod. Heathcote suggests they start over, coming down the corridor, finding her again, and helping her learn to play; they go away in a hum of enthusiasm. Heathcote has handed them a gift, a chance to show her the one thing they know how to do best—to play.

When they come back, their faces show the eagerness of a shared decision. They are going to teach her a game. She greets them sadly, her whole body drooping with discouragement. "I didn't think you'd come back," she says, looking up at them briefly and then returning her gaze to the floor.

"We came to teach you how to play."

"Remember, you wanted us?"

"The first game we can play is called *hiding*."

"Hiding?" One bright-eyed blond boy explains to her how to play hide-and-go-seek.

"I hide all my life," sighs the ghost.

Several of the children propose changing to another game. One girl hits upon a different solution. "You could be the seeker." Heathcote looks up at her bewilderedly. "The *seeker*—you find us."

Another girl corrects her, "No, she wouldn't like that; she's been hiding all her life."

"But I've not been seeking all my life," the ghost says, with a glimmer of interest in her eyes. "You mean you'd let me look for you?" They nod. "But

I'd never be able to find you," she says, resuming her despairing pose and plaintive tone.

"Yes, you will."

"We'll help you."

"We'll hide in some dumb places like the curtains." Nods and giggles accompany their glances at one another.

"You mean you'll let me be clever?" Heathcote asks, ironically mirroring what she is actually allowing the children themselves to be.

"Yes."

"No one ever let me be clever before," she muses. Then, in a frightened tone, she presses the class further, "I don't know whether I'll like looking for you." There is much talking among the children at this. "But will you run?"

"Yes."

"Do you always obey the rules?"

"Yes."

"I don't think I'm good at rules."

"We could teach you how."

"Teach me how to do the rules then. What do I have to do?"

"Well, you have to find us, try to find us, and if you don't find us and you want to give up, you can just say 'I give up.' "

"And you've got to count to a number, like five or ten, twenty— anything."

"Why do you have to count?" asks the ghost.

"So we'll have time to hide."

"Oh, I see. I wouldn't mind trying it. Is this called a game?" They nod an affirmative. "And is it playing?" More nods. Then she introduces a new perspective. "Seems kind of strange. Hiding to be found?" More nods and murmured yeses. "All right. I'll count, shall I? How many do I have to count?"

The children decide on ten, to make it easy for her. She asks them to show her slowly to count, and they all count in unison. "One. . . two. . . three. . . four. . . ."

"I've got the idea. All right," Heathcote says and counts slowly to ten. The children scramble, giggling. Most of them hide together in a rather obvious place under a line of tables at one end of the hall. When Heathcote finishes counting, she sighs wearily. "I don't know if it's worth it. Should I look?"

From their hiding places the children call eagerly, "Yes, yes!"

With another deep sigh the ghost worries, "I'll never be able to find them." She walks slowly in the opposite direction from their hiding places.

"Yes, you will! Yes, you will!" urge the children.

The ghost listens. "They're over here somewhere," she says, moving towards the curtains. The children behind them can't wait; they jump out. "You let yourself be found!" she says in amazement. One child takes her hand, and they go together to other hiding places. A boy points to some shoes beneath the next curtain. "Oh, there's one!" says the ghost in triumph. As the children who are found help her, she finds another, then another. Finally, she says, with a note of her old despair, "But I didn't find everybody."

"But you found a lot of people," says a boy consolingly.

"Oh, there's one! You really do obey the rules," she says, finding a boy behind a pillar.

"Where's my brother?" asks a girl at the ghost's side.

"I don't know," the ghost answers.

"I know!" come several voices.

"Where?"

"Here!" come several voices from under the tables at the end of the hall.

"I'm sure I haven't found everyone. There were more than this."

"I know where they are!" say some of the children at her side.

"Can you help me come and find the others?"

So they help her find the rest of the children. In their role as orphans they have identified with other children who are unlike them in their family pattern but much like them in their capacity to play. Heathcote has deftly led them to be very clever indeed. By withholding her expertise, she has led the children to teach her how to play, then how to win.

10. PLANNING

Three stages of planning are needed for classroom drama—before the first session, between sessions, and during sessions. Each stage poses a different set of possibilities and problems.

When you begin your initial planning, you first decide what is at the center of the lesson. Do you want to modify the behavior of a class in a certain way, expand their awareness, get to know them, or lead them into a specific area of the curriculum? Whatever your goal is, you will need to concentrate all your efforts on reaching it, so discipline yourself not to mix up your plans by pursuing several aims at once. At least for the beginning of the drama, plan for every signal to zero in on your target.

When you have defined your ends, you can go on to discover your means. First of all, whether or not you know the class affects whether or not you can go ahead and plan a drama based on specific material. If you don't know them, you may just make a guess about their interests and behavior. On the other hand, you may want to assess an unfamiliar class by asking diagnostic questions like, "What do you want to do a play about?" In this case, you do not choose any material prior to the first meeting. You plan only that you will not reject whatever the class chooses, and that you will try to get them to reflect on their situation in some way. Heathcote often uses this approach when she knows nothing about a group prior to meeting them.

When Heathcote knows a class, she usually plans and sets up a drama beforehand. Knowing the class enables the teacher to choose material and devise strategies that will catch their interest and at the same time modify where they are.

There are some kinds of plan that you must make before the first meeting with the class, regardless of whether you know them or whether you will be introducing them to a specific subject:

1. You need to get their attention.
2. You want to give them an opportunity to make some clearcut decisions.*

---

*See the discussion of branching questions in Chapter 6, "Leading Through Questions."

3. You need to use something of what the class already knows to contribute to the drama. To do this, you will plan to seek information in some of your questions.

4. You must bring the class to a moment of reflection on what is happening. All of your planning will be geared so that this goal is not bypassed, no matter what the class chooses to do or how they handle the drama. You need to decide whether you are going to approach this goal by taking a role in the drama or by stopping the drama.

In making these plans, write down each teaching strategy you can think of that might lead to your objectives. Beside each, list in two columns all the reasons *for* using it and all the reasons *against* using it. Then you will have a basis for choosing the strategy that has the most effect and the fewest limitations for the specific class you'll be working with. Heathcote urges you to be as realistic as you can and weigh each advantage against a disadvantage.

When Heathcote is setting up a specific drama, she often plans the first session elaborately and precisely. She will plan which role she is going to assume to heighten the emotion of the drama, and perhaps set someone else up in role.* At this stage, she can also assemble props. Heathcote is committed to showing the class nothing but the best reference books, artifacts, or art objects she can find. Even with very young children, she uses adult materials more often than children's. For example, when she was doing the drama of the seventeenth-century sailing vessel, she took pains to find an old model of a ship of the period and samples of scrimshaw carved by sailors. She also collected paintings and photographs that would help the students identify with the conditions of work and life aboard a sailing vessel.

Just as important as planning what you will do is knowing clearly which bits of the drama you dare not plan if you expect to harness the drive of the class. Classroom drama calls for defining a particular moment and assuming an attitude—and not planning beyond that. To decide on an outcome is to reduce the drama to "just pretend." The goal is to live a particular kind of life at life rate in an unpremeditated way (as one does in most of one's life); that way, surprise is not precluded by planning, but can shock an individual into new awareness. Instead of planning what a group *will* do, you lead them to act and then discover what they *have* done. You must not try to predict how the class will respond to what you set up beforehand, nor must you care which of the alternatives they choose. All of your signals should be as open, bland, evocative, and non-directive as is consistent with the goal you have chosen. Early in the drama you want to elicit the class's ideas, unbiased by yours. This is especially important because most groups of students have been programmed to expect the teacher to tell them, not ask them, what to do. All

---

*The next two chapters give more ideas on how to set up a dramatic situation that combines the elements of theater with ambiguity. The former keep the focus, while the latter provides a lure, stimulating the class's curiosity and evoking a response.

too often, the only questions a teacher asks are merely thin disguises for directives: "Here is what we're going to do, OK?" It's only a very brave child who will dare say, "No, it's not OK."

The content of your initial planning will be affected by the goal you have chosen. Suppose you want to test out a class you do not know and discover what you can about them. In that case, you plan nothing else but that, so you can base your subsequent lessons on what you find out in this one.

If you want to change the behavior of the class, you approach planning a little differently. It may be that you want a class to learn how to confront one another with language rather than with the blows that are usual for them. In that case, you set up a situation which calls for a verbal battle. This gives the class the confrontation they are seeking, but it also pushes them to discover a new way to contend. You may plan a drama to get a group to stop kicking the furniture. This does not mean you can guarantee that when the drama is over, they will not go back to kicking the furniture: to do that would be to play God. You can, however, get them on a see-saw between kicking and not-kicking by planning a drama—about, say, caring for and sorting eggs for market—which just might help them lean in the direction of not-kicking. Your job is to try out different lures until they take one and stop kicking, if only for a few seconds.

You will want to plan differently still if your goal is to get the class into a particular subject. Suppose you want to make the events of the American Revolution come alive and to stimulate an interest in that period of American history. Then your plans will all have to do with finding just the right symbol for colonists. Will it be having to pay still another tax; being served with a billet to quarter an arrogant stranger, a British soldier, in a small cottage; or organizing a militia of minutemen? You will need to make sure to frame your questions so that the class stays within the general subject.

If you also know the class, you can plan to meet their needs as well as the demands of the curriculum. Sometimes, in fact, you face a conflict between the two. When that happens, Heathcote, without hesitation, opts for meeting the students where they are. She calls this realistic planning. Far too often, we cram in history or geometry or science or literature as if we assumed that once our students graduate, they will never again have another chance to learn, never again converse with an intelligent human being. What Heathcote looks at first is not the subject matter but the youngsters who see no point in knowing all that. She starts with them, not judging them, knowing intuitively that it is their right to be where they are, to reject what they feel they must and to affirm their own interests, no matter how different these may be from the ones the school would like them to have. Heathcote meets regularly (as all of us as teachers do, at least some of the time) with classes that do not care to learn. Her first goal is to hook them with a lure they cannot resist. The more she knows about their interests, the more likely it is that she can spot the little thread of interest that can be pulled out of them and woven into a drama that is a part of the curriculum area she is expected to introduce. She makes no pretense of "teaching it all." It is quite enough if the students have found a way in. They have the rest of their lives to read and explore; they must begin by discovering that in a book they can find someone just enough like themselves so that they can begin to identify.*

For any drama, no matter what her goal, Heathcote's plan is to work slowly, to take time for the class to become committed and for belief to be built. This does not mean she stands still or repeats work. Instead, she thinks of as many different ways as she can to stay in the same place while seeming to move forward. She employs rituals** and group assessments of progress to help a class stay with a problem and become aware of their feelings in a situation.

To see how Heathcote's mind works in planning before the first day of a drama, let's look at the strategies she thinks of in response to a specific goal. She is working with a team of student teachers who are planning a drama for a group of seven- and eight-year-olds they have not yet met. As usual, she pushes her adult students to plan, as she does, so that everything they do on the first day of a drama will aim at moving the class towards a chosen goal. Therefore she urges the team to begin by writing down what they intuitively perceive to be the essence of the drama, the significance of this work for this particular group of children.

In this case, the heart of the drama, the central goal the teachers choose, is the children's realization that they have a common problem to solve, that there is no one to rely on except themselves, and that they alone must find a solution. Heathcote then helps them think through alternative strategies. She reminds them that they first must consider the size of the group and the available space in the classroom. She suggests that their first decision will have to be whether the drama would be factual truth or a fantasy truth. Heathcote herself starts with practical, factual material when she wants both kinds of truth, because no practical material avoids fantasy, but much fantasy never gets to the practical.

Then she suggests that the problem they give these children should be a very big one, since persons this age seldom find any problem hard to solve. From the several problems she proposes, the teachers select that of recovering a ship full of gold ingots sunk in the deepest part of the sea.

The team's first job is to define the task and figure out who is going to pay for the retrieval of this ship. Heathcote makes some suggestions: One of the teachers can enter in role as the owner of a big company and present the class

---

*See Chapters 16 and 17, "Code Cracking: Literature and Language" and "Code Cracking: Other Areas," for ways to move from where students are into curriculum areas.
**See Chapter 8, "Dropping to the Universal."

with a chart that is fairly ambiguous. It defines the difficulties, but it gives no clue about the historical period of the ship. Thus, it does not mention material such as wood or steel; it may simply say that this ship is one of the largest of its kind or period. The teacher-in-role can also bring in some old-looking documents, singed at the edges. These might include an old assay of the value of the gold ingots, with the modern equivalent in dollars added in modern ink; half of a chart of the tonnage of the ship; and other musty, stained papers—all stamped with a modern stamp of the date they were found. The company owner can explain that this chart and papers were found in cleaning out an old building. Looking very up-to-date and efficient, he or she can carry them in an actual, not imaginary, contemporary briefcase and press the class for modern business and technical efficiency in solving this problem; yet, with these documents, the class may well go to the Spanish Main.

When in need of historically evocative documents, Heathcote has frequently gone to a class of older history students and challenged them to make up some documents that are true to the period. She lets the students know she trusts them to put together papers that are as authentic as possible, by telling them that she will not be looking at them before she opens them in front of the class. That way, she says, she and the children can examine the papers and make discoveries at the same time.

The sunken ship drama might begin in the company owner's office. (In this case the teacher gets the class to meet in a very small space.) The teacher-in-role asks for volunteers. If there is no response, it may be necessary to hold out the lure of quite large rewards. This would be a last resort strategy because it would militate against the main goal of this drama—the inner feeling of accomplishment in solving a difficulty on one's own. If the class commits itself only in response to a large monetary reward, one of the teachers might try to extend their idea of reward with a question: "Have you ever held solid gold in your hand? If you shut your eyes, it's just a brick like any other, and yet there's a lot of blood in it, isn't there?" Now Heathcote doesn't know when a teacher would use this comment; it may not be until the children have actually found the ingots at the bottom of the sea. She suggests the student teachers plan it, nevertheless, because it means reflection; it's a probe they can use at some apt moment in the drama.

Another thing she mentions is a strategy to get everyone absolutely committed to getting the ingots, to figure out why they need to bother about getting them. One such strategy might be to have each child sign a document that demands that its signers are trustworthy and will not try to steal any of the gold. The ritual of signing will give the teacher a chance to look each person in the eye and make a demand that requires personal commitment.

The next thing Heathcote brings to the teachers' attention is the available space. It is important that there be a lack of space to connote "shipness," so she recommends staying in a small classroom. She looks at the tables in the room and asks, "How can we perceive shipness with these tables?" She experiments then with turning them upside down; then sideways, end to end—this, she feels, gives the best effect of cramped quarters and of going from compartment to compartment.

At this point she rethinks the plan of having this ship sunk in the deepest part of the ocean. The disadvantage is that the children will be wearing diving equipment with helmets and pressurized suits which will separate them from one another. No, that will not work, so she decides the ship will be sunk in shallow waters where they can scuba dive to explore, but the underwater terrain will be rocky, and the ship will be partly buried. In other words, the problem will be great, even though the water is shallow. So she decides that the teachers will need good pictures of scuba equipment and that they should plan to give the children some choices; for example, these fins or those? They will need to do some research about the deepest water into which scuba divers can safely go and the hazards they might face, such as the bends or nitrogen narcosis. This kind of information she knows the teachers may never use, for the children may not take them into it, but they'll have it ready for a possible postdrama discussion if not for the drama itself. Heathcote knows the scuba diving situation reduces the children to communicating in pantomime, so she suggests regular sessions above the water. There the class can share what they've found, tabulate and make estimates of what is there from what they've seen, check to see whether each diver is honest, and so on. She recommends exploiting the experience underwater to develop spatial cooperation.

If a leader arises, she suggests giving him or her plenty of room to develop—but not to become a dictator or keep the others from feeling that they, too, are involved in solving this problem. If that happens, the teachers might "cripple" the leader in some way—maybe by helping the others make an effigy or plot a rebellion.

One thing Heathcote would plan to get to when the divers reach that sunken ship is this reflection: "You know, it's incredible that men have learned to build bastions against water." What a teacher cannot or dare not plan is how that class is going to take the challenge and get to the ship, and what ship they will find when they get there. Whatever it is, the teacher must plan to accept and build on it for the next part of the drama.

If there is only one hour for this drama, the teacher can start in role on board the ship: "Are you the people who have come to do it? Right. Come over here. She's lying in four fathoms. I've brought the documents for you to look at. You did get the message, didn't you? I see you've brought your scuba outfits as requested. These will all have to be inspected over here." The next goal will be to get to the point of asking, "Can you plan your dive in teams?" and the divers will soon be ready to go down under. If, on the other hand, four days are available, the teacher can begin by cutting out ships and drawing pictures of scuba diving outfits.

When Heathcote does a drama herself, she goes through the same "for" and "against" listing of strategies that she asks of her adult students. We can see this process in her planning for a drama to help a class of fifth and sixth graders sense the spirit of inquiry that lies at the heart of an archaeologist's career. In this instance she asked us, her adult students, to join in the planning. She and all of us began by collecting a set of artifacts fashioned of natural materials—wooden vessels without nails or metal of any kind; wooden paddles and mallets; clay pots without glaze; large uncut beef bones, boiled and bleached to look very old; seeds of various sizes and shapes; pressed leaves; a primitive drum; an old, frayed fishing net; a carefully knotted pattern of cords that might be "discovered" to be a record-keeping device in a primitive society; a crude spear made of a sharp stone bound to a wooden shaft; a gnarled tree crotch; gourd bells; an antique polished bead necklace. She wanted to bring the problems of the archaeologist, the expert, into the classroom. She admits, however, that this kind of teaching is only second best. Her first choice is to take a class away from school and let them work alongside real experts, as part of a team of archaeologists actually at work on a site. This she does in England whenever possible.

In this case, she decided to use as a lure the Big Lie that in the large hall where the class met, the children would find a tomb from which they might get a clue to a culture long since dead. Through probing and looking, they might discover the values, the beliefs, the core of that culture. She knew this kind of pursuit would quickly move into research, recording, museum exhibits, information to report to the public, so she planned to have plenty of paper and drawing and writing equipment handy. She also assembled a limited library of resource books—not enough to overwhelm the young researchers, but full of enough detail and illustration to answer some of their questions about how a primitive people might have lived their daily lives. A book like *The Epic of Man** or *The Ascent of Man*** is the sort of thing she wanted to have on hand.

She directed her adult students to the task of setting out the tomb, suggesting that the absence of color might be a way of symbolizing the notion of the primitive. She made sure all of the artifacts were of earth tones and asked us to dress in subdued hues the days the children were there. She brought in several yards of a roughly woven black and brown fabric and some old stained and faded rags to be used for gravecloths. We cut a large, coffin-shaped piece of brown burlap to put under each of the bodies. A young man and woman and two children agreed to be corpses.

---

*The editors of LIFE Magazine. *The Epic of Man.* Englewood Cliffs, N.J.: Prentice-Hall, 1961. 307 pp.
**Bronowski, Jacob. *The Ascent of Man.* Boston: Little, Brown & Co., 1974. 448 pp.

Then we were given the problem of deciding where to put this tomb. Our first thought was to put it under the cupboards which ran along the front of a raised platform about three feet higher than the main floor. Heathcote evaluated this in terms of its advantages and disadvantages. Its obvious value was that it would force the children to work under the awful, cramped conditions under which archaeologists often do work. Its major disadvantage was that on the first day the children would have to wait to see the tomb before they would have any commitment to it. Therefore, we rejected this plan, at least for the first day of the drama.

Next, we tried putting the bodies fanned out in a semicircle in a corner of the hall. This way we gained a feeling of enclosure, yet the corpses would confront all the children at the same time. The only problem here was that the corner had stone walls, which created the feeling of a church. (This was only natural, because in fact it was a church where the class was meeting.)

We tried putting the bodies onto tables. This made them more accessible, but Heathcote quickly rejected this plan because bodies on tables give the feeling of operations. Her instinct was to keep the bodies less accessible so the class would have to do more to get at them.

We tried setting them up near the door where the children would be coming in but rejected this because it, too, would make the tomb too accessible. Finally, we chose a spot on the floor far from the door; there we arranged the bodies in a circle around some carefully laid-out wooden leaves and a primitive drum. The heads were toward the center, propped up on upturned wooden bowls which were placed on the burlap grave markers. We streaked the faces and bodies of the swimsuit-clad corpses with yellow chalk and wrapped them in gravecloths. The man's face was partly bound with a gray cloth; the woman's eyes were covered with a strand of her long hair. Around each body we carefully arranged the artifacts and bones. Next to the man lay the spear and knotted rope, next to the woman a bowl of seeds and a decorated pot. Heathcote decided this arrangement had the most affect. By being far from the door, it would hold its essence longer, and yet when the class gathered round it, everyone would be able to look into the mystery at the same time.

When the plan was carried out, the advantages and disadvantages of Heathcote's choices were tested; she made further decisions as she worked with the class. Right away, the presence of the dead bodies provided a powerful lure for the children. Its only disadvantage proved to be that at first it initiated more inquiry into the cause of death than into other aspects of the culture. The fact that two of the bodies were those of children caused the class to speculate that a plague or disaster might have overcome the tribe.

Heathcote decided she would try to move the class into an examination of other aspects of the tribe's culture. Accordingly, when the class assembled, she asked them whether they would like to take up the artifacts and examine them. This they did, individually and in small groups, drawing and labeling each for an exhibit; thereby they got more deeply into the archaeologist's role. This strategy had the additional advantage of letting the children determine their own pace and level of involvement without too much teacher interruption or pressure. At the same time, however, it had two disadvantages: it prevented Heathcote from getting to know the children except as she could observe them from a distance, and it prevented the children from feeding on one another's discoveries.

Next Heathcote decided to set up a communication system in order to learn about the tribe. The great advantage of this was that individuals could come to her without feeling threatened; the disadvantage was that the rest of the class was denied each person's discovery. There was also the distinct disadvantage that no matter how the drama might be limping, Heathcote had set it up so that she was not in a role to help it along or introduce tension when needed.

Another strategy Heathcote had chosen for use throughout the drama was to assume the attitude of the archaeologist and the casual tone characteristic of experts in approaching artifacts. This had the advantage of giving the students something they seldom, if ever, get in their other studies—the presentation of a culture as totally undefined, with only clues as to what is significant.

The class was faced with the problem of growing a new culture out of nothing but artifacts and a burial site. They had to posit a theory about the social life and values of a people on the basis of what was found with the dead and how the bodies and objects were positioned. They were starting in the middle of a mystery, but because the tone was casual, they took the artifacts away and drew sketches of them, presenting theories about their use. This had the disadvantage that the whole was broken up and the mystery of the gestalt no longer worked on them. The children treated the artifacts as archaeologists would—examining them, arguing over their use, arranging them in a museum-type display with labels. They lost the sense of mystery they might have developed had Heathcote's tone been one of awe in the presence of the holy and untouchable.

Even though she knew it might work against the establishment of the attitude of the archaeologist which she was after, Heathcote decided to ask the class whether they would like to become the people living in this culture and using the artifacts instead of viewing them as experts would. This meant they would assume roles suggested by the artifacts. The advantage of this strategy was that it offered an opportunity to elaborate a more complex culture than they might be able to do if they stayed in the roles of researchers. Heathcote knew, too, that even when the class was assuming the roles of the primitive people, she would continue to press for the spirit of inquiry she wanted to develop, using questions like: "What have we now discovered about the relationship between the leader and the people?''

Thus, whatever teaching strategy you choose, you have a price to pay. Heathcote says, "To feel this balance between for and against is one of the securest things you can find in yourself, because there need never be guilt about your task and the way you set about it; you have weighed up the pros and cons and have risked those strategies that seem to have the greatest gain for the least loss. If it doesn't work, you cannot blame yourself. You cannot possibly foresee everything."

No matter what you do, once a drama has begun there is no way to go back and start over. That experience has to become a platform for everything that follows, so you have to devise a strategy that takes account of what went before.

Heathcote repeatedly advises teachers not to waste energy in self-recrimination or regret. That is self-indulgent. Instead, take account of your blunders and admit them to the class without incriminating yourself: "I thought this might lead us to the problems of the spacecraft, but maybe it isn't working. What do you think? Would you care to try it again and this time have us all be part of the *same* ground control?" There is no apology, simply an open acknowledgment that the work is not going well; nor is there any attempt to ignore what they have just been doing. If the relationship between the teacher and the class remains healthy, the work can go as wrong as anything, and they can all recover. If the relationship is bad, or if the teacher or class waste energy affixing blame, there is no way to recover dramatic work that is faltering.

One thing Heathcote will not do: she will not shrug her shoulders and imply that whatever work the children are doing is worthless and can easily be cast aside. This is why she acts on each suggestion they seriously propose and takes responsibility for making it work dramatically. She feels that far too often we reject a child's contribution or even our own ideas, throw them away and say they don't matter. If an idea is the best you can think of at the time, it should be valued, not thrown away; it is the platform on which you build your next idea.

In real life it isn't possible to throw out what you've just done and live as if it didn't happen. You've bought this shirt, spilled that grease, lost your wallet, had this child—and there's no changing it. You will always be affected by the experiences you have had. To split life into sterile little atoms and see no connection between one and the next is to lose the power that is present when the tensions within one's life are held together in a whole. Heathcote illustrates it this way: when she goes out to buy a new bedspread, she looks for something of what she liked in her old one, or else she tries to get one that's totally different. In either case, what went before has a part in the choice of the moment. We cannot recover a tabula rasa, so why pretend? The only way we ever mature is by recognizing that something carries over from the last thing we just finished to the next thing we move on to. Once we accept this in ourselves, we see the absurdity of pressing a class to forget who they are and what their values are at the moment—regardless of how much we might personally regret that they have these values—and pretend to be totally different people. This is asking for phony pretense, for giving the teacher what she wants to see, at a cost in personal integrity and mental health that is awful to contemplate. People can't turn themselves inside out. We are at any given moment the product of myriad experiences, and we have to begin by accepting that wherever we are is an acceptable place to be. Once we've done this, we are comfortable enough to extend our range of experience a bit. People should never be made to feel that where they are is not all right, for if that happens, they haven't the courage to do anything but hold in terror to the only place they know.

When Heathcote's adult students hand in a lesson plan, it includes one central aim; several strategies, with arguments for and against each; and a list of materials needed:

1. Aim

2. Strategies   for   against

    a.

    b.

    c.

3. Materials

She asks them to show her their materials before they meet with their class. Sometimes the "materials" include another person dressed to indicate some role.* They may also include recordings—storm sounds, rolling waves, bird songs, train whistles, babies crying, wild beasts fighting.

Heathcote's critique of a lesson plan points out the difficulties that may arise as the teachers use the strategies they have chosen. She helps them decide which strategy holds the most potential for effective drama and poses the fewest difficulties: this is the one to start with.

So far we have looked mostly at the planning that precedes the first session of a drama. Now let's concentrate on the other two kinds of planning: between-session planning and planning that goes on while the drama is taking place. Between sessions, after you know the direction the drama is taking,

---

*See Chapter 11, "Using Role in Teaching."

you have time to fill in the gaps in your own understanding. For example, if a class has chosen to do a drama about the American Revolution, it is good to come in the second day with some alternative historical events to give the class as choices for direction: for example, the Boston Massacre or Tea Party or Paul Revere's ride. You need to have facts at your fingertips to use if the class feels the need for them. These facts may be unnecessary, of course, because the class may have another idea.

After the first session, you assess the degree to which the class is nearing the goal you originally set out to achieve. If they seem to have moved very little, you try to figure out why. There are many possible reasons. Their belief may not be firmly established yet. Perhaps they have ignored the lure you thought would entice them. A small group may be spoiling it for the others. It could be that you haven't actually found the right "content level"—that is, the desired simplicity or complexity in approaching the material—for this class. For some reason, they may feel insecure in their roles or in participating in the drama. Perhaps what they thought would be exciting has turned out to be overwhelming and so they have gone "weak" on their roles. They may not yet have seen the advantages of cooperating in a group task. If one of the participants is assuming all of the leadership, the others may not become involved and take responsibility for decisions. It may be that as yet this group is merely talking cool rather than living hot through the events of the drama.

When you've figured out the reasons for your difficulties, you will be able to plan strategies to modify the children so they can overcome the limitations of the day before. Be very honest about your own points of discomfort in the previous lesson. Decide whether these are just sore points with you that should be ignored, or responses to genuine problems in the drama. If the group has been flippant, sharpen your wits and see whether you can think of a dramatic way to shock them into a more serious attitude. You may decide to begin a session by assessing the class's commitment to this particular drama. "Did you think about this drama at home? Were you hoping we'd go on with it?" If they say "no," you must be prepared to start a new drama, of course.

A good way to begin any session after the first is with questions that will evoke a summary of what has happened in the drama so far. "I can't quite remember what happened yesterday. Can you help me?" What the children remember will be a clue to what was significant or interesting to them; this will give you guidance on what you dare not ignore but must build on in this day's session. You can also use this review time to find out more about what individuals were doing. "I saw you drawing something yesterday, didn't I?" is a good bland question that leaves it up to the child to tell the class what it was, if it was relevant to the drama—or to simply shrug and say, "Yes." You might say, "I saw you two crawling under that table there. What did you find?" Don't push for an answer if one is not forthcoming. After all, the worst way you could begin a second session would be with a sense of failure about the day before.

As you plan your strategies between sessions, you make the same two lists as before: arguments *for* and arguments *against* each. When Heathcote was deciding how to set up the second day of the tomb drama, she kept the same aim: to develop the spirit of inquiry that is central to the archaeologist's career. The alternative strategies she considered were totally different, however, because the children clearly were serious about the drama, curious about the possible meanings that lay behind the arrangement in the tomb, and committed to finding out more about this tribe. One strategy she considered was to say, "There are those who are responsible for the various times of the day—for the food-preparation time, the teaching time, the ceremonial time, and so on. Therefore, will you apportion the time around the clock and write in the time of day that you are responsible for?" For this, she would need a large construction paper clock with no numbers on it. The advantage of this strategy was that it was a crude way to put pressure on the children she had not had a chance to talk with the day before. If she felt she dared press into the verbal area, she planned to ask each child to tell the others the myth attached to the task that child had chosen. She also considered setting up a ritual in which each individual would interpret the values of the tribe as reflected in his or her job. Another possible strategy was to have each member of the tribe take on two apprentices from the large class of adults who were watching this drama and teach them how to become a part of the tribe. Another possibility was to have a drummer drum hours of the day. As the drum tolled each hour, the tribe would move to the appropriate activity for that time of day or night. Another, more difficult strategy would have been to symbolize the dark and light sides of life; the tribe members would define these in terms of their particular tasks. Heathcote also considered having the children devise names for each segment of the day and develop appropriate rituals to symbolize those segments. She thought of setting up a strophe and antistrophe of the tribe and the archaeologist: the tribe would live their lives, but from time to time the archaeologist would say "Stop." Then they would freeze and answer the researcher's questions about the meaning of what they were doing.

This is the way Heathcote plans—proliferating all the possible strategies she can think of and then choosing one that best suits the needs and the potential of the class. Like the process of segmenting, this listing of all the alternatives you can think of provides you with a wide range of choice and assures you flexibility in planning. In choosing a strategy for the tomb drama, Heathcote never forgot her primary aim; she selected the strategy she felt had the most implications, so it would lead to the most reflection.*

---

*If you want to find out what happened in this drama, see Chapter 17, "Code Cracking: Other Areas."

With another group, Heathcote's planning after the first session concentrated on finding ways to get the group more committed to the drama.
The first session had been disappointing—part of the group didn't seem to
care much about what was going on, another seemed overwhelmed by what
was expected of them, and a third seemed to have very little interest in
cooperating on a project that involved the rest of the class. Therefore, all of
Heathcote's strategies focused on ways to develop personal commitment. She
considered having each person make a commitment to be personally
responsible for some piece of machinery. This is one of the crudest ways to
get people to work. She considered rituals. The three groups had chosen to be
in three different countries, so she weighed the possibility of bringing them
all together for a conference to make a report to the world about their
countries. She thought of pulling them all together to work on a common
task that the whole world had to solve together, such as bringing down an
unknown space ship. As part of this strategy, she planned to ask the class
whether they wanted the visitor from outer space to invite them to a new
world or bring them to a new recognition of their own world. Naturally all
her strategies for this class involved as much soliciting of their opinions and
their decision taking as possible, for they badly needed to see their ideas at
work. She carefully considered the hazards attendant on each strategy. If she
decided to have a space ship, choosing a crew would create a problem.
Because the children had already chosen other roles for themselves the day
before, choosing a crew might militate against the entire class's feeling good
about staying with their roles. (If the space crew could jump out of the
challenge of the roles they had chosen the day before, why couldn't everybody?) One of Heathcote's rules in drama is that when you choose a role, you
don't drop it lightly. You at least try to stay with it as long as you can. She
may make an exception when the role is a very big one—Moses leading the
Israelites, for example. Even then, however, she does all she can to shore up
the role for the volunteer, having him or her stand on a table, perhaps, or
letting someone else be deputized as leader while Moses goes off to confer
with God. All the while she's helping the volunteer explore the role more
fully, and she asks the group to help with it as well. This stance is consistent
with her conviction that our lives have a continuity that we deny at our peril.
We can't just throw something down if we have committed ourselves to
it—not without psychic cost, that is. On the other hand, if a whole class
decides not to go on with a drama at all, she is prepared to let that happen.
As for the space ship idea, she decided not to use it unless some new children
came in the second day. Then they could be the crew, and the rest of the
class could continue in the roles they started out with. This actually
happened on the third day of the drama, so she used this strategy then.

Sometimes the problem that needs solving is that for some reason, one
individual is impeding the progress of the group. If the problem is belief,

Heathcote deals with that very swiftly.* The problem, however, may be simply that one individual is too eager to solve all the difficulties a group faces and to solve them before anyone else has a chance even to reflect on the matter. In this case, the teacher has a challenge Heathcote tactfully calls "managing the leader." Those of us who studied with her one summer at Northwestern University remember vividly a forceful and verbal nine-year-old named Ken. Ken was a slight lad who knew all the answers. When his group decides to do a drama about the American Revolution, Ken is right there with facts and solutions; before the drama has gotten under way, he is issuing muskets to his minutemen; he is quite prepared to start the war and end it in the next 10 minutes. Heathcote's challenge is to let this eager leader assume his aggressive role for long enough so she can focus his energy on the group task. Then she works gently to win him to a new kind of leadership, the slow gathering of evidence and proof to convince a nation that the time for rebellion has come. She "promotes" him from the role of rabble-rouser and plot hatcher to Samuel Adams, the leader who coolly collects data, keeps records, and writes letters; the thoughtful leader, choosing his words with care. Most of the strategies she considers between sessions are ways to keep Ken under control but give him enough status to sustain his interest. She cannot deny him a role where his information and expertise, which is considerable, will be valued. Heathcote decides that if he were to prove that she, as governor of the colony, has been cheating the people and overtaxing them, this proof would have to come slowly. His merely shouting it would not do. So she plans to prepare some documents with a different color of ink over an erasure in several credit columns and to keep these on her desk in her governor's house. There Ken can find, study, and decipher them and then use them as evidence against her in role as governor. Before she has a chance to use this strategy, however, Ken is defying her, refusing to pay a tax although he has the money to do so.

The governor has no choice but to put the rebel in the stockade; this limits him physically, but of course the villagers can come to the stockade and listen to his ideas. Heathcote is pleased with this development, however, because at least the initiative to ask for Ken's leadership is now in the hands of the rest of the group. Ken puts his head through the back of a chair in which he sits backwards and manages to look very uncomfortable. Heathcote sets up two volunteers to be his British guards with their muskets in hand. The villagers try to bring him food, but the soldiers forbid it. All this time, Ken keeps hurling unrepentant invectives at the governor and soldiers. His classmates are amused and laugh; obviously, Ken is in a familiar role as class clown. Heathcote stops the drama and says, not to Ken but to the group: "We're falling into a trap here. Now let's do this and not laugh. Of course, he's saying

---

*See Chapter 7, "Building Belief."

things that are amusing. It's easy to call somebody a stinking rat in a school classroom with a green carpet on the floor, but it's not so easy to say that when you could be shot in a minute. This is why you mustn't laugh." This plea to the group as a whole sobers Ken as well; soon he is politely requesting that the soldiers free his hands so he can feed himself; they refuse, so he sits dumbly while a girl slowly spoons him his supper. We all watch Ken grow a tremendous control under his hot-tempered bravado.

Heathcote's problems with this leader are not over, but his growth is beginning. In subsequent dramas she "promotes" him from defiant leader to the rebel who is shot, from a doctor who is animatedly directing the entire staff of doctors and nurses in a hospital to a patient "who is deeply unconscious." "Promoting" Ken to these passive roles is not as difficult as it might appear: all Heathcote needs to do is ask for a volunteer for a role that sounds exciting, and Ken is the first to apply. She uses the word "promote" with her adult students; with the children, however, she is careful not to give any indication that she is favoring one child above another. One of the hallmarks of her teaching, as a matter of fact, is her refusal to compare children. She will critique the work as a whole, but she will usually congratulate any child she feels is trying in any role, no matter how large or small it is.

Heathcote plays to the natural leaders of the class most of the time. Some of her adult students have questioned her about this, suggesting that a more "democratic" goal might be to rotate important roles and bring everybody "up to the same level." Heathcote rejects this because it is not realistic. A person who is shy in a certain type of situation is going to continue to be shy in most similar situations. Leaders cannot be leaders without followers who acknowledge their right to lead; why not recognize that this is true in every group of people, and let leaders arise in a natural way? This is consistent with Dorothy's conviction that we bring to any new situation all of our previous experiences.

In every group there are one or more people who tend to stand apart and watch, who are reluctant to get into the center of the action. Heathcote's challenge is to find a way for people like this not to try to stop being the loners they are, but to find loner roles they can identify with within the drama. Let them make their contributions to the group effort in the role of outsiders, observers, or reluctant participants. If one of the children stutters, let that child be the person who refuses to speak. Then put on so much pressure that this stubbornly mute person can't help speaking out; at that point, stuttering won't matter.

On the other hand, quite often in a drama a child will volunteer for a role that he or she at that point is not up to handling. Heathcote does all she can to help such a child feel success in the role and grow through it. She never hints to anyone, "You cannot manage such a big responsibility." On the second day of the Revolution drama, for example, Ken's quiet, unassuming sister volunteers to be the British governor—the role that Heathcote played so strongly the session before. She is not up to the role in an external sense, but Heathcote never acknowledges this. She sets her up behind the big desk and gives her a paper and pencil. Who knows what image of governor grows inside that slight frame as the girl quietly writes the letters to King George and in her soft voice demands the tax payments?

In summary, a great deal of the planning between sessions is based on what Heathcote has found out about the group and how it functions. She sets up environments, brings in documents or materials for research, plans strategies that will help this particular group of children move from where they so solidly are to a new awareness, a richer understanding of their experience. Sometimes her strategy is to bring in a person from the community who can answer questions that have been raised by the experience of the drama. A group of children who are in the middle of a drama about mines are ready to listen to a pit worker. They are ready with questions that brew from the inside, like "What does it feel like to come out of the pit every day when the sun is going down?" They're not interested in school-baked questions, like "How deep is the average mine?" This does not mean that a school visitor has to be someone special. Any adult has had experiences that children whose curiosity has been aroused by a drama are ready to ask about. One of the mothers might come in and meet with a group of primary children to answer questions like "What is marriage really like? What do you do about money if there are two? Doesn't it seem kinda strange to find yourself with a new name?"

So we have predrama planning and between-session planning; we also have the third kind: on-your-feet planning. While a drama is going on, especially when it is going well, Heathcote's mind is racing to plan the next happening or to find a way to drop the level and examine implications. She thinks through her next verbal statements, deciding how to word them sensitively and carefully so that they will signal to the class exactly what she wants. Whatever the class does, she's going to be ready with the next move. She's burnishing up her tactics in her mind all the while and looking at the implications of what the class is doing. As she puts it, "There is no luxury in the profession of teaching except the luxury of thinking, and, my God, what a luxury!" She thinks about her teaching all the time—in the classroom during the drama and at home at the kitchen sink.

If the drama is limping, Heathcote decides whether it's better to let the class go on and get through this problem on their own or to intervene and help them. She will try to intervene before the class senses that a rot has set in. She never wants a class to spiral into failure. This does not mean that they cannot look at work that is going wrong, but when Heathcote stops to look at it, she takes a full share of the responsibility, suggesting that it might go better if they approached it differently. She will often interject a fresh face into the drama, introduce an unexpected element, or ask a branching question to elicit a new commitment. She doesn't hint that the class has fallen down; instead, she tries to quickly help them assess where they are and examine some of the alternatives they face. If Moses loses heart and does not know how to stand up to Pharaoh, Heathcote will say something like this: "It seems to me that here's where we are now. There is this new element, isn't there? This king is deciding to harden his attitude. He's saying, 'No, Moses is not going to get that piece of papyrus he's been wanting. Anybody can see that the river is turned back to water; I'm all right. He's not having it.' So, how does anybody handle a problem like that?" She solicits suggestions from the group, asking them to help Moses decide what to do with this new development. Thus, Heathcote puts her thinking at the service of the class, always alert to their needs during a drama.

When the children are doing something that detracts from their involvement in the drama, Heathcote tries to find an appropriate way within the Big Lie to modify that behavior. For example, if a group of primary school children are going down to the bottom of the labyrinth to hear the voice of the oracle, she may find that they are butting each other. Then she will suddenly discover that there is a priestess who conducts each one separately down the dark winding hall. This way she attacks the problem of butting without stopping the drama.

If you start a drama with a pudding of feelings,* you will have no initial planning but you will be pressed to plan very quickly once the drama has begun. It is your task to provide the tension within each situation and plan the transition from one emotion to the next.

Although Heathcote makes use of books as she plans, she does not read "how-to" books and follow their formulas (although she would go along with the views of Winifred Ward, Caldwell Cook, Peter Slade, and others). Her greatest resource is not explanations of technique but literature and history, sociology and anthropology, biography and psychology, mythology and fable, poetry and art. She wants to spend her time outside of class reading books that tell her more about the human condition, for that is her storehouse of material. Her wide-ranging reading includes books on how learning occurs: *Contrary Imaginations* by Liam Hudson, *Guiding Creative Talent* by Ellis Paul Torrance, *New Think* by Edward De Bono. She also reads Marshall McLuhan, Jerome Bruner, Rachel Carson, Joseph Campbell, Carl Rogers, Sigmund Freud, Susanne Langer, Robert Graves, Pierre Teilhard de Chardin, Alfred Korzybski, Herbert Read, William Glasser, and Norbert Wiener, to name just a few. She seldom reads textbooks—she feels that they do little to illumine inner experience, and it is inner experience that she thrives on.

*Described on page 69.

She looks to books, not for plans, but for nourishment for her own growth. She reads out of felt need. Because her drama plans begin with a clear idea of what the drama is *for*, its center of meaning, everything she does is calculated to reach that center. She is convinced that drama teachers have gotten by with very shabby planning in both Britain and the United States. All too often, they cannot tell you what they want the children to achieve in a particular lesson. This kind of fuzzy-headedness will never win respect for drama in the schools. Without a clear center, there can be no sensible planning.

11. USING ROLE IN TEACHING

One of Heathcote's most effective teaching ploys is her skillful moving in and out of role. She goes into role to develop and heighten emotion; she comes out of it to achieve distance and the objectivity needed for reflection. Thus she helps participants stir up and express emotion and a moment later set it aside and look at it coolly, growing what she calls a "cool strip" in their minds.*

Heathcote goes into role more actively early in a drama than she does later. Talking about emotion is no substitute for reacting to it, so Heathcote's characteristic stance at the beginning is to step into a role and play it in a highly charged, often aggressive way. This sets the stage for the class's response. Once their drive is strong, she can play down her own role. If she comes on in role as a threat, her action promotes a reaction that unifies the group against her, harnessing their emotional energy in a very effective way.

Because she can be such a dynamic and forceful leader in role, Heathcote often startles or even frightens a group. When this happens, she immediately jumps out of role and addresses the class as the teacher again. For example, she once gave a group of six-year-olds a drink at a party they were dramatizing. Suddenly she said in a very witchlike voice, "Aha! You drank my drink, didn't you?"

"Yes," they murmured, for they had.

"And now you nice, kind American children are my slaves. Aha-ha!" She saw that this forceful utterance had a strong effect on them, so she quickly came out of role and said with a warm smile and her normal teacher voice, "Would you like to be my slaves just to see what happens?" They agreed, so she went back into role again.

The roles Heathcote takes are those that give her the greatest maneuverability. Her favorite ones are middle-rank positions: the first mate, the foreman in the factory, the police officer who is just following orders, the radio

---

*See page 136 of this chapter for discussion of a teacher's own cool strip.

transmitter on a submarine, Caesar's messenger, the doctor's assistant. This way she is not the final power, but she is the effect of that power. She tries not to take the role with the highest rank—she wants ample power, but not the power to make final decisions. These she wants to leave to the class, and she assumes that in most classrooms there will soon be a volunteer for the highest-ranking position. If she has too much power, the class will look to her for leadership; if too little, they'll mow her down until she comes out of role to manage the situation. In a middle-rank position, she can simply refer them to a higher authority, saying, "That's all I know," or "I've done as I was told," letting the class take it from there and decide what happens. In the middle rank, Heathcote is in a position to communicate freely to those of both higher and lower rank. She can impose the limits that create tension and even work to raise a group to a feverish pitch of anger against her; then she can step out of role and congratulate them for their unity and convincing expression of feeling. Through opposing her in role, the children develop a sense of their own power.

In the drama of the American Revolution, Heathcote chose the role of governor. Although he was the highest ranking person in the colony, his authority derived from the king and his laws. Heathcote played him, moreover, as a loyal and obedient servant to His Majesty, King George. She therefore did not have sufficient authority to make any significant changes. These could come only when the colonists chose to rebel; thus Heathcote forced them to unite.

To effectively go in and out of role in situations of high emotion, Heathcote needs to give the class absolutely clear signals as to when she's in and when she's out of role, so they'll have a clue as to how to respond. At other times, she may deliberately assume a bland "shadowy role," in which she doesn't set up an opposition to the class but rather joins them. In this case, she can facilitate their working through a situation, sometimes in role, sometimes out of role as teacher. Then her signals do not need to be so clear. She steps in and out of role at the service of the class, as we shall show later.

When she is in role, Heathcote never takes more than one decision that indicates a direction for the drama. Out of the response of the class to that one, she will take another, but her goal is the same as the goal of her questioning: to get the class to take responsibility for what happens in the drama. She may begin a drama by saying to a group, "It's expected of you. Weren't you briefed?" Then she stands expectantly for their response. A class member might begin to define the teacher's "it" by saying, "I had no message that I had been chosen for this mission to the moon."

One time Heathcote began a drama in role as a man of middle rank from a different group. She did not indicate who she was except for a hint of military bearing; from a little distance away, she walked purposefully toward the seated class. When she arrived, she paused, looked at all of them arrogantly, and demanded, "Take me to your leader." The children looked at one another questioningly; finally, more and more of them began to look at one particular boy. He acknowledged their choice by standing. Heathcote said, "You have never seen a man like me before." Still she did not define her role or circumstances.

The standing leader did it for all of them with the words, "We do not like Romans here." This set the tone for what lay between the two of them. He responded to the nonverbal signal that what was said was a threat, and he was willing to throw it back to her.

Heathcote said with a sneer, "There are many of us; you'll just have to get used to us." Her next problem now that the child had told her who she was, was to decide why this one Roman had come upon this group of non-Romans. Again she did it with as few words and as much ambiguity as possible, so that the class could make what they wanted of her words. She gave herself some rank with the words, "I have left my horse down by the river. He was thirsty. Have you met a man you can trust who can bring the beast up here?" Heathcote knew that in Roman times ordinary soldiers did not have horses, so the animal gave her rank; at the same time, she wanted to make it clear she was not the tribune of a legion. The leader sent two boys to get the horse. While they were gone, Heathcote threatened, "Are you sure you can trust those men with my horse? It will go ill with you if my horse suffers."

Then she told them why she had come. "I have been sent to find what the skills of your tribe are. Are there any skilled arrow makers in this tribe?" she asked in a sarcastic tone. Some of the children stood up, but their leader motioned them to sit back down. It was clear he didn't want this. Heathcote reached out her hand, but the arrow makers, looking tentatively at their leader, wouldn't shake the Roman's hand. She looked to the leader and waited, saying in gesture, "What about this?" It was a moment of pure theater. They looked at the leader; he nodded; she smiled and shook hands with each of the arrow makers.

The Roman asked the arrow makers to show her their work. She looked it over carefully, then said, "Hmm—the workmanship here is better than the metal." This upgraded them as workers, was true to the times of the Romans, and in the same breath kept her authority as a Roman who was competent to make such a judgment.

She asked for more information about the skills of the tribe, and the arrogant tone of her pressure united the group against her. The leader said stubbornly, "We're not tellin' ya." They all started murmuring agreement. Then Heathcote came out of role, asking, "What have you done?" in a tone that was clearly congratulatory. They had achieved an identity as a people who would let this Roman go only so far. Heathcote never asks a group, "What are you doing?" That is a teacher question that implies that they are up to something. Instead she asks them what they have done, a question that implies an achievement on their part.

The rule of thumb seems to be never to hold onto a role any longer than is necessary to get the emotional energy of the group going. Heathcote always leaves a door open so she can slip out of role, give her role to another person, or take the part she is playing out of the drama altogether.

Another rule about assuming a role seems to be to give a prodigious amount of information nonverbally but to actually say very little, giving each word weight and importance. Heathcote started one drama about a strike by entering in role, standing with her hands on her hips, looking petulantly over the class of seated children, and shouting, "Not another bloody laydown, is it? Where's the foreman?" Then she stood there until they did something.

At the beginning of another drama, Heathcote went away from a seated group, then came back and stood apart from them, concentrating on the feelings she wanted to project: fatigue and helplessness. She sighed, waved a signal to them in the distance, and called wearily, as if from far away, "I have been as far as the mountain top, and I can find nothing. We are in the same position as yesterday. I could see your boat. There is neither shelter nor habitation here." This message, although it left further definition to the class, clearly set up a predicament, defined them as all part of one group, and put them in a boat. Thus the verbal and nonverbal signals provided information, although Heathcote appeared to be merely assuming a role and calling to the group.

A third rule about going into role is to use the authority of the role to keep the whole group functioning as one, at least at the beginning of the drama. If the group splinters, the teacher's influence in role is diminished to the one group she finds herself a part of. Once she had a group of teenage girls who wanted to do a drama about the effect of an out-of-wedlock pregnancy on a community. The boys were not particularly interested in this problem. Heathcote came in very firmly in role as the father of the pregnant girl, demanding, "Who *is* the father of this baby? We can't help but speculate." She looked squarely at the group of boys.

At this all the boys put their heads together right away. "You know, this could mean real trouble! Is it one of us?"

Two minutes later Heathcote noticed that the boy who had chosen to be the vicar was having trouble finding a way into the drama. Still in role as the girl's father, she looked at him and said, "I don't know, but when it happened to my Maggie things were said in public."

The vicar replied defensively, "I said nothing in the pulpit about it," and he was in.

"No, well, you may not think you did, but I remember feeling it at the time. Perhaps I was reading it wrong," said Heathcote.

By concentrating on getting all of the boys into the drama, she made the problem theirs, not just the girls'. Before long, the girls were saying, "I don't care who's the father; it's nothing to do with him now."

The boys disagreed, putting pressure on them, "It's all very well for you to talk in this high-handed manner and to go on about how she's done nothing wrong. There's a child coming that needs a father." So those flippant-seeming boys found themselves considering the needs of an unborn baby.

In role Heathcote can move into a small group that is having trouble with the Big Lie and contribute positively, making suggestions that help their belief: "I'm getting very tired of this work. Are you? Ask your leader if we can have a rest."

A fourth rule of teaching in role is to use the role, whenever possible, as a way to get the group to explain what they are about. Heathcote's favorite roles for this purpose are the visitor from outside, typically a very non-aggressive person from outside the community who wants to find out how they do things; the reporter who is getting facts for a story; the person in authority who needs to know what this group has been doing; the messenger who must make a report to the king; or the television or radio interviewer. Another outsider role is the person who will not go along with what the group has chosen. In this role, Heathcote pushes a class to persuade her to go along. Her skepticism is a challenge for explanation and argument.

The great advantage of a teacher's assuming a role is that it takes away the built-in hierachy of the usual teacher-class relationship. When the teacher is in role as a participant in the drama, there is no reason for the students to show undue respect or deference. This, for most teachers, is a new stance, one which allows for a real exchange to take place easily and spontaneously. In role you can be far more harsh both verbally and nonverbally than you dare be as teacher, thereby heightening the drama and feeding the class cues in a way that is not possible as teacher.

In addition to the two clear stances of teacher and of participant in role, Heathcote has a third stance which is deliberately not so clearly defined through verbal and nonverbal signals as are the other two. This stance we shall call *shadowy role*, a bland and ambiguous projection that is so much like the teacher in personality and authority that the class often has no clue that it's a role. When Heathcote takes on a shadowy role, she defines for herself an interest, an attitude appropriate for the situation, and she projects this clearly. At the same time, it is apparent that she is the teacher. Of course, she is also free to drop the shadowy role and, without any clear signalling, act as teacher whenever the drama seems to demand it. If the class takes her into an area where she needs to go into role, she will signal this clearly and go from the shadowy role into an unambiguous one, showing this by a different posture and expression. The value of the shadowy role is that it provides a way for you to project an attitude before you commit yourself to a role that may well be one a class member wants to assume. Still you remain free to move more firmly into the role at any point you choose. Heathcote uses the shadowy role whenever a drama is limping, whenever she feels the class is not quite ready to do without teacher leadership, or whenever she wants to leave the options for direction as open to the class as possible. She does not want to move into a strong role that will determine direction if she senses that the class is strong enough to respond to a blander leadership and to clues that are more subtle.

Let's look at Heathcote in shadowy role at the beginning of the drama about the American Revolution. First, she helps the class establish belief in their village and in their role as colonists. She asks, "What work do we do in our village?" Saying this, she is assuming the attitude of one of the villagers and yet half in role as teacher is also directing them. She takes on her own shadowy role next, "As governor, I send papers to England." Then she asks as teacher, "What do you do? Write your job on the blackboard beside your house." She goes on as teacher directing them to fill out the diagram of the village on the board.* Then, still half as teacher and without changing her tone or gestures, she asks, "If I wanted to talk to all of you, where would I go?"

"The well."

Then Heathcote goes more into the governor half of her role, saying with authority and power, "Today I shall wait for you at the well because I have some news for all the colony." She stands tall and holds her scroll out in front of her, clearly in role and in a one-who-knows register. The class is not ready to respond to these nonverbal signals. They look confused, so she drops the governor's posture and asks in a warm teacher manner, "Do you call yourselves British?"

"No, colonists."

"This chair will stand for the well. Will each of you go to your house again and then come to the well? What time of day should it be?" Although at the moment she's clearly teacher, helping them get this first moment right, she is standing beside the well where they know she will be as governor. She's not yet in role, but still working to establish the setting in their minds. "People have found this village a good place. Who knows what it might be 200 years from now?" Then in a narrative mode, "On this summer morning people are going to get water for their farms." She wonders, still in the teacher half of her shadowy role, "I'd carry mine in a pitcher. I'm not sure what it would be made of." Then after a pause, she decides, "My pitcher would be wood. You think what you'd bring." She leaves herself open to move into role, but she stays in the teacher half as long as is necessary to get the class ready to respond to her in role. She begins by helping them believe in their pitchers and buckets, and she doesn't rush this stage of the process. She continues, still as teacher-leader, "Go to the well where you see all your friends. This is

---

*See Chapter 7, "Building Belief."

no holiday. This is a working day. Find out what you'd say to each other and how you'd get along." Immediately a small group start scuffling at the well. Heathcote moves firmly into the governor half of her shadowy role. "Excuse me, you're wasting time. I need to get my water." She pantomimes pulling up a rope and then says angrily, "Who's in charge of the well? Three days ago I reported that the rope was in need of repair." The class is still not ready to pick up the challenge of Heathcote-in-role. A few boys as villagers start hurling insults at her and uncommitted ones giggle. Heathcote immediately addresses them as teacher, "Would you dare laugh at a representative of King George?" Then, half in role, she goes on, "I shall have some news for you, so try to be careful about what I said."

Another occasion for a shadowy role is when you are team teaching with another teacher who is in a clearly defined role. Then your job is to focus the class's attention on the other teacher-in-role and alternately as teacher and in the shadowy role of participant to keep the drama focused on a response to the person in role.

So far we have shown how Heathcote assumes a role or shadowy role; now we shall look at how she uses another person in role. She puts such a person or persons into a strongly fixed role, one for which there is an immediate emotional response. Heathcote's goal is to set up the person-in-role in such a way that she or he can cast an emotional net around the class long enough to catch them. She works toward developing a communal concern for or sense of mystery about the one-in-role.

Heathcote hit upon the idea of bringing in another person in role as she was struggling to find a way to arrest the attention of groups of retarded children or adults who have difficulty holding any single focus as a group long enough for anything significant to happen. She finds it effective to set up the person-in-role before the group arrives, and bring the group into a room where this person is standing waiting to confront them. It is effective also to costume the one-in-role. This helps both the one-in-role who can then concentrate on adopting the attitude suggested by the costume, taking on that mantle, and the class, who are presented with strong nonverbal clues they can respond to. Heathcote instructs the person-in-role not to speak first, but simply to answer all questions as one in that role would. She or he need not have had any prior theater experience.

Heathcote joins the class in approaching the one-in-role, but she, not the person-in-role, is leading the drama. Typically, she uses one of her adult students or a teacher in the school where she is working as the person-in-role; he or she usually has had no prior theater training. The one-in-role simply stands and provides a focus and a tension; where the drama goes is in the hands of the class and the teacher. The teacher can feed clues to the person-in-role with words like, "I don't think he's going to want to eat that," or "She may be angry if we tell her," or "He may run away if we talk right to him; should we risk it?" The teacher also keeps the attention of the class firmly on the one-in-role; she coaches the person before the drama to maintain poise and mystery as long as possible. Then, as teacher, she can say, "Listen to what he says," and the few words of the one-in-role can take on weight, fullness, and intent.

Heathcote's goal in working this way is to expand the class's awareness of what it is like to be the person-in-role and to lead the class to discover their range of responses to such a person. She has found that a person-in-role actually does capture the attention of retarded groups, and this is the first essential if anything is to happen. Such a person can even, in some cases, hold a class's attention for an hour or more, so that the drama actually has time to go somewhere.

She has also found that using a person-in-role makes it possible to lead the class either into archetypal experience or into tasks associated with a particular role. Roles that lead best into archetypal experience are the stereotyped ones—a conventional fairy princess, nun, ghost, king, inventor, gardener, fortune teller, vagabond, clown, sea captain, derelict, pirate, ice queen, or rent collector. Some roles that tend to lead a group to perform tasks and to use the appropriate vocabulary are—a helpless adult tied into a ball, a limp doll, an astronaut, a blind or wounded person, a wild man in an animal skin, or a recently arrived immigrant who cannot speak or read English. Heathcote chooses the role that has the greatest potential for leading a particular class into a new area of reference, into new experience. Although she prefers the archetypal role because of its potential for "left-handed learning,"* she will choose a task role when her goal is to develop an awareness of the attitude, job, and language of a particular kind of worker.**

I watched Heathcote use another adult in role with a group of eight- and nine-year-olds who were dramatizing the life of a group of early settlers. Her goal is to edge this very verbal and active group into an archetypal experience of confronting someone who has a sense of mission and commitment. She asks one of the adult class members who is actually a nun to wear her conventional nun's habit but gives her no prior instruction except that she is to stay in role as a nun and tell the group that she must get to the Indians. She is carrying a large cross made of two tree branches and a big, heavy Bible. When the nun admits that she is nervous and doesn't know what to do, Heathcote reassures her that she need do very little. She can be the dumbest nun known and can play it nervously, if she likes. What Heathcote is after is what the role symbolizes. Heathcote suggests that she herself, in role as one of the settlers, might say, "She's so naive she doesn't know about the Indians." Then she could see how the children cope with that naiveté and what they do to help. She tells the nun-in-role to decide how she knows

---

*See Chapter 14, "The Left Hand of Knowing."
**See Chapter 17, "Code Cracking: Other Areas."

about the Indians and what her mission is. She also needs to figure out where she's come from and what difficulties she's had so far. Heathcote won't let the nervous nun talk this out with her and the adult class before the children arrive; she assures her that she and they will discover this together. This is a typical approach of Heathcote's; she resists planning out plot details before a drama begins. The less she knows about what will happen, the more alive she is to respond at the moment of discovery. However, she assures the nun-in-role that if she dries up, she need only signal for Heathcote to help her out.

Then the children arrive. After some discussion, they decide to begin their drama in the early evening when they are all at the waterhole in their little settlement. They begin working together, drawing water and filling buckets. Then the nun walks in. Heathcote introduces her, "This is Sister Margaret. She tells me she needs to reach the Indians."

The nun says softly, "I don't know where I am."

The children tell her that if she goes to see the Indians, she'll be killed by the time she reaches them. They try to dissuade her. They ask her to come eat with them, and she does, blessing the food and telling the settlers about her journey. One of the men draws a map to show her where she is. He tries to explain how impossible it would be to reach the Indians alive. Heathcote interjects, "Although she seems gentle, she may be stronger than she looks."

Ken, that particularly vocal member of the group whom we've met before, tells her she'll need a gun. "What we really should give her is a gravestone," he asserts firmly to his fellow settlers. "The law of averages says she's not indestructible."

Heathcote suggests, "She may not worry about the law of averages."

When the nun goes off to rest, the community discusses the problem she poses. They comment on the fact that she blessed the food. Ken says disgustedly, "People don't do that around here." Then the group starts mocking the crazy way the Indians do their praying. Before long they are talking about the threat of the Indians, about how they will kill anyone on sight, about how they have no law. Heathcote doesn't interrupt this sharing of their prejudice. Instead, she says to herself, "I've got my next play, brother. It'll be about those Indians you don't understand."

Deliberately restraining oneself from an involved response or argument when a group is clearly wrongheaded, as in this instance, is what Heathcote calls working from inside one's "cool strip." She urges teachers to grow their own cool strip, a part of themselves that can hold off from involvement, reflect on what's happening, and plan an appropriate next step for the drama. Without a cool strip, teachers become too immersed in the drama to lead it effectively. The danger of losing a cool strip is greatest when the teacher either disagrees strongly with the values of the group or is in role and so is concentrating on her or his own feeling and response. However, it is at the height of the dramatic action that a cool strip is most in demand. Part of

Heathcote is always cool, detached. It became a joke among us adult students: we would ask each other, "How is your cool strip growing?"

In the drama with the eight- and nine-year-olds, the nun-in-role works for the girls, but the boys are bored. Simply dismissing the nun as a "kook," they decide to go off to their hunting. Heathcote delays them only long enough to be sure that they are committed to being responsible hunters. They have only two guns to share, and only five bullets each, which she carefully passes out. Despite this, the hunters quickly get into a skirmish with the Indians. As they carry on without Heathcote's leadership in a fairly superficial drama, she works to deepen the belief of the girls. They ask Sister Margaret a great many questions and finally decide to give away the village's only mule to help her on her journey to the Indians. In the meantime, the men come back from the hunt with one of their company seriously wounded in the leg. They grab Sister Margaret's cross to use as a splint, thereby demonstrating that they have little or no regard for it as a symbol of a different set of values. When the men discover what the women have done with the mule, they decide to hold a village court. Although the women defend their gift to the nun rather persuasively, the men put pressure on them, arguing that they cannot plow without a mule. The women respond that they'll just have to learn to plow without it. Ken is shouting by this time: "We need that mule for something important! Send her away on foot!"

The women point out that the nun just might bring them peace with the Indians. One of them even notes, "You can't blame the Indians for not trusting us; after all, we took their land."

Another remembers, "They taught us to plant corn." The girls are united in defending their gift. Heathcote in role as a citizen of the village asks those who are in favor of the gift to stand up. Eighteen do so; Ken and three other boys remain seated to vote "no." By having the "yes" vote stand, Heathcote effectively reduces Ken's power; the mule goes with Sister Margaret.

After the drama is over and the children leave, Heathcote tells her adult class that a person-in-role needs to stand longer and say less than Sister Margaret did. The longer a person-in-role can take the silence and wait to let the class make the first move, the less time it takes for the drama to get deeper. By talking early, Sister Margaret missed the first beginning of the children's thinking. Heathcote feels we need to train teachers to rely more on what they are and less on what they know. They need to find a way to get through without always depending on words.

It is often the needs rather than the competencies of the person-in-role that call out the most compellingly. For this reason, Heathcote frequently confronts the class with a person who has a helpless quality, like the derelict* or Sister Margaret.

---

*See page 139.

Once Heathcote brought a smartly dressed man into a group of five- and six-year-olds and told them he was going to be Granddad. The children watched as he took off the wig he always wore in real life (an act of no little courage on his part), then his jacket, tie, and shoes. He took off his neatly tailored trousers, revealing an old pair of baggy pants with suspenders underneath. He put on some slippers and glasses and became Granddad, who lived with the class all week. He was a regressive sort of Granddad; he kept losing his specs and dropping things. His presence provided an exercise in caring. He became quite real to the children: even though every day Heathcote said, "Good morning, Mr. Richards," and then he went through the ritual of transforming himself into an old man, the children still went home and told their parents there was an old man in school. That is what they wanted to believe. They spent the week helping him and came to like very much having him in class.

Heathcote once brought into a class of very tough teenagers a student teacher-in-role as a large, old woman with a big handbag. She wore a shapeless dress, a man's jacket tied around the waist with a string, men's shoes, and a very good felt hat that had seen better days. Sitting beside her was a fairly complete stack of newspapers of the past two months and a cracked teacup with a used teabag on a dish beside it. Into the large handbag Heathcote had put a collection of clues: some 1906 check stubs, a few photos from that period, half a tin of cat food, a little book on English wild flowers, an old ring with a signet stone, half a pie in a paper bag, two National Assistance (welfare) books, a pension check, an old comic book, and a letter signed "Ben." The letter is written in a rather bad hand and tells about the trouble Ben's been having with his bad back.

Heathcote asks the class to come meet this woman, reminding them musingly that she has a history and that someday she will die and her rich past won't be known. As they come close to her, she says nervously, "You've not let the cat out, have you?" They reassure her and find out that her name is Annie. Then Heathcote turns them into archivists who seek to find out how this woman has lived. Annie remembers little and can give them only vague clues. From this and the contents of her handbag, they piece together her past life. They decide she lives in one room of a three-story house that looks like the one on the next page.

She goes to the bus station every day to tidy it up. She brings home a newspaper to read. The class finds out that in the last burglary, the lock on the back door got broken. Since then, she has used a string to tie the door shut. They decide no one should know about this. They start very tentatively to care for her, respecting all the while her need for privacy. When a group of fifth graders are invited in to meet Annie, the class of difficult and hitherto bullying high schoolers defend Annie. They won't let the little kids get too close or ask idle questions.

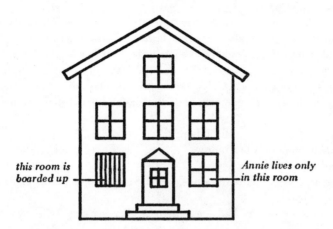

this room is boarded up ——— *Annie lives only in this room*

Another vulnerable person-in-role whom Heathcote has used is a small Chinese girl who can speak Chinese. Heathcote stands her under a clock in a classroom. In her hand are a Chinese passport and a much folded letter that says in English, "When you get off the plane, wait under the clock and I'll be there." When the group come in, their first problem is how to approach somebody if you want to help her. They agree, "You can't just walk up to somebody and say, 'What are you doing?' " It is obvious that she has been there with her big suitcase for a long time. When they speak to her, she answers in Chinese. Most groups of children do figure out a way to solve this Chinese girl's problem, for they cannot bear to have her come so far and be let down this way. She has come on the wrong day; she is in the wrong place; there's another clock. In any case, there is nothing she can do to help it, and the class has a problem. This is another exercise in caring.

In Nottingham, Heathcote was faced with a group of children who had a propensity for tough, violent behavior. Some of this may have sprung from the sheer frustration of their daily lives. A large number were victims of poverty and neglect. One, named Ozzie, had never spoken a word in school. Heathcote decides to meet violence with violence. She brings in a big man with crew cut hair. Like Granddad, he comes in first in good clothes and then takes these off in front of the class, revealing prisoner clothes underneath. Heathcote introduces him as Tom Crow, a tramp; she says, "I wonder what people like that think about. He gives me a funny feeling."

The class doesn't hesitate, "People like that are tramps and murderers, and they kill people."

"Do they really?" Then she turns from the tramp and asks the class what they do when they are not in school. They tell her they play, so she says, "Here's my house; I live on your street." She draws a picture of her house on the board. Then she says, "You go play on Miss Brown's doorstep today."

"Who's Miss Brown?"

Then Heathcote jumps clearly into role as one of the members of the neighborhood. She says with the authority of one who lives there, "She lives in Number 41, doesn't she?" When they look at her in puzzlement, she goes on, "Oh, you have not seen her lately? Well, her dog's about; I hear it barking. Get yourselves off and play on Miss Brown's doorstep."

The children go to one corner of the classroom and then call back, "She's there."

"What do you mean, 'she's there'?"

"We knocked on the window."

"And there's this fierce dog."

"Is there?" Heathcote responds, helping their belief. "How big is it?"

"It's a big dog!"

"I didn't know she had enough to feed a big dog," she says, feeding in information.

"Well, it's a medium big dog."

"I wonder where she gets the money from; she's on a pension, isn't she?" one boy asks, picking up the cue that she's poor.

Heathcote presses him, "How can you tell?"

"Aw, you can tell by the washing on the line."

"Can you?"

"Yeah, it's all women's clothes."

"Really? Does she ever go away?"

"Never."

"But she seems gone now."

"Then why's the dog still there?"

Then Tom Crow appears, coming around the side of the house. As it turns out, this violent class doesn't want him to have done any damage. When they speak to him, they ask without suspicion, "You don't come around here often, do you?" He answers with a gesture. The adult playing the role of Tom is actually a psychologist; he has decided to use the boy who never speaks, Ozzie, as a go-between, so all he will say is "Ozzie." When Heathcote hears this, she too puts pressure on Ozzie, asking the group, "Do you know him?"

"Yeah, he never talks," one girl says, looking at Ozzie's impassive, strong face. Ozzie edges close to Tom Crow, who touches him and begins to whisper in his ear.

Soon the whole class is pressing Ozzie: "What's he saying? Has he seen Miss Brown? Go ask him."

Heathcote stops the drama to build up an image of what Miss Brown is like. She gives each child a task: Can you explain where Miss Brown's family came from? What hangs on Miss Brown's washline on Monday? Can you tell where she got her dog? Can you explain where she gets her money? What does she wear on Sunday? What is her favorite meal? (She can afford only one serving, of course.) Here is a sample of the stories they write with the help of the adults who are watching. These children had been labeled "violent," but there is not one violent thought in any of their papers. It is all very gentle.

Miss Brown's washing.

She washes her dress and coat.
She doesn't wash very often, because she hasn't much money.
She just washes clothes in the sink because she has no washing machine.
Some clothes have holes in.
She likes clothes but has no needle and cotton to sew them up.

What Miss Brown thought about her dog.

She bought it dog food, Bounce every day. She took him for a walk every morning and every dinner and every night. She took a ball with her for the dog on the field. He sometimes carried his food in his mouth, and he carried the newspapers the Post and the Daily Mirror. She had to go to the shop every day. She did not have a lead for the dog. She loved her dog because he did what he was told. She had had him a long long time, when he was a pup. She got him from a pet shop. He slept in a basket downstairs because it was warm.

What she does all day.

She used to take the dog for a walk every day.
Made the dinner.
Used to call the children in to go and shop for her.
Every day she washed the plates up.
She watched the Telly, she loved Tom and Jerry.
Every night she would go to bed at 7 o'clock. She got up at 5 o'clock.
The dog barked at 5 o'clock.
She always liked custard pie, and the dog liked chicken. The dog loves the old lady, and the old lady loves the dog.
The dog's got a room for itself.
They always go next door to see a friend, another old lady.

How Miss Brown got on with her neighbors.

She had some neighbors.
There were two.
One an old woman lived next door on one side. She liked to drink tea and she got on very well with Miss Brown. She was a widow and she helped Miss Brown with jobs such as shopping.
On the other side of Miss Brown lived Mr. Chilly who made a noise. He played the radio loudly.
One day Miss Brown saw Mr. Chilly in the street.
She said to him Don't make a noise I cannot sleep at night because the radio is on too loud. He replied "All right" went in to his house and kept the radio switched off that night.

Heathcote has the children read their papers aloud, so that gradually a picture of Miss Brown is built up. One of the adult teachers who is watching says, "Get that tramp out of there," but instead of taking up the idea, the children begin to defend Tom Crow's right to be there.

"People have a right to have a place to be," one child says to the adult observer. "He has a right to be here when Miss Brown's away." The whole group join her in resisting his being arrested or taken away. They spend two days looking for Miss Brown.

Finally, Heathcote asks a branching question, "Do you want to find Miss Brown alive or dead?" They say, alive. "Well, where might she have gone and left her dog here? You know she never leaves her dog."

A little girl says, "I'll be Miss Brown." She goes a long way off from the group and sits down.

The children decide she has gone to her old house; according to one of the children's papers, it was slated to be torn down because it was old. Miss Brown had had to move against her will. The class goes to the spot where the girl is sitting, and there they find Tom Crow as well. He's camping out in Miss Brown's old house. Again he whispers to Ozzie; Ozzie leads them up the stairs and on up to the attic. Higher and higher they go in silence. Heathcote's flesh is crawling by this time: what are they going to find up there? Finally Ozzie and Tom lead them to the little girl with her eyes closed. Heathcote whispers, "Is she all right?"

"Yes, she's just asleep," says one girl, who is touching her. Miss Brown opens her eyes.

"Miss Brown, we have been worried sick over you," says Heathcote in role. She is shivering and can't remember much.

"Is Tom Crow downstairs?"

"Yes."

"He always watches," says Miss Brown. So they come down the stairs, leading her gently. By now Ozzie and Tom Crow are great pals and are talking to each other.

"Come on and have a cup of tea with me," she says, and they all walk back to Number 41 and sit in her living room.

She tells them why she was in the attic. "Oh, I always go there on the anniversary of my daughter's death." This child is actually a starved-looking waif, deprived in real life of many material things; still she is capable of giving the class this great gift.

"Did your daughter die there?"

"Yes, she was little, you know. So I always go and sort of sit there for a bit." She looks at Ozzie, "Fetch him in." Ozzie goes to get Tom Crow and seats him. She says, "I've an old suit of my husband's which'll fit 'im." So the children dress him gently in his own clothes and stroke him as they do so.

Some of the school staff come in and watch at this point in the drama, but all they can say is, "Ozzie's talking!" This makes Heathcote angry. A "violent" class is caring for a disheveled adult in a way that few adults in that school are actually caring for those disheveled children, and the staff cannot assimilate this fact.

Here is the story that group wrote after the drama was over:

THE STORY OF MISS BROWN.

All the children knew Miss Brown.
She lived in a street near to them.
They played in the street outside her house.
Her dog liked to play with them.
One day she left her dog in her house and went away.
She left her washing on the line.
The dog barked and the friends heard it barking.
They looked everywhere for Miss Brown.
Upstairs and downstairs but she could not be found.
They remembered she used to live in another very old house the other side of the field.
They went to seek her and they found TOM THE TRAMP.
He looked hungry. They gave him milk, and some sandwiches.
He told Oswald that Miss Brown was upstairs in the attic of her old house.
The children found Miss Brown—she was cold and shivering and couldn't remember anything.
They took her home with TOM THE TRAMP and they all sat round the fire.
They had a cup of tea.
Miss Brown gave one of her husband's suits to TOM.
She told all the children that her daughter had died in the attic of the old house and that was why she liked to go there to remember her little daughter sometimes.
The children look after Miss Brown and do her shopping and get the dog meat from the butcher's.

To demonstrate how to set someone up in role, Heathcote has each of her adult students dress in a costume that she or he thinks has potential for use by a person-in-role. She then comments on how that role might be used. She is always looking for ways to use the faces and costumes in the class as a way into archetypal experience. Thus, she urges her students to find a length of cloth, a hat, or a bag that symbolizes a way of life.

For example, she will see in a young, slim, pretty woman with long, straight, blond hair the potential to become a mermaid for a group of young children or mentally handicapped people. Heathcote makes her a big, beautiful, crepe paper tail which she can move in a sinuous manner. She sets the mermaid up on a rock with her comb and mirror, adding bits of rocks and pebbles about her tail. She tells her to be combing and singing when the class comes in. Heathcote sets this part up very carefully, but she does not plan what the class will see; if they see a seahorse instead of a mermaid, she will let that happen; it is not her job to decide how the class will respond. Her goal is to set up a person-in-role in an evocative yet bland role. She plans what to do if the flimsy tail breaks, of course; then she can ask the class whether they want her to be a woman with a tail attached or a mermaid with a woman inside. The fact that the one-in-role stays there and confronts them and will not go away provides the tension for the drama. Heathcote will not rush them into seeing what she intends with eager questions like, "Do you see the mermaid?" She tells the mermaid to find their questions confusing: If they ask what her name is, she'll not know about names. Heathcote may plan to have a man in a fisherman's outfit come in and carry a big net towards the mermaid. He will do this at a point in the drama when the class has decided they like the mermaid. Usually the class will then attack the fisherman and try to stop him. Once a group of mentally handicapped people put the fisherman in his own net. When the mermaid's tail came off in the struggle, they decided to take it to the shore and throw it into the sea. "We must return it to Neptune," they said.

When Heathcote is setting up another person in role, she starts with her or his physical aspects. The quality of the gaze, the set of the jaw, the size and posture—all are starting points for deciding how this person might be used. Once she saw a tall, proud, somewhat stubborn young black woman as a sunflower. She used her for a group of mentally handicapped children as a tall sunflower that simply could not hold up her head. The long, lovely neck became a stem; twelve heavy golden petals ringed her face. When the class first saw the sunflower, she was drooping. Her petals weighed heavily on the children. It was so hard to hold up that beautiful bloom when the stem was so weak. The class had to face the problem of getting the sunflower to stand up. They built a fence, and they took the beautiful, falling-down heavy flower and lifted her and leaned her against it. In every way they could, they encouraged her to stand. The girl stayed in role, a weak flower that was just barely managing to stay alive. The children prayed over her; they put food into her hand. This was wrong in fact, but it was right in feeling: they were nurturing the poor sunflower. After all, it was caring, not photosynthesis, that Heathcote wanted to develop in the class.

If a person wears glasses, Heathcote emphasizes this aspect of physical appearance. If she wants to emphasize vulnerability, she'll find an adult with the thickest lens and the smallest physique to work in role. To symbolize that here is a person with a lot of thinking to do, the frames might be enlarged with dark paint. A monocle can be translated into an eye that sees differently. She might put dark sunglasses over a person's real eyes and add a third eye with a monocle. This might be the eye of memory; Heathcote could use it if she is working with a group of mentally handicapped who are convinced they can't remember things and her goal is to help them discover that they can. To high school students, the monocle might be a symbol of madness or of what seems madness but may not be so. The glasses might be extended to a telescope: then the class is plunged into the brotherhood of all those who use tools to see more. Suddenly they resemble Galileo, who was the only one with this kind of instrument.

One tall, slim woman powdered her face white, curled up her dark hair, and put on a doll's mouth. In her long, white stockings and red-and-white checkered dress, she became a limp doll. It was the children's challenge to get her to stop flopping and sleeping and find a way to get her to open her eyes and stand. With young children, Heathcote has used a doll tied in a box. As they stand around the box all tied in a ribbon, the children can hear a faint tapping and soft "Let me out, let me out!" One of the appealing things about a doll is that it is quite adult in size but totally inadequate.

Heathcote looks for a person-in-role who needs the group for some reason. This does not mean that the person-in-role must be unduly helpless or vulnerable, but that the person must have the power to draw the class in. Once I stood on a table in a long, black flannel cape and black cap. Heathcote decided I could be the guardian of a treasure or mystery, a seeker who needs information, or a messenger who brings information. In any of these there is some lure for the class that they won't want to ignore. Heathcote urges her adult students not to look at the person-in-role theatrically, in terms of all the things that might happen now. Instead, she says, look at the role as a way of evoking some kind of involved response, and then trust that the drama will go somewhere. It doesn't really matter where it goes: the main thing is to give the class time to find a response, to be patient with their groping attempts to understand and act. As teacher, you keep your attention fixed on the role and say, "Come, have a look at him," "Do you think we dare move closer?" or "Why do you suppose he's here?" Keep your questions bland so that the class is free to make their own interpretation of what they see.

Over the years, Heathcote has developed four major rules about using a person-in-role, guidelines for making the experience vital for a class.

First, the teacher must stay in charge of the role; the person-in-role responds to the class and to the teacher but stays in role at all times. The teacher protects the one-in-role from drifting (since the person-in-role is not used to acting) and from being treated with disrespect by the class. If the one-in-role is sitting beside a treasure chest or holding onto a large bag, the teacher must protect the right to privacy, make sure that personal property is shared only when the possessor chooses to share it. The teacher also give clues to direct the one-in-role's response when necessary.

Second, the person-in-role must look within for the meaning of the role. How to project the attitude of the chosen role is the person-in-role's own affair. The teacher who coaches this person too much beforehand throws away the opportunity to spontaneously react to the one-in-role along with the class. The person-in-role's job is to discover her or his identity and feelings and then project them all the while the class is there. The teacher has to sensitively pick up this attitude and figure out how to use it with the class to move towards a moment of reflection that drops into the universal. The person-in-role should maintain a single attitude and unmixed signals. It's best to stay close to just one central effect. You want the person-in-role to be as restricted as it is appropriate to be in that role. This does not mean that the effect might not be ambiguous (Heathcote works towards ambiguity), but if the one-in-role decides to project an unwillingness to give up cherished beliefs, for example, then that attitude will prevail no matter who the class decides the person is.

Once, with a Latin class, Heathcote set up a drama in a Roman home. She asked a student teacher who knew Latin to wear a long flowing robe and bring along with her everything she could find that implied a Roman household: a bowl, jar, handmade broom, mirror, low bench, wax tablet and stylus. Then, when this Roman matron invited the Latin class into the classroom she had set up as her home, they could examine each of the items. Since the goal was to cement the language, they of course did all this in Latin. The woman-in-role assumed a Roman name and concentrated on projecting a person who was as Roman as she could make herself. She answered questions about the items of her household, and Heathcote exploited the role to get at the quality of this woman's life for the Latin students. The one-in-role concentrated not on the class's learning, but on projecting Romanness.

Heathcote's third guideline is that the role has to exemplify a way of life. If the person-in-role is engaged in a task, that task should be considered less important than the purpose to be served. The task should grow out of the role. If a role remains too firmly limited to the job, it cannot move to the universal. An inventor can be struggling to solve a problem, but his struggle also exemplifies his inventor's eye that never sees anything for just what it is but for what it could be.

Once when she was working with a group of mentally handicapped children, Heathcote set up a blind market woman in a long African gown. This role did not work, because it was so strongly task oriented. The market woman was sitting down with a sack of potatoes she was trying to sell. Because she was blind, she had to trust those who bought from her to pay enough. The children responded to the task, not the role. They eagerly set about helping her locate the potatoes, finding them very interesting, and helping her sell them. They never got to the universal of blindness.

The fourth guideline is that although the person-in-role concentrates on just a single attitude, the role itself must not be fixed too firmly. There needs to be an ambiguity, a mystery, a strangeness that holds the class. Your goal is to move into the "left hand," into archetypal experience.*

---

*See Chapter 14, "The Left Hand of Knowing," for more examples of this use of role.

12. THEATER ELEMENTS AS TOOLS

Classroom drama uses the elements of the art of theater. Like any art, it is highly disciplined, not free. Like painters, sculptors, or dancers, the participants are held taut in the discipline of an art form. Thus there are rules of the craft that must be followed if the implicit is to be made explicit, if the classroom drama is going to work so that, as in theater, a slice of life can be taken up and examined.

Drama is never doing your own thing. Everything each person does must be in context of the others in the drama and the Big Lie all are committed to believing. In a classroom, each individual must agree to be open to others and to stay with the challenge of responding relevantly if the imagined moment is to take on the texture of real experience. Ironically, by disciplining themselves to respect the rules of drama, the participants become more free to discover all of the possibilities within the art form.

The difference between theater and classroom drama is that in theater everything is contrived so that the audience gets the kicks. In the classroom, the participants get the kicks. However, the tools are the same: the elements of theater craft. As Heathcote sets up a classroom drama and trains teachers, she relies on her theatrical sense.

However, she is not in theater, ever. She thinks we tend to press children far too early to grow the art form of theater—the making of an overtly explicit statement with one's gesture and body and voice. It is enough to press children to believe. Belief belongs to both classroom drama and theater; making overt explication belongs to the theater alone. Heathcote puts all her energy on what is at the heart of not only theater experience, but all of our life as well: the process of identifying with the experience of another person. Whether her students ever go into theater is irrelevant to Heathcote. Her concern is that they use drama to expand their understanding of life experience, to reflect on a particular circumstance, to make sense of their world in a new and deeper way.

What the play looks like from the outside does not matter to Heathcote unless it bothers the class. What she is after is not a play that is accurate or looks right to an audience but an experience that feels right to the participants.

One element of good theater is focus on a particular moment in time that captures the essence of a broad, general human experience and shows its implications. In the theater the playwright does this for us by taking sides in an issue, selecting a central character, and revealing the tension of his situation with carefully contrived explications within the theater tradition. In the classroom, the teacher does this by simplifying the general subject to a single moment and using sensory details to sharpen the focus for the class.

At the beginning of the "killing the President" drama, Heathcote takes the big idea of assassination and makes it work dramatically by giving the class enough sensory details of one particular spot so that they can build a clear image—though not necessarily the same image—in each of their minds. She asks the boys to close their eyes, saying, "I want you to see this place where this gang lives and always meets when it's on a job. Nobody would ever dream as they pass it outside that inside there a group of men hatch all kinds of destructive plans. Trucks come and go, load up and leave things; inside, packing cases lie all over the place. But there is one very special packing case, and I would like for you to see it very clearly. It has a door, and you can go through the packing case; and behind it is another door. Through that door is the meeting place for this gang."

To this imagined place the boys come, with all their prior experience about similar rooms, and begin to talk as they believe men would under these circumstances. The Big Lie has been swallowed—they are "in." Their concentration has been heightened by Heathcote's clear focus. In real life, we are bombarded with such a wide range of unrelated stimuli, at such a fast rate, that we are often distracted from concentration and reflection. In drama, there is only one thing to attend to at a time. The world is made smaller and more comprehensible by this isolation of a single factor. In drama, too, we can play out the consequences of a particular act and not have to really live forever with its effect. We can literally have our cake and eat it too because after the drama is over, we can go back and do it again differently. This never happens in an absolute sense in our lives: as Heraclitus reminded us, you can never step into the same river twice.

Once belief is established, Heathcote works to develop another of the tools of theater craft—tension, the pressure for response that is at the heart of a dramatic action. Tension is the "third dimension," what the drama is really about—not the story, but the cliff edge on which the participants find themselves. The teacher's main task after getting the Big Lie accepted is to lead the group to a cliff edge and then leave them there. They must struggle to find their own way back to safety. The teacher doesn't tell them what will happen, because that's up to them. This is where the excitment in drama lies, where energy is released to power the class forward to new discoveries. A drama is a trap into a particular time, place, and circumstances. This is the fixed moment, and there's no escaping it; it can only be worked through. This fact alone, once the class perceives it, provides a tension; the class is under a real pressure. This pressure can be the suspense of not knowing, or it can be the desperation of sensing a crucial limitation which one has to fight to overcome. Tension is at the heart of good drama as Kenneth Tynan defines it: "Good drama for me is made up of the thoughts, the words, and the gestures that are wrung from human beings on their way to, or in, or emerging from a state of desperation."*

How does the teacher inject this element of desperation into a human situation? Sometimes Heathcote does it by stepping into role as someone who won't let the class off the hook, who demands a response. With immature classes she often sets up a very blatant opposition to the class, thereby creating a conflict and making it easy for the students to respond.**

She may provide tension simply by introducing a surprise question into a firmly established scene: "What is that crawling over there?" Or, "My Lord, have you seen the boy? We have lost him."

Heathcote sometimes supplies a transitional narrative as the children pantomime the action. This gives them a feeling of continuity as she leads them to another cliff edge. "Night came, and the tired band of explorers laid out their sleeping bags before the fire. They climbed into the welcome warmth of the heavy bags and slept soundly until sunup. When they woke up, they looked around their camp in horror; all their food was gone." After the children have worked themselves back from one cliff edge, they often need a period of repose before they are ready to take on another challenge.

Another way to introduce tension is to define a relationship between people that is fraught with complication. For example, if two male doctors are discussing the technique of a brain operation, the situation is not necessarily a dramatic one. If, however, the same two doctors are discussing a specific operation on a particular woman and in the course of the conversation discover that they are both in love with her, a tension is introduced that makes the situation dramatic.

The suspense of not knowing always creates tension. The longer you have to wait to find out, the more tension you feel. So, whenever a class is in a position of waiting to see what will happen, Heathcote does all she can to keep them concentrated on the anticipated event and get them more and more worried about the possible outcome. For example, on that sailing ship of 1610, the captain disappears after the first day. The girl taking that role

---

*Wilson, Colin, and others. *Declaration.* (Edited by Tom Maschler.) New York: E. P. Dutton & Co., 1958. 201 pp.

**Examples of this are in Chapter 11, "Using Role in Teaching."

has in fact gone on vacation with her family. As time passes, the crew feels increasing consternation because the captain does not come out of his cabin. Finally, after two days, they decide to break in the locked cabin door and see what is wrong. Speculation ranges from "He doesn't care about us," "He is ill," "I think he's insane," to "He's been murdered." Five boys are ready to storm down the door and find out. Heathcote wants to set up the drama to heighten tension, so she won't let this small group of boys instigate the break-in just yet. A few girls in one corner have been talking about a mutiny; others are more concerned with their tasks aboard ship. Three of the crew are earnestly talking about whether they can take up the captain's mission if the captain himself is dead—whether this ship can go on and follow a dead man's dream. "Did he give his chart to any of the crew?"

Heathcote stops the drama to effect a dramatic focus. "If the captain is dead, then what? The second mate would take over. If he's not dead but mad, then there would be some point to that mutiny you are talking about. Which will it be?" is her branching question.

They decide they want the captain to be dead. The boys are as eager as ever to break down the door. She reminds them that if they were aboard a real ship, they would not be allowed to do this on their own. They'd have to report the locked door to the first mate. As the teacher, she sums up their situation: "The captain has not been out of his cabin since this ship set sail. Some say the captain has gold, but that is just a rumor. I don't know and you don't know about this yet. We may decide we like the idea of the gold and produce it. But for the moment let's make the opening of this cabin door happen to all of us at once. Out of this will come our choice of what to do next." So she slows the pace and builds the tension. In role as the domineering and loyal first mate, she addresses the assembled crew in a raucous voice: "Attention all seamen! I've heard the rumors that are going round about the captain, and I'm gonna prove to you that he's a good man. This Alan is his personally chosen cabin boy. So Alan and me and the second mate are gonna go personally down and at the risk of the captain's anger we're gonna push open that door. Now you stay here as witnesses. Neither Alan, the cabin boy; nor I, the first mate; nor Bill here, the second mate, will enter the captain's cabin. You can watch from where you stand. So turn yourselves around and look at the captain's cabin. Don't take your eyes off it. OK?" She continues, in a louder and slightly petulant voice, "Now don't let anybody say they were not in a position to see. There will be no more rumors aboard this ship; there will be fact. . . .Put your shoulders to that door. Is it locked from the inside? Then push. Go on, keep on." Then she turns to the second mate: "Better give him a hand, Bill. And neither of you set a foot over that threshold, hear?" The two boys push again. "Go on. It seems to be giving. Push again. Take a run at it. Do you feel it giving a little?" Before long, the boys are actually panting from the effort of running repeatedly against the imagined door. Out of role, Heathcote coaches, "It's a big door. No captain's gonna have a little flimsy plywood door in those days. It'd be a thick door of heavy oak. It's got an iron lock. Don't get it open 'till you feel it's right." Then, clearly back in role, she says roughly, "Do you hear anything in there?"

"Sharks!" shouts a boy who has all this time been standing on a chair as the poop deck lookout. He has been unaffected by Heathcote's attempt to focus the group's attention. She looks up at him. Without showing any irritation at his irrelevant outburst, she says, "We'll watch for the captain; you watch the sharks." As long as his private vision of the scene doesn't dissipate the intensity of the action at the captain's door for the others, she lets him go on with his spyglass. To the two boys she says, "Try again. See if you can feel your way to the moment when both of you know the door gives way." They continue until they make it. Heathcote shouts, "Everybody stand back! The door is open!" Then she orders the cabin boy to walk in and look around, but not to touch anything. He walks back slowly, looking a bit awed. "What do you find, Alan?"

"The captain's lying in his bed . . . ."

"Well?"

"He looks dead!" The group gasps. Suspense has been built while the group waited to find out what was behind that door. Although the class had decided they would find the captain dead, they didn't know exactly when the break-in of that door would come. As they all (except the lookout on the poop deck) silently watched the two boys arduously run against that door, their anticipation became more intense. That final gasp is real.

One of the easiest ways to build up tension is to create a situation in which something is going to happen, but no one knows exactly when: the police are going to raid the place; the ghost is going to appear; the doctor is going to get the plague; Pluto is going to swoop down and grasp Persephone; the mountain lion is coming to maul one of you; you are to be interrogated in your turn, and you know you're the one who will be found guilty. Everything is set up so that this *must occur*, but none of the participants, except the one who is in role as the protagonist, knows when or how it will happen. This creates the tension of waiting and not knowing how you will respond. To plan a response in advance is to wash out the tension. Suspense is the press of *not* knowing.

Another way to create tension is to introduce an element of desperation caused by a limitation of some sort. It might be that one of the vital necessities, such as food, water, or air, is in short supply: "You three have the responsibility of carrying the water for the trip across the desert. It's up to you to see that it's shared fairly. No one dare simply take a drink when he likes."

A limitation of space can create tension. Heathcote remembers facts that hold dramatic potential: The dimensions of the quarters for Africans carried unwillingly to the New World in a typical slave ship were 5 feet 10 inches deep by 16 inches wide by 30 inches high. To know this is to have a clue to the tension felt by those captives.

Sometimes Heathcote will use the tension of not being able to get out; for example, in a mine disaster, a sunken submarine, or a stuck elevator. Once a group of New York teenagers decided they wanted their play to take place in the New York City Public Library. Heathcote quickly assumes the role of a minor official, walks into the room holding an imaginary walkie-talkie and begins saying into the transmitter: "This is the New York City Library. You want me to lock it up right now? Right." One of the students asks her why she is locking the door, and she says, "I don't know; my orders are to lock the place up and nobody's allowed out."

She goes on pantomiming locking each door. After watching her a few moments, somebody says, "We want out of here; you've got to give us that key."

"If you attempt to go, I'll throw this key out the window," she says, brandishing it in front of them. By now they are earnestly discussing the situation. They sense there are more thrills in accepting this Big Lie than in denying it, so they obey the rules. They don't try to leave the library.

Finally, a boy says, "Can I use your walkie-talkie?" She lets him have it; he says, "It isn't working."

"It is, too!"

"It isn't."

"Christ! You're right! Well, if you must know, all I know is there's some sort of scare out there. That's all I know, and I've said more than I should have already." The group guesses that an atomic bomb has exploded. They keep coming to Heathcote, who continues not to know anything. Finally they decide she should go out and find out what is going on. She resists, "Oh no, my orders are to stay right here." Then they forcibly take her key out of her pocket, unlock the door, and push her out, grabbing her walkie-talkie in the process. She stands away from the group as they start to talk together. They begin to worry. What have we done? One of the boys begins to repair the walkie-talkie. At this point, Heathcote decides to be the police head-quarters.

However, before she can do that, one boy shouts that he's leaving the building. He bursts out the door, comes straight to Heathcote, and says, "This is fascinating! I never dreamed drama was like this!" and so the two of them have a little chat about how exciting it all is.

All at once the others get the talkie-walkie going. Heathcote hands over a transmitter to the boy next to her. "You better take it."

This he does, but he doesn't answer their particular call. Instead, he says, "We are clearing Forty-Sixth Street." The students look at one another: the library is at Forty-Second Street. They know they are not to be cleared yet.

"I repeat. Will all other areas stay put; your turn will come. If you have enough water, bear up." He keeps applying pressure, moving up a street each time.

Heathcote walks up the library steps and says, "Let's suppose it's three hours later." This intensifies the pressure. They discover that there is very little water left in the cooler and the faucets don't work. They start to argue amongst themselves. After a little while, Heathcote has them move to 12 hours later, then to the next day. The situation gets more and more tense. The limitation of having to stay in that place under those difficult circumstances heightens the dramatic impact.

After the drama is over, they reflect on the situation. One girl says, "You know, I just realized I haven't thought about anyone but myself for three days!"

Another limitation that causes tension is not being allowed to do what you're committed to doing. One group of children has decided to be a medical team taking supplies to Russia to help in an epidemic. They meet Heathcote in role as a customs official who blocks their entry and again as a mother who won't allow blood tests on her daughter. This frustration creates tension because the doctors can't get on with what they are committed to doing.

In another drama, a nine-year-old King Ahab decides that Jezebel's temple can be built only in the center of the city. This means tearing down something that the people are very committed to preserving: their homes. They plead eloquently to him to spare their homes, because their children need shelter. Their pleas are disregarded. They dare not rebel against the king, but they also feel the agony of losing their homes, which by now symbolize their powerlessness. In the tension of desperation, they finally hit upon one reason for not razing their houses that the king dare not ignore. One child says bravely, "Your majesty, King Ahab, there's a leper in my house, and you better not go in there." King Ahab says, "Then we'll burn your house down, not tear it down." The child says back to him, "Do you think that that would kill leprosy on this spot?" She has won; Jezebel does not get her temple built because that clever child, under the pressure of desperation thinks of the one thing the king can do nothing about.

Another pressure Heathcote uses is a limitation of time. If the students are archaeologists at work labeling and preserving the artifacts from a tomb, she might suggest that this site is going to be inundated in a dam-building project in three weeks. The challenge is to save the tomb for posterity. The team dare not work so fast they risk breaking irreplaceable artifacts, but they must make the deadline.

We have seen how Heathcote uses tension to heighten drama. She also uses the three spectra of theater craft in a classroom drama. With them, she can create artfully some of what seems to be magic when it occurs on the stage.

The spectra are:

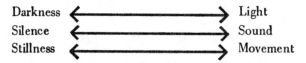

For thousands of years the human family has been employing these spectra in the development of theater, in devising ways to affect an audience. The result is that theater craft is flexible and adaptive. In the classroom, the teacher can shape it according to the needs or interests of the class; the children need not be twisted around the medium.

Theatrical tools need to be adapted not only to the children, but also to the room. In the average classroom, it is often difficult to use the spectrum of darkness and light. The simplest way to overcome the fact that many classrooms are designed to be light but never dark is to have the children close their eyes and pretend it is dark. Heathcote frequently asks children to do this. In a drama about an orphanage, she wanted to create the feel of bedtime in a room that could not be darkened. She had the children lie down on the floor and close their eyes while she lighted a real candle and held it high. Then she softly beckoned the children to leave their imagined beds and come to the light of the candle. As they actually stirred from a state of stillness to movement, they moved in their imaginations from darkness to light. Heathcote's words emphasized the change from one end of each spectrum to the other. "In that dark bedroom, the orphans came to the glimmering light of a single candle." In a room that cannot be darkened, Heathcote often uses the magic of a candle or lantern, either lit or unlit, to create the illusion of darkness. If she can get real darkness, of course, she uses that to create the drama of a glimmer of light in the night.

She might begin a drama about Beowulf by using the darkness-light spectrum. As the soldiers gather around the welcome warmth of the fire in Hrothgar's dark hall and are chilled with talk of the monster Grendel, Heathcote might say, "I gain comfort from these flames in the night." Then, as the fire dies down, the challenge might be, "Who will dare go out into that dangerous dark for more logs?"

If a group of primary children want to do a drama about a monster or dragon, Heathcote knows she's going to have to use darkness, even in a bright room, to make that monster come alive. In one drama she decides to hide an angelic-looking, curly-haired, blond volunteer monster until she can build up his belief in himself as the monster and the belief of the 43 others in him. She finds a piano to hide him behind and works back and forth between him and the class. "What does he look like?" she asks the class and gets a description of his teeth and claws. She goes back to the monster's cave and says, "You've no idea how scared they are of you!" Then back to the class, "What time does he come out?"

"At night."

"Let's go to bed then." She helps them set up their beds in the castle and lie down and close their eyes. Finally they all believe in this monster they cannot see. Then the little boy behind the piano comes out of his cave, making the fiercest monster sounds he can muster, and it doesn't matter what he looks like. By that time he is a big monster to everyone in the room. By manipulating the children to believe in the darkness, Heathcote has led them to believe in the monster.

The silence-sound spectrum can be employed in a variety of ways to heighten a drama. In the monster drama, when it comes time for that little blond boy to threaten the victims, he senses that his voice cannot do the job. Heathcote asks him, "Why do you keep coming around our castle?" She hands him a piece of chalk. Enveloped in a rapt silence, he writes in a very large circle on the floor:

Although he is not yet able to move effectively from silence to sound, he has grown into such a big monster in his mind that he can fill the silence in that classroom with a very big threat.

The silence-sound spectrum lends itself well to dramas about theft. One class decide they want to steal the queen. Heathcote first works on the looks of the castle. The children tell her it is a big building and the queen is at the second window on the right; ivy grows up to that window. The challenge then becomes, "Who can be quiet enough to climb up that ivy?" It is a contest of silence; the only sound is the queen's muffled scream.

Often Heathcote finds it helpful to simplify a situation by deciding to have an event unfold in just one of the three spectra. For example, a group of 10-year-olds decide to live in 1646 and to have something happen that poses a mystery. They start the drama on the village green at noon on a summer day. All labor has stopped because the sun says it's time to eat. They decide that at that moment a coach should drive into the middle of the village; the horses will stop, but nobody will get out. This is the mystery. They then decide that the coach will arrive in sound alone. Most of them go back to believing in their lunchtime lethargy and their cheese and bread, while one group goes off to build the right sound for that coach. In the slow struggle to get the noise right, the coach becomes real. When the children play a rhythmical pattern on some coconut shells, everybody knows the coach has come into the village and is standing in their midst. That sound which has begun and stopped has silenced them all. They now believe the coach, and are ready to tentatively explore it. Inside, they find a sick man. They decide he has the plague, and so are plunged into theater.

A group of fourth and fifth graders were doing a drama about building a nation. When one of their strong young men is mauled by a mountain lion, the community decides the animal must be killed. They set up an elaborate lookout system, stationing themselves at intervals around the room. One boy volunteers to do the sounds of the lion, but his attempts come out weak and catlike. In order to make the snarling lion sounds effective, Heathcote maueuvers with the silence-sound spectrum. The hunters must watch in silent guard through the night, ever alert for a short, low, bird-like whistle—the signal that the lion has been sighted.

Suppose you find yourself setting up the drama of Beowulf's battle with Grendel in a noisy, clumsy class. You may as well start with noise, as Heathcote did, asking, "What does a Viking do when he's been out all day, and he's hot and tired, and he has this steel helmet and steel breastplate on?" The class will probably tell you he takes them all off. Then you may say, "Yes, and what a clatter of the shedding of the day that would be!" With this response, you have suggested not only the action of removing the heavy metal, but also the feeling of shedding the cares of the day. This is not to say that the class will pick up on both, but both will be there in case they can handle them. You say to this class, "Make as much noise as you like in taking off that armor; meanwhile, I shall watch to see how you show that you are weary." A child may be saying, "By gum, look at the blood on my sword—crash!" as he flings it to the floor. Because you have planted a seed earlier, you can stop all the clatter after a bit and say, "I see you are shedding your arms, men. Will you now shed the day? Tell us what you really think. Show me how you feel when you pull out that sword and lay it down. One man might say, 'This sword has done a real battle today' and throw the sword down with force and verve; another might wonder if this sword would ever be any good to him since he failed in battle today." Then you can have the class show their feelings as they pull out their swords. Heathcote chooses to lead a noisy class into noise, because in so doing she is saying to them, "You can do what you're good at—being noisy and boisterous." After she has won them through the noise, she is ready to impose the silence. They won't have a Grendel come until the last sword is dropped and they are in bed. Then its growl can be heard—and with a class of noisy ruffians, this growl will be a big one.

On the other hand, with a quiet class you might start with a near whisper: "I have a feeling he will come tonight, don't you? Let's mark the place each man will take for his bed. Who will be near the door? How shall we choose? Shall we draw lots? Does anybody remember, does he take the first, or does he come forward and turn and take another?" Then the class will tell you their vision of Grendel. There'll be no question.

"He takes the sixth."

"Where is the sixth place?" They'll tell you, and so you'll know where they think the door is.

There will be no army yet, just a group of men deciding what to do with their swords when they sit down. "Can we sit quietly in our chain mail, or will it creak?" You know the Grendel for this class will make a very little noise in a very big quiet.

In the same way, the spectrum of stillness to movement can be put at the service of a class. The monster behind the piano might begin his effect by leaving the stillness of his cave and striding around the castle, the only moving creature in the middle of a still night. If a whole regiment of soldiers are at attention, the breathless messenger who runs in with his torch becomes the focus of the drama. If, on the other hand, everyone is moving, the sudden still one who enters and stands apart may arrest attention. If the goal is to establish the feel of a ballroom, it might all be done with movement—whirling couples and elaborate bows to the king and queen. Then comes the moment when all movement stops and the prince stands to address the revelers, holding one lone glass slipper in his hand.

Once Heathcote's goal was to make a shy, tall lad into the martyr Thomas à Becket. She decides to use the stillness-movement spectrum to make something happen so everyone will believe he's Becket. She tells the boy to kneel toward the front of the classroom as if it were the altar of a cathedral; then she takes her own winter coat and drapes it around his shoulders. So he's a kneeling, still figure at the front end of the class. She tells him he need only stay there and pray. She puts him into stillness and takes the rest of the class off to the far end of the room. She whispers, "He's no idea we are here. How far will he let us come before he turns around?" She gets them to make the stamping noise of knights in armor as they move toward the kneeling figure. She knows that with all that noise behind him, the boy himself will turn around without her having to tell him to do so. Nobody with any sense could help turning around when 35 pairs of marching feet are coming up from behind. At the point when this still figure turns, Heathcote's going to get those noisy knights still and stop the drama. She has prepared for this moment by marching at the front of the group because she knows that if she doesn't stop them, they won't stop. In this particular group there are boys who might go right on and try to strangle Becket. With the drama stopped, they can talk about the situation. Becket's at bay now even though he's a bishop. They all know it, and they know they've come for him. They are in the theater. Like a playwright, Heathcote has structured the situation dramatically so an emotional explosion must occur. She has deliberately set it up using the stillness-movement and silence-sound spectra.

You use these same spectra when you say to a group of kindergarten or primary children, "I don't know what's in that box." Something says you must not let them all crowd up to it, or the experience cannot happen. They have to stand back and stay quiet. Then they can experience the impact of the tiny sound of a soft rustling of newspaper inside that box.

Heathcote employed the stillness-movement spectrum when she set up the drama of a police officer's entry into the gang's headquarters after the attempted assassination of the President. The police officer comes in to find the guilty person. All but he know who that person is: the man who is wearing a second jacket over the checkered one the radio reporter has described at the scene of the crime. Heathcote makes sure that the gang members are sitting expectantly when the officer enters and that he comes in the farthest door. Thus he has to confront all those faces the moment he enters. She doesn't say anything to him about walking slowly; rather, she helps him recognize what a threat the gang members are to him. She sets up the drama so he will feel this keenly as he walks through the long room and they watch his every move. The stillness holds; he is the only moving figure, methodically going from person to person, never turning his back on any of them, caught tense in the danger he feels.

In the course of most classroom dramas, Heathcote uses all three spectra. For example, if she is doing the capture of Persephone by Pluto, the drama might begin with sound and movement—the voices and actions of the children at play. Pluto arrives with thundering horses, with sounds and movements unlike those of the children, and they are frozen into silence and stillness. Then Pluto and his captive might depart with movement of yet a different quality and in an awed silence. Persephone's friends may leave the field in a slow-paced movement unlike their earlier play; the silence may be broken only by the sound of Persephone's weeping. Her journey to the underworld may be a change from light to darkness.

Heathcote uses these three spectra when she wants to set up a focus to begin; when she faces a difficulty in getting the group to sense the dramatic potential of a situation; when she wants to expose a conflict more explicitly; or when she wants to change the direction of a drama. In every classroom drama she employs the tools of the theater: trapping a group into a particular moment, developing tension, and exploiting the three spectra.

13. MOVEMENT

In addition to playing the spectrum from stillness to movement, Heathcote evokes a wide range of nonverbal experience whenever she feels it can elicit a more meaningful and profound participation than she could get with verbal exposition alone. She gets classes to live through an experience without using words in order to develop a kinesthetic sense of that experience, a rhythm of the act that builds from the inside regardless of the way the process may look to others. All of her dramas have a significant nonverbal part. For example, if her goal is to help children feel the enormous burden of settling in an inhospitable land, she spends what may seem to observers an inordinate amount of time lifting heavy imaginary rocks and stacking them into a wall. The process may go on relentlessly until the children are actually puffing from the exertion. Only then will Heathcote stop the work, complaining in role that her hands are bleeding and her feet are aching in this cold.

In addition to evoking the nonverbal, Heathcote consciously employs it herself, sending out to the class very precise and intended nonverbal signals. She calls this "going into the movement area"; to avoid confusion with the stillness-movement spectrum, I shall speak instead of "nonverbal experience."

The great advantage of a nonverbal approach is that it stays at the universal level of understanding. It introduces a class to holistic human experience that words haven't yet broken up.* Movement gives you an entrée into the universal, but you need language to explain what the experience is all about. This is why ballet programs are so full of explanatory materials. Movement alone cannot explain *why*, and we live in a heavily verbal culture where not to know the drift of something, not to see it in terms of cause and effect, is to feel at a loss. For example, dance will very graphically show you the killer and killed in a single flash; the feeling is effectively and economically portrayed. However, only words will give you a profound insight into why this act took place.

Movement will tell you that I'm tired, that I'm old, that I carry a heavy burden, that I feel helpless to cope, that I'm waiting, that I'm patient, that

---

*See the next chapter, "The Left Hand of Knowing," for more on this.

I'm poor. However, to tell you in a flash the *why* of all this, you need words. To do it in movement would take a very long and complicated ballet.

Verbal		Nonverbal
Why?	have cleaned offices all day	tired
Why?	am 48	old
Why?	am taking home a load of groceries	carrying a heavy burden
Why?	my children keep running away	helpless
Why?	for a No. 9 bus	waiting
Why?	I love my children	patient
Why?	widowed	poor

The crucial thing to know is when it is more efficient to use the nonverbal and when it's better to use the verbal. No teacher need ever feel terrified of using either.

To Heathcote, it's anathema that a person can say seriously, "I am a teacher of movement only" or "I am a teacher of words only." Everyone who is breathing is quite capable of teaching both, since everyone uses both all of the time, whether consciously or unconsciously. Heathcote is opposed to the artificial splitting up of movement and words, and in training teachers she works simultaneously on the development of both in each student..*

Not only do all teachers use both verbal and nonverbal experiencing and signalling, but so do all children, beginning long before they come to school. They learn to read nonverbal signals sooner than verbal ones. Heathcote uses this example: "If I'm standing with my daughter trying to indicate that if you don't come really soon now, you'll have to walk two miles to school, I might go very firmly into movement rather than words: I'll take up the car key, get my bag, put on my coat, and say by every nonverbal means I know, 'Now, Love—or else you're walking.' " We interpret the "doing" things much more deeply than the "saying" things, because as children all of us have depended

---

*See Chapter 19, "Teacher Training," for the types of exercises she uses.

for survival on reading nonverbal signals rather than listening to what someone is saying. To avoid trouble, a child must recognize that the sparks are going to fly any minute; so the child learns to read the nonverbal signals most swiftly. This ability is one of the great strengths children have. For this reason Heathcote frequently moves into a role so she can communicate simultaneously with both verbal and nonverbal signals; the latter play right to the children's strength.

Heathcote diagrams the two ways of experiencing and signaling this way:

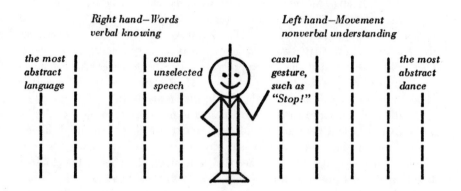

Right hand—Words
verbal knowing

Left hand—Movement
nonverbal understanding

the most
abstract
language

casual
unselected
speech

casual
gesture,
such as
"Stop!"

the most
abstract
dance

On the basis of her goal in the drama, she selects a mode somewhere on this scale from verbal to nonverbal. The further to the right hand of the figure she goes, the deeper she is into highly selected and compacted verbal experience. At the extreme end is the most economical and abstract of the verbal—the language of lyric poetry, from haiku to sonnet. Here words say the most they possibly can and need the fewest nonverbal signals. An experience is rendered in as completely verbal a mode as possible. The further she goes into the left hand, the more stylized become the gestures. The communication of a mime like Marcel Marceau through highly selected and stylized movements belongs far to the left-hand of the figure. At the extreme end of the scale is the most abstract dance form that can express the essence of an experience through the most refined movement.

In an ordinary social environment, each of us is a blend of verbal and non-verbal experience. Children tend to be more nonverbal than adults. In Britain, Heathcote knows, she lives in a society that relies heavily on the verbal and is not given to extravagant gestures. The average English person views her or his body as an instrument primarily for getting about, so the English have developed a wider range of verbal than nonverbal expressions. For this reason, Heathcote often concentrates on training British teachers to expand their range of movement. She has a quarrel, however, with teachers of movement or drama who do not see the importance of moving back and forth between the verbal and the nonverbal. To isolate movement from words is to set it apart from other experience and thereby make it artificial. Every teacher must move back and forth along the word-movement scale.

Because most children find a nonverbal response easier than a verbal one, Heathcote often sets up a drama so that the class can respond by action rather than words, at least at first. She will say to a shy King Arthur at his banquet table, "Will you give the best pieces of meat to your most gallant knights?" This lets him show in gesture what he may not be ready to say in words. Your task as teacher is to hone your questions so they evoke a response in the mode you are seeking. If your goal is to lead into movement, don't ask questions that require language. Also, your goal must always be to lead in such a way that the drama progresses. Heathcote never reduces movement to a mere exercise that is just a way of practicing for the drama. It is always a part of, a way of proceeding with, the drama itself.

Heathcote's response to nonverbal drama is the same as to the verbal. She will often stop and ask the rest of the class to watch as one child moves. "Say, look at this one! What a marvelous thing you have said with your hands!" Thus she upgrades the nonverbal statements, showing all the children that they can say things without words. She works to build an experience, like a verbal expression, from the inside first: she captures the essence before she worries about what the outside looks like.

Movement stays with the whole and stays in the present; it takes longer than words (to rush movement is to destroy its power); it demands a commitment to struggle that the verbal often does not; it gets at a deeper understanding. The essence of a funeral may be slowly picking flowers to strew on the casket, or it may be marching in a deliberate procession through the center of the village. In either, the essence is ritualistic movement, a patient, slow taking-in of experience.

To get at the abstract quality of a rocket, you don't start by worrying about whether you are showing any motion. You think about the essential quality of a rocket and stop thinking about the fact that you have arms and legs. You may decide that the essence of a rocket is the steady thrust of power. If you concentrate on feeling that, you won't worry about what you may look like on the outside.

If a drama calls for falcons, as it may if it is set in the Middle Ages, Heathcote's instinct is to use the nonverbal mode to set up the mews where they live. She needs to help the class establish the essence of birdness. What stance do you take on the perch? How do your eyes move? In what directions will your head move? How do your claws look on the perch? What can you do with your body to show that you are a highly trained, proud, predatory bird? How long a chain must I give you so you won't hurt one another? The responses that come will be nonverbal.

After the children have set themselves up mimetically, they can move into a moment in the daily life of the mews. What alliances or friendships are there among the chained birds? How can you show this without words? How do signals pass among falcons? What sounds are there in the night when no human hears? Is there a hierarchy among birds? What determines status—wing span, beak, hunting skill, power in flight? How does your supremacy show? Once the children are into the power element, they are nearer dance than mime. They will start to glare and peck at one another. What happens when you are unchained and free? To get flight, the children will go into an even more abstract movement, to express flight's essence in a dance. It may help to talk a bit about the nature of a feather. The tail and wing feathers have a strong center and firm surface. The feathers under the breast are soft and downy. What do you do with your strong feathers as you prepare to fly? To answer this, of course, is to move into dance. The class may find that they are no longer birds but rather flight itself.

Once a class is into abstract movement, the dance of flight, you are close to sculpture like that of Michael Ayrton. You might then open a door, ironically enough, into the extreme opposite end of the diagram, into abstract poetry. You might take the class from their experience of abstract flight and say, "You understand flight, and you have made others understand it. You are like Icarus and Leonardo da Vinci, and the Wright Brothers. Now listen to how this man has captured flight's essence in 16 lines of poetry." The most abstract of movement can thus be shown as akin to the most condensed of language.

Heathcote acknowledges the influence of Rudolf Laban, the seminal dance theorist and teacher who provided the intellectual foundation for the development of modern dance in Central Europe. Laban was intrigued by the various movements of the human body and formulated a system for categorizing and recording them. His work influenced not only dancers but teachers of movement as well. He provided a language for describing the different textures or qualities of various movements.

Rudolf Laban was born in Bratislava in 1879 and studied dance, drama, and theater arts in Paris, but his interest in movement began in his boyhood. His father was an army officer, and as they moved from place to place he was able to study not only the patterns of life in countries bordering Czechoslovakia but also cultures in Western Asia and North Africa. When he was 15, he was profoundly moved by a sunrise he saw while walking in the mountains. He felt the urge to express his feeling, so he danced. As a result, he began to wonder whether different cultures caused people to have different movements in response to common or similar experiences. He finally concluded that they didn't, that the elements of movement are the same in all cultures, that each movement is made up of one or more of eight different kinds of effort:

1. Float	5. Dab
2. Glide	6. Thrust
3. Slash	7. Flick
4. Wring	8. Press

Each of these kinds of effort has a characteristic tempo, direction, and degree of weight. Any movement can be sudden or sustained, direct or flexible, and heavy or light. Direct movements are made toward a target; flexible ones have no specific aim. The eight kinds of effort listed above can be characterized this way:

	TEMPO	DIRECTION	DEGREE OF WEIGHT
1. Float	sustained	flexible	light
2. Glide	sustained	direct	light
3. Slash	sudden	flexible	heavy
4. Wring	sustained	flexible	heavy
5. Dab	sudden	direct	light
6. Thrust	sudden	direct	heavy
7. Flick	sudden	flexible	light
8. Press	sustained	direct	heavy

Each of us has our own movement style, made up of a combination of kinds of effort. It is important to be aware of your movement style so that you can consciously work to expand the range of kinds of effort you use. If your tendency, like Heathcote's, is to make quick, direct, and light movements, you will want to develop movements on the other ends of these scales.

Certain kinds of movement typify certain cultures. If you want to get the essence of the Egyptian, all your movements should be direct, to reflect the style of life and architecture that we associate with the culture. A characteristic movement shown in Egyptian sculpture is the direct movement with the right arm and the right leg working together; this is an aggressive movement. Turning the face to the side also reflects a characteristic of Egyptian sculpture. If, on the other hand, you want to capture the essence of the Greek, use the right arm with the left leg; this movement is much less aggressive.

Movement can be a way to get the mentally handicapped to respond in a new way. If you are working with mongoloid children, you will try to find a way to break through their characteristic movement, which is heavy and slow. Heathcote once put a little man under a table to get a group of mongoloids to stop making so much heavy noise with their feet. The little man was frightened and would not come out until they rose on tiptoe.

Theater, dance, and movement training all help you move into the non-verbal mode of drama. They help you know where you are in space and how you can move in order to create a new dimension in the drama.

Movement gets at what you cannot state verbally. It produces what all persons hold in common. It also produces all the rituals of a culture. Movement gives you more than one image at a time; it is not linear. Like photography or graphic art, movement brings you juxtapositions and relationships that explode into new revelations.

14. THE LEFT HAND OF KNOWING

Dorothy Heathcote is not out to cleanse experience of its bewildering variety or mystery. She reminds us that the information available at any given moment is never neat or linear—it comes at us in a swirl of images and sensory data. In this chaos Heathcote discerns structure and pattern, but always the structure is subject to transformation in the next moment. She relishes the possibilities available in any particular situation and thrives on the dynamics of subtle changes in relationship.

Heathcote is not tending a fenced-in garden of "right-handed" knowledge. Instead she is always leading an expedition into the wilderness of the left hand*—a region where interrelationship is what matters, where everything grows together, living in terms of, taking account of, but not destroying everything else; where there is no distinction between weed and flower, useless and useful.

The fiction of academic orderliness, the notion that information should be presented in only an isolated, linear, right-hand way is something Heathcote solidly rejects. This kind of information is not all there is; it is not *knowing*—understanding emotionally as well as intellectually. It denies the richness of our experience, buying a "tortured orderliness"** at the expense of wholeness and subjective reality. Linear thinking takes the world apart and outlines it. Left-handed knowing takes it all in and makes of it a synthesis, a vision of the whole. Although the vision is synthetic, the wholeness is not a fiction: it is the nature of reality. "As proclaimed in a space-filler in *The Last Whole Earth Catalog:* 'We can't put it all together: it *is* all together.' "

---

*See Bruner, Jerome S. On *Knowing: Essays for the Left Hand*. Cambridge: Harvard University. Press, 1962. 165 pp. This book has influenced Heathcote's analysis of the way her own mind works.
**Meeker, Joseph W. "Ambidextrous Education, or How Universities Can Come Unskewed and Learn To Live in the Wilderness." *The North American Review.* Summer 1975. This article provided a provocative framework for assessing Heathcote.
The passage citing *The Last Whole Earth Catalog* is also taken from this article.

Joseph W. Meeker reminds us that university education, skewed to right-handed thinking, is often confusing because it relies on only half of the human brain. He refers to linear, right-handed thinking as functioning with "the left half of the brain" because the left half of the brain controls the right side of the body. The right hemisphere of the brain synthesizes—it affects left-handed knowing. He notes that most university scholars today—

> are found to be overwhelmed by the abundance and complexity of their pursuits. . . .Facts are everywhere, but they fail to come together. Perhaps that is inevitable when minds are confronted with as many new questions as our time provides. Linear factual knowledge must accumulate in the labeled bins of the left brain for a long time before its integrating threads can be woven together into a colorful whole cloth by the right brain.

> The trouble is that education, hooked as it is to linear functions, fails to encourage rightbrained weavers. Balanced mentalities are easiest to find among those who have never attended universities or who have recovered from their influences through several years of post-educational living in larger contexts. By denying higher education to some people—women, racial minorities, the poor—we have managed to keep their brains [lefthanded knowing] in working order, even though they may lack status, power, or adequate learning. The left brain's dream of social unity arising from universal higher education has never been realized. That may be the luckiest break we've had in recent centuries. Those who are innocent of universities and those who have convalesced from their effects are perhaps the best hope for the future of higher education.*

Dorothy Heathcote is one such person. Denied by poverty the mixed benefits of a university education, she is endowed with an insatiable curiosity and a capacity to open up for herself vast vistas of aesthetic and historical experience. Heathcote has used both halves of her brain unceasingly to take in truth in its myriad manifestations.

I have never seen her isolate or deny any part of human experience. For example, when her daughter was born, the baby became part of Heathcote's professional life. Graduate students, male and female alike, fed the baby and walked beside the pram as they had their tutorials. As the baby grew, she was invited to join the groups of children in Heathcote's drama sessions, whether they were in England, America, Israel, Hawaii, Australia, or Canada. Sometimes Heathcote's husband was on vacation and could accompany her and entertain their daughter during classes. The rest of the time, little Mary Ann—and one of her friends as well—constituted part of the experience of the class. Heathcote felt no conflict between her roles as mother and lecturer, so neither did her students. When a lecture was interrupted by "Did you bring the food, Mummy?" she would stop to put her arm around Mary Ann and assure her that indeed she had it in her bag.

Ibid., p. 45.

For Heathcote, everything that the human race knows now and has ever known and believed to be true exists side-by-side in an unsettling tension and ambiguity. Because she rejects nothing, she views the knowledge and myths of our age in light of those of the past, and vice versa.

An example of this approach is the way she introduces a group of five-year-olds in Hawaii to two kinds of truth. They have been studying about holes—caves, cavities in teeth, holes in the road. Heathcote decides to go from there to volcanoes, placing the scientific and the mythical side-by-side. She considers this an efficient way to learn that modern man has a scientific explanation for these manifestations, but that ancient man had another explanation. She knows the scientific truth will be the one these modern youngsters will go away believing, so she gives the Hawaiian guardian of volcanoes, the Goddess Pele [Pélē], the stronger signals by having a 17-year-old student dress in the role. Heathcote meets with her before the drama begins and tells her the stories of the Goddess. Then she hands her two saris, one red and one yellow: "Do what you can to make yourself into the Goddess Pele." She has her daughter copy in a child's printing 14 different letters to the Goddess, such as—

Dear Goddess Pele,

When your hot ash falls on our fields, think of our hard work in the sun.

Your faithful people

Dear Goddess Pele,

When the molten lava flows down into the valley, remember our houses lie in your path and spare them.

Dear Goddess Pele,

When you make the sea boil with your hot ash, remember we need the fish.

Dear Goddess Pele,

Thank you for the new soil you have made. Please remember next time to give us warning that your flames are coming.

She rolls up these letters and gives them to the student who will be the Goddess. Then she meets with the children. She has seven cards, each with one of the letters of the word V-O-L-C-A-N-O on it. She sits down with the children and says, "I can't seem to make this into a word at all. It doesn't sound right no matter how I put it." So the children help her; they arrange the letters different ways and decide it says "volcano," but they still cannot spell it. They keep working at it for half an hour, all the while talking about what a volcano is and what makes it form.

At this point the Goddess Pele comes storming in, looking all frizzled. Her feet are covered with ashes, and she has soot on her face and arms; she looks as if she's been in the fire just a bit too long. Gesturing with the bundle of letters in her hands, she shouts angrily, "Are you the people who keep sending me these letters? I haven't time to be reading these all the time. You've no ideas how hard it is being the Goddess of all that lot!" She sweeps her hand back towards the door she entered.

All the time, Heathcote is giving the children the scientific explanation for volcanoes—for example, "It's caused by a crack in the earth's crust." Pele interrupts with, "Of course, it's a crack in the earth, but where do you think I come in? 'Cause I'm real; look, you can touch me. The story about volcanoes is about me." The Goddess lives in the classroom all week while the children see a film of the 1972 eruption, make a model of a volcano, draw a diagram of the earth's layers, and learn facts. The Goddess Pele stays disgruntled. "Have you any idea how hot it all is?" she asks. The children give her the answer in degrees, but the Goddess gives them an answer in story. The two kinds of truth live simultaneously; the children experience both. Heathcote wants the class not to find them incompatible. The left hand of knowing can encompass both, for nothing is untrue if people have at some time believed it. Both the scientific and the prescientific are attempts to make sense of the mysteries that surround us. There is no need to sort out and reject part in order to make sense of the whole. Both world views are part of what it means to be human.

Heathcote's instinct is to keep the forgotten language of image and dream alive and powerful as she sets it next to scientific facts, which must then withstand the pressure of the old truths. A high school student assumes the attitude of a modern scientist delivering a lecture on forest ecology to an assemblage of learned colleagues—and in walk the Druids, dressed in white. They challenge his truth with theirs, which is based on their observation, experience, and belief.

In another drama, an American researcher is photographing the sun. Prometheus enters, asserting that he was much more daring back when the world was new—he stole fire from the very hearth of the gods. In the dramatic confrontation, students are pushed to weather ambiguities, to carry incompatibles side-by-side. Heathcote reminds us that we must be able to live in the worlds of both the scientific right hand and the mythical left hand. We must be able, as she puts it, "to be bi-real."

Heathcote deliberately seeks contraries, believing with William Blake that "without contraries there is no progression."* By presenting scientific, verifiable, objective truth—which itself leaves out much—along with a contrary view, Heathcote makes progression beyond the present truth an available option.

*The Marriage of Heaven and Hell. This passage occurs in the Argument.

In presenting the above examples, I have implied that Heathcote presents just prescientific truth in a left-handed way. This is not the case. Whatever the material, Heathcote tries to get inside it, into the left hand of knowing. For example, if her goal is to help students understand the commitments and tensions of the scientist, she will ask them first to assume the mantle of the scientist. They are simply to try to see the world the way a scientist would and to take on an unsolved problem, as any practicing scientist must do. One group of children decided that as scientists they wanted to take on the problem of drought in the Sahara desert. In their roles, they discussed the problem at length. They finally decided that if they could blow a cloud down to the north part of Africa, they would stand a good chance of making rain by seeding it there. So the problem they tackled next was to design a giant fan to blow the clouds from Europe down to the Sahara. They had to determine the height of the clouds and the intensity of the sun at that altitude, then find a metal that would withstand that intensity. They consulted science teachers, textbooks, and encyclopedias to find out what substance would be best. One girl found herself arguing, for example, "Asbestos is no good; it's not strong enough."

Too often, educators assume that children do not know enough to do anything about such a massive problem; the truth is that no one ever knows enough to tackle something that has never been done before. The most knowledgeable scientist in the world is not different in kind from this group of children; both can only guess at ways to proceed and sort them out by trial and error until they hit on a new way to solve a problem. By tackling the challenge of the unknown and previously unsolvable, children in drama function as scientists, experiencing the feel of the role and thereby left-handedly understanding something about the drive for information that must necessarily impel a successful scientist.

Often Heathcote is not sure just what the children will actually experience; her goal is simply to get them into the left hand and see what comes of it. For example, when she was teaching a group of about forty adults in Hawaii, she asked them to wear deep, soft colors and to arrange themselves together in a shape that they felt to be a giant tree. The tallest are in the middle, and the others are entwined about them. In the middle of the tree Heathcote hangs a bright shawl with a naked doll the size of a human baby cradled in it. The tree then begins to rock slowly, while the adults softly sing, "Rock-a-bye Baby." Heathcote's only instruction to them is not to let her get the baby. This is the scene a group of mentally handicapped children face when they enter the room. As the tree sways and sings, Heathcote says, "That's my baby. Would you like to see it?" The children nod, so she reaches out and tries to get the baby. As she does so, the tree swings the baby up out of her reach, hissing. The sound is, "Rock-a-bye—SSSSS!" whenever she reaches for the baby. The children have a problem to solve. "I thought when I put the baby in the tree, it'd be safe, and it was—as long as I didn't try to get it back," Heathcote says mournfully. So the children, who are actually quite little, muster up their courage and venture into that tree to try to get the baby. They get braver and braver and beckon Heathcote in, but she says she dare not come into the tree. They assure her it's safe, and she goes into the tree with them, and they all are rocked gently with the baby. Finally the children decide they must chop the tree down to get the baby, so they take on the formidable challenge of hacking down all those adults. Then they let it grow up again. To these Hawaiian children, this is a banyan tree with all its entangled roots above the ground.

When Heathcote uses this with a group of older retarded children, they decide, "You can't chop this tree down, because if we do that, where will we get our fruit?" So they woo the tree; they find its spirit in the trunk. It speaks to them. They say to the tree, "Do you realize what you are doing? It's not a bird, it's a baby." So the tree gives up its baby and mourns because it has no child now. The question then becomes, "Dare we give the baby back to the tree?" They finally decide to lend the tree the baby as the tree lends its fruit to them. As Heathcote admits, this drama has a center to it that she doesn't understand, but it has something to do with people's needs and plants' needs, nurturing and wanting, giving and taking. When she has tried it in mental hospitals, the doctors have been very excited because it has touched on something the children have a memory of but very little experience with—the maternal.

Let's look at one more example. I watched Heathcote deliberately lead a group of five- and six-year-olds into the left hand one hot July morning when they were doing the drama of the orphanage.* Supper is over, and it is time to go to bed. Heathcote has laid out pieces of colored paper, one for each child, in a large horseshoe shape. Here, she tells the children, are their beds. Then she asks us adults who are watching to take places at the heads of the beds and be their guardian angels. Our first task is to write the children's names on their beds. Then Heathcote tells the children to arrange their angels in the position they wanted them to be in—sitting or standing, and in a particular posture.

After the children have positioned their guardian angels, they stretch their warm bodies against the welcome coolness of the stone floor of the vaulted church hall where the drama is held. The humid summer morning is transformed into a stilled bedtime in a strange house: sighs, a few faked snores, then giggles. Heathcote pulls them back into the sense of darkness and night: "Don't confuse snoring with sleep. As you sleep, should I sing?" She lights a large, real candle, sets it on a table, and sits beside it in a chair at the open end of the large circle of beds. She begins to slowly pull a needle

---

*Described in Chapter 9, "Withholding Expertise."

through some imagined material, up and away, as she rocks back and forth. Softly, she begins a bedtime song: "Good night to all the little stars; Good night, sweet moon so high. . . ." The snoring dies away. The children stop wiggling. The hall is quiet except for Heathcote's soft and soothing song.

Then she muses, "I wonder what all those orphans are dreaming of? Will the guardian angels bend low and listen to what the children tell them in their dreams?" She continues to hum the lullaby, the angels bend low, the children smile up at them, and a few start to whisper their dreams. One remembers the happy times when her father and mother were alive. Another sees Frankenstein's monster coming out of his grave and jumping on people. One girl is a queen welcoming visitors; she thinks they are her friends, but she isn't sure. Her guardian angel asks whether they are her pretend friends or her real friends. She says, "Let me go ask them." She lies back down and closes her eyes. Then she opens them, saying happily, "They're my real friends!" Another one sees the orphanage burning down, but the endless corridor and ghosts are still there. One girl is in a field of flowers on a spring day, and it is very cool. She pauses a long time and then adds, "I wish it were winter instead of summer. I had my Mommy and Dad then." So by slowing the pace and letting the children dream, Heathcote gives them a chance to identify with orphans.

After the dream telling ends, Heathcote says softly, protectingly: "And so the orphans sleep their first night in the orphanage, and the candle burns all night in their room. It grows quiet and very still; even the angels sleep. . . ."

Thus it is that into our fact-flooded psyches Heathcote comes splashing with her left-handed paddle. She's headed for a truth where mere facts are not what matter, for the deep knowing that makes information come alive, for experience that breeds energy. Her adult students are moved by the felt truth of her work and have become committed to developing their own left-handed power.

Heathcote's wilderness beckons. One nine-year-old summed up the feelings of many of us. He and his classmates were journeying back into time on an imagined Halloween night, and they became frightened. Heathcote said with concern, "Should we go forward, do you think? I feel very responsible for all our safety." "Yes," came the boy's strong voice, "We must go forward now to find out all there is to know. We owe it to ourselves."

15. CLASSIFYING DRAMA

As a drama is proceeding, Heathcote can classify the various responses she is getting from the class according to several different classification systems.* One of the most useful is to analyze student responses in terms of their mode of exposition—in terms of the way the drama is projected. All dramatic projections can be located on a continuum from the most "classic" or highly stylized to the most "domestic" or casual. A new dimension of experience can be very quickly reached by shifting from one place on this continuum to another. As a teacher, you want to achieve the utmost flexibility of projection, so that you can change the face of the drama at any point where you think this would bring a new source of energy and awareness.

To be free to classify at all, of course, you will have to phase out of your consciousness—as much as possible—any evaluation of student response. If you are busy rejecting what the students give you, you haven't the perspective to classify and find a way to put their input to use.**

If a class has great trouble believing and are in fact tempted to laugh nervously, you can sometimes help their belief by deliberately stylizing the action—moving the drama from the domestic to the classic. You might do this by entering in a stereotyped role such as the prison guard, the judge in court, or the conductor of an orchestra; thereby you will require of the students a stereotyped response that will serve to get them into the drama. All you have done is take the dramatic net in which all are caught and cast it into a

---

*As we noted in Chapter 8, "Dropping to the Universal," one such system is to classify according to implications.
**This has been discussed in Chapter 7, "Building Belief."

different water, into a mode where the demands and potential are different, though the goal of the drama may remain the same. If the new water into which the net is dropped is a classic rather than a domestic stance, a more highly stylized and carefully selected gesture and behavior are appropriate. The classic mode calls for the most economical and effective expression possible and for a projection that is larger than life.

To most teachers, the domestic mode looks easier; it is casual and akin to everyday human relationships. Although it is the mode most Americans choose for nearly all of their daily affairs—certainly for their marital and social relationships—it is actually the more difficult mode to get into, because it demands great belief. In this mode, gesture and language are not consciously selected. (At the unconscious level there is no such thing as a completely unselected or random gesture or word, however.)

If a class is doing a drama about a tribe showing their young how to carry on the traditional procedures of work, the tone of the tribe member may be casual: "We take three buttercup leaves and grind them with this bone . . . ." This casual tone may be hard to sustain because all of the familiar gestures and words are available. Ironically enough, the very limitations imposed by the classic tend to free the participant. Because so little can be chosen, the act of choice itself is easier.

In the highly stylized classic mode, posture is determined by the role; gestures are dictated by a stereotyped norm; actions are based on a cultural expectancy; and even tone and diction are prescribed by precedent. This is not to imply that the classic is always formal or stiff. Rather, it is stylized; stereotyped; stated both verbally and nonverbally in the broadest, highest, and most blatant fashion. A cardinal in procession to the altar is in the classic mode, but so is a first mate shouting, "Come on, you lubbers! Hoist that mainsail!" or a seated, humble beggar stretching out a hand for alms. The classic simplifies experience; one characteristic is heightened at the expense of the complexity of human feeling, thinking, and behavior. What is gained by the classic is a clear, clean look at one quality, one aspect of experience. What is lost, of course, is the ebb and flow of human feeling and mood, the oscillation and complexity of ordinary human responses. If this latter is what you are after, the domestic mode is the more appropriate; if the quality of a single stance is what you want to examine, choose the classic. Young children have trouble making sense of complexity because their capacity for abstracting into categories and concepts is limited; they find in the classic an ordering and simplifying that they much need.

Stereotyped characters frame a quality before children have a concept or word for it. Not only young children, but also older students with little or no drama experience find in the classic an easier entrée into assuming a role. Even if the role is unfamiliar, the classic stance imposes a structure and dictates a style. The discipline of stylized gesture, action, and language limits and, at the same time, frees. When Heathcote uses another person in role,* she sets that person up in the classic mode, not only to simplify the attitude the one-in-role is to project but also to simplify the signals so the class can respond more easily. The classic mode projects a more powerful signal than does the domestic.

I first experienced the classic stance in one of Heathcote's classes when we were asked to use as our frame, or limitation, a chessboard; we were to assume the roles of chess pieces and in those roles improvise a drama. My previous experience in theater was virtually nil, and the idea of actually "acting" terrified me. However, the command to assume a stance on the chessboard sounded simple enough, and before I knew it I found myself stretching up to a posture both regal and stiff. I stood poised as one of my classmates placed an imaginary crown on my head; I held out my elbows to sustain my royal garments. Behold, I was a rigid chess piece queen, ready to attend to the demands of the role.

I could move rapidly—and in any one of eight directions—across the chessboard we had drawn on the floor. I could capture any opponent on contact. I was very proud. Only then did I discover that I was continually blocked by the other pieces on my side—my own people. Only as they chose to move was I granted power; I could not run them down. I was limited by one of the most rigid of all classic stances—that of a mere object in a game with time-honored and inviolable rules. The very limitation had plunged me, quite without my trying, into a new area of awareness about the restrictions a head of state faces.

In my case, the imposition of the first Big Lie plunged me into a classic stance. In some other instances, it is the participant who chooses this mode. I have seen students choose a classic stance within what is otherwise a very domestic drama in order to help themselves to belief. Once a group of junior high students were taking on the roles of members of a primitive tribe. One of the girls stretched herself up tall, limited her gestures to the most stylized, and began lifting the water pot from her erect head and pouring it into her bowl, without any random movement or idle chatter. Everything she did had an order and concentrated respect for form. She moved quite intuitively into the classic mode to capture the essence of the tribal task and its significance. Her choice led her into belief and into a sense of the primitive. Her whole body expressed her isolation in a personal experience as she concentrated on precise gesture.

Although the classic seems simple as a way into drama, it is actually the mode that demands the greatest discipline over the long term. One simply may not drop back into the natural and normal for respite. The press for style and form is continuous, and to sustain it requires great concentration and control. The classic is always larger than life and more highly selective in

*See Chapter 11, "Using Role in Teaching."

gesture, tone, posture, and language. In most groups, no matter how compellingly the drama may cry for the stylized, there will always be some students who simply cannot sustain the classic mode for more than a few minutes. This few minutes, however, is enough to turn some of those who usually just mumble into eloquent speakers.

In every drama I have seen Dorothy Heathcote lead, there is at least one moment when she moves into the classic in order to upgrade and give dignity to what the children have done. For example, when a group of sixth and seventh graders have spent most of an hour as the members of a primitive tribe going through the first activities of the morning, she calls them all together to share what they have been doing. She doesn't just say in a domestic language, "Let's all come over here now and tell what we've been doing," even though it is in the domestic mode that most of the youngsters have been working. Instead, she sets a tone of dignity by lifting the language at the same time as she calls them together: "Can we gather now to tell the essence of the morning?" After they move to where she is kneeling by a big drum, she says slowly, "For me, the essence of the morningtime is arising early to see the world anointed by the sun. I feel myself anointed by the day. What is the essence of the morningtime for you?" One child, still clearly in the domestic mode, ventures, "I start getting the food ready."

Heathcote repeats slowly, upgrading a little, "The morning is a time pf preparation." She goes from child to child, asking, "What is the essence of the morning?" Before long, the answers are taking up her language and serious tone: "a time of preparation"; "a time of sharing food"; "a time to watch the wild creatures wake up from their sleep"; "a fresh, happy time"; "a new beginning." Heathcote repeats each response, even if it is itself a repetition. The answers move slowly from descriptions of what the children have been doing to descriptions of the mood of the time of day. The children begin to pick up the classic style, lifting their language, slowing their pace, and deepening their tone.

The further removed is the dramatic material—the further in time and place from the present condition of the class—the easier it is to lift it to the classic. The closer the material is to the present condition and real circumstances of the class, the more likely it is that the youngsters will work in the domestic mode. Every child has some relationship with the material of the drama, and that relationship can be located somewhere on the continuum from the highly selected (classic) to the unselected (domestic).

For example, when Heathcote was working with a group of adolescent boys who were actually in prison, they chose to do a drama about prisoners of war. The prison camp would move most groups of youngsters into a classic mode because of the distance from their own experience the setting would provide. However, to these boys, already in prison, the situation is theirs. They know what it is like to live behind locked doors while all the authority

and power are in the hands of someone else. When Heathcote says, in role as
a threatening German officer, "Thirty-six standard British rifles out of there,"
her own tone is in the classic mode. She is assuming the stance of a stereotyped
officer in relation to a group of captured enemy soldiers. Her gun is pointed
at them, and they have surrendered. They have no choice but to obey.
However, this group of boys don't respond in the classic mode. Because they
are prisoners in real life, their daily life is in many ways not unlike the life of
prisoners of war. Thus, when Heathcote takes a classic stance as the
authority of the enemy government, their response is in the domestic mode.
They are bringing to the drama their own wide range of experience in prison.
Heathcote knows that by using their own material, in this case a prison, they
will drop naturally into the domestic. She knows, too, that the material is
good for winning them over to her but difficult to use to get them into the
classic or more highly selected mode. Yet she wants to use the classic mode to
get the boys out of their own experience and into a new one that can shed
a light on their present condition. Changing the mode of projection from the
domestic to the classic is often a very effective way to get a drama deeper, to
get to a reflection on universal human experience.* In order to move the boys
into the classic, Heathcote decides to take the domestic aspects that they
understand and then drop them into a problem that demands a reflective
response. She chooses to examine the time in the prison camp when the
soldiers are getting their letters. During her coffee break, she painstakingly
writes 33 letters for the 36 boys. She is careful not to put any implication
into the letters that are not there in the room already, so she writes things
like this:

> Dear Son:
>
> I hope this finds you as it leaves me at present. The war seems long
> over here. How is it with you?
>
>   Mom
> P.S. The cat has had two kittens.

She put in this last line in case the reader wants to latch onto a bit of
loving.

By writing too few letters to go around, Heathcote gets the drama from
the domestic to the classic. She resists any temptation to play funny games
and say: "You've got one, you've got one, you've got one, you've got one,
and you three haven't got any. Now deal with it." Instead of that kind of
self-indulgent role playing with the class, she just throws the letters on the
floor and says matter-of-factly: "They're all for them in this lot." She does
not plan which three boys won't get letters, because that is precisely what the
group must decide. The way they deal with this problem demands a

---

*See Chapter 8, "Dropping to the Universal."

selectivity and focus that their ordinary domestic behavior does not necessarily call for, and it is this challenge that extends their area of experience. She knows she is taking the chance that the ones who don't get letters in this imagined prison camp might well be the same ones who don't get mail in their own prison. In that case, she will quickly bring in a "late mail." The problem she drops provides a press out of the domestic mode, however, and some of the boys are in fact ready to respond in a more selective or classic manner.

Heathcote cannot magic a boy into giving his own letter to someone else. She has no right to do that. All she can do is to use drama as a tool to make a new extension possible. Drama puts at the center human beings struggling with a problem; Heathcote's goal is to get them out of the muddles of uncaring or "anything goes" and enable them to think about a problem in a new way and begin to examine different ways to deal with it. When this happens, the language changes and there is a greater understanding of how people can relate to one another.

A useful way to think about classification is to combine mode of expression with the 14 areas into which Heathcote divides any culture: commerce, communication, clothing, education, family, food, health, law, leisure, shelter, travel, war, work, and worship. We have already seen how Heathcote uses these areas to find a moment of beginning for a drama.* If we reflect on how we would project them dramatically, we can discover in each area examples of modes of expression that illustrate the classic and the domestic, as on the chart on the next page.

The classic-domestic continuum classifies the way a drama is projected, the stance the participants take as they assume and develop their roles. Heathcote also classifies the source of authority for the decisions a person in role makes within the drama. Borrowing the terminology Edward T. Hall used in *The Silent Language*,** she calls her three classes the *formal, informal,* and *technical* levels. These are the terms Hall uses to describe three levels of functioning that take place in every culture. To avoid confusion I shall call the three sources of authority within drama the *unquestioned assumption, reliance on experts,* and, using David Riesman's term, *inner direction.*

The first category, *unquestioned assumptions*—what Heathcote calls the *formal*—is the level of culture that everyone agrees on, acts on, and takes for granted. The system made up of these assumptions, never seriously challenged in daily life, is the basis of all the other elements of the culture. No matter how "liberal" or "modern," every society and every subgroup (professions and institutions, for example) has a mass of customs based on unquestioned assumptions. Such customs are taught by example and warning, by tone of

---

*See Chapter 5, "From Segmenting to Dramatic Focus."
**op. cit.

MODE OF EXPOSITION
or
THE WAY YOU PROJECT A DRAMA

voice rather than explicit explanation. Those who ignore them are ad-
monished or punished. Eating with silverware, washing oneself, toilet
training children, examining evidence in scientific procedure, assuming that
there are psychological norms for sanity, protecting and nourishing all viable
infants, voting—all are based on largely unquestioned assumptions of
comtemporary U.S. society.

When she works at the level of unquestioned assumptions, Heathcote
(either in or out of role) gives each person a task. "You will be a potter; you
will be a weaver; you will grind the corn." Here there is no questioning of the
authority. This level meets the needs of an immature class. It has these
advantages: it gives the class an instant focus; a limited view; a chance to use
all previous knowledge about, for example, making pots; and the possibility
of getting started without having to make a lot of decisions. It has these
disadvantages: you as teacher must set up the communications between
individuals; and you will never know what the group's idea of how to set up
this situation would have been. If you plan to set up tasks, you plan only two
things: how to get each individual going, and how to get these individuals
back into communication. In classes with poor social health, you will
probably use crude strategies like calling them to meetings. If you sense they
can handle a less crude approach, you might ask, "Can you find a way of
needing each other?"

The second source of authority is *reliance on experts*—in Heathcote's
terminology, the *informal*. This is the level of functioning in which a person
has a right to question an assumption, to debate whether or not a certain
cultural pattern is right, but in which there are authorities who can provide
expertise if one chooses to seek it. When Heathcote sets up a drama at this
level, she will move into role not as an expert, but as a person with the power
to bring in the expert if one is needed. If possible, she lures a class member
into assuming the role of the expert. If the class decides to solve a certain
problem, there is an authority who must be consulted for this type of matter;
they dare not make up the rules themselves.

The third source of authority within the drama is what I'll call *inner
direction*—what Heathcote terms the *technical*. This is the level of functioning
on which each participant has an equal opportunity to lead. When she wants
to get a class to work by inner direction, Heathcote doesn't set up tasks for
them—she lets them find their own tasks, their own way of responding to the
situation. There can be no appeal to experts, nor to any unquestioned
assumption. The class members by themselves have to find the solutions to
problems. As in a democracy, each citizen is responsible for what happens.
When Heathcote has a class working by inner direction in a drama, she presses
them to analyze a problem and solve it without relying on her or anyone else.
They are the ones who make all the decisions.

The unquestioned assumption creates atmosphere very fast, because you as teacher create it; inner direction relies on the group to create atmosphere. Heathcote will risk having a class work at the inner direction level if their social health, the quality of interaction, is good. When Heathcote introduced the sixth and seventh grades to the tomb drama,* she quickly assessed their social health as she watched them approach the tomb. She decided that it was good. They treated the tomb with respect and interest; they looked her straight in the eye; and they were able to share sitting space on the floor easily. So she decided to let them function at the inner direction level, assuming the mantle of the expert, the archaeologist, and examining the artifacts on their own. She imposed no rules; whatever structure the class gave to their discoveries was of their own devising. The atmosphere was established by the tomb—not by the teacher in role, as it is in a drama based on unquestioned assumptions.

If a class's social health is poor, working by inner direction won't extend them; they will fall into the same interpersonal traps that characterize their out-of drama relations. At the unquestioned assumption level, on the other hand, there are rules. The teacher, in role as a person with authority, can impose these clearly defined limitations, and the class members have to commit themselves to working within them. If the class in the tomb had been less mature, Heathcote would have moved to the unquestioned assumption level and come in as an expert on bones.

If a class is doing a drama about making cars in Detroit, you can begin at any of the three levels. If you assess their social health as poor, you choose the unquestioned assumption level. You start in role as foreman, and no one can do anything before checking in and seeing the foreman for orders. You are the one-who-knows—and who will tell them—how to make cars. The unquestioned assumption level demands the greatest commitment to letting you, the teacher, lead.

If you decide to work at the reliance on experts level, you begin as one of the workers. "I don't know what's wrong with these damn things, but all these chassis are coming out square, and they should be comin' out oblong. Let's go ask the foreman. Hey, you, come on over here and look at this. What's wrong?" Heathcote is a worker guiding other workers to an authority who will show them, probably largely nonverbally, how to do the job. "You should have done this. . . ."

If you think the class is socially mature enough to handle the inner direction level, you can start with, "Well, where the hell *is* the manager? If he's still out, like he has been all these weeks, we'll just have to get on by ourselves. Do you think we can manage it? Can we cope? Will we be responsible?" This is the level that demands the greatest individual decision taking by the students.

---

*Described in Chapter 10, "Planning."

Heathcote once set up this situation to illustrate the three levels—unquestioned assumption, reliance on experts, and inner direction: She, a member of a primitive society, is sweeping the house of the women, when in walks a man, an anthropologist. If the action is to be based on unquestioned assumptions, she knows that if anyone finds out he has been there, she will have to die and so will he, because a pattern has been broken. The rule need not be explained, because "Thus it has been and thus it shall be." All she can do is run away and try to get to a place of refuge before she is caught; from now on, her life will be burdened with this event. The anthropologist, of course, may never know why he is killed. If the action is to be based on reliance on experts, it's dreadful for the anthropologist to enter the house of the women, but she can go to the priest and get purified. If the action is to be based on inner direction, here she is sweeping, and she says to the man who walks in, "Don't you think you're in the wrong place, sir?"

Heathcote uses these three levels as a way of tripling the potential for dramatizing any situation. The unquestioned assumption level looks most like "real drama," because it gets to the spectacular very fast; Heathcote's instinct is to resist it, however, when she finds a group that can handle inner direction. This does not mean she won't allow the group to decide to take it into the unquestioned assumption level, but she tends not to lead them that way herself.

When the class can handle inner direction, they are providing the energy for the drama; they are making it theirs; they are deciding. When the drive is in the students, they can run the show. This usually doesn't look as interesting from the outside because the participants are talking directly to one another, often too softly for observers to hear. Nevertheless, this is when drama is really happening in the classroom.

As we combined the classification of the 14 areas of culture with that of the two modes of expression, we can combine it with Heathcote's classification of drama according to source of authority: unquestioned assumption, reliance on experts, and inner direction. The examples on the chart are from contemporary U.S. culture; of course, they would be different for another culture or for this culture at a different period in time.

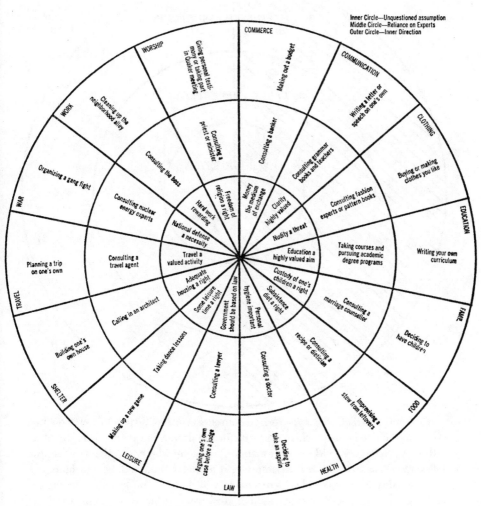

SOURCE OF INFORMATION

We can put the two classification systems presented in this chapter together in this way:

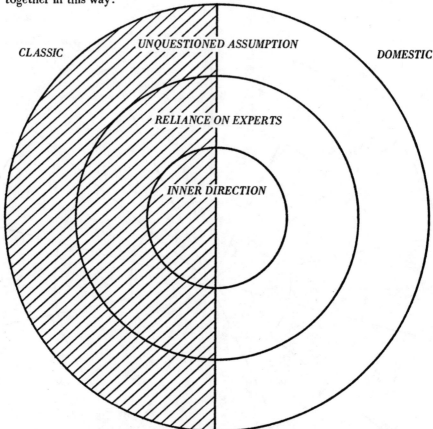

A teacher selects the appropriate source of authority for a drama on the basis of the needs of the class. Any role in the drama can then be projected in either a classic or a domestic manner, or somewhere on the continuum between these two poles. For example, if a drama about skiing is to be based on inner direction, each class participant will decide how to act in the drama and the teacher is clearly not leading. However, within this drama based on inner direction, a student has the further choice of whether to project the role in a classic or a domestic mode. Either way, the student is still operating on the basis of inner direction. Suppose a boy is in the role of ski instructor. He might say, "You must never let a pole out of your hand," projecting his directive in a classic manner. On the other hand, though his role as instructor is the same, he might choose to keep his manner in the domestic, saying, "Will you come a little closer, you guys?" The language and gestures and posture differ, but the role and the level of the drama—in this case inner direction—remain the same.

Roles at the unquestioned assumption level tend to call for a classic stance more frequently than do those at the other levels, but any role at any of the three levels can be projected in either a classic or a domestic manner. Heathcote prefers to start a drama at the reliance on experts level, especially when she does not know a class well. If she sees they can manage well, she can move them to the inner direction level; if they cannot, she can go to the unquestioned assumption level. At the reliance on experts level she assumes a strong role to get the class's belief going, and then she looks for ways to move them to inner direction. In the sailing ship drama described in Chapter 1, Heathcote assumed the role of first mate and projected that role in a classic manner in a drama that was at the reliance on experts level. Through this role she fed the class a ship, a rope, a horizon, a mission, and a mainsail which became a task. Every signal she gave was classic, highly selected to evoke shipness. Because the group handled reliance on experts well, she could later move them to the inner direction level with the musing, "I wonder how rumor spreads on board. Let's just see when we know there's a murderer on this ship." She asks questions that will lead them to inner direction because she senses their readiness. Her leadership can diminish as theirs swells forth.

Classification systems provide you with a way of thinking about what's happening in a drama. By using them, you can be more flexible and avoid being trapped in your plan. At the same time you have a handy way of not getting lost, because you can know at which of the three levels you are operating and think about the gains and losses of changing to another level. You may decide that the best way to extend a class's area of reference is to move from reliance on experts to inner direction at one point. At another stage the nature of the situation may call out for the unquestioned assumption level. Changing levels or changing modes of projection from the domestic to the classic is often a very effective way to get a drama deeper, to get to a reflection on universal human experience.* If you know where you are in terms of level and mode of expression, you can concentrate on sending out clear signals and not mixing them up. All of your energy can be focused on evoking the desired response from the class. Classifying is an effective way to keep a drama from drifting.

---

*Described in Chapter 8, "Dropping to the Universal."

16. CODE CRACKING: LITERATURE AND LANGUAGE

Not surprisingly, some of Dorothy Heathcote's most enthusiastic followers are not teachers of drama at all but teachers of other subjects—especially literature, social studies, and history. She has shown how the discipline of theater can be harnessed to the service of other academic disciplines. No matter what their academic expertise, teachers find in Dorothy a kindred spirit, a person steeped in the rich heritage of Western civilization and curious about, appreciative of, and conversant with a wide range of academic disciplines and creative arts.

If we think of any material stored in books as an unpalatable beef bouillon cube, to use Heathcote's metaphor, then some means must be found for releasing this dense mass into a savory broth of human experience. In educational circles, this process has been called code cracking—breaking the code so the message can be read. Heathcote guarantees that her lessons will do this.* She will lead a class to want to know. In a drama she deliberately immerses a class in the mystery of not knowing and shows them that the impulse to research is born of this tension, that the process of discovery is joyous and exciting. When her students start asking for and poring over big dictionaries, art books, examples of illuminated lettering, adult texts of all kinds, Heathcote knows the drama has done its work; it has created a need for information. The code has been cracked, and the learners have found they have power over material rather than its having power over them.

She doesn't care how much a child has read. What's important is not to collect a few more titles or vocabulary words, but to be modified in some way by what one has read. Has reading been a means of relating personal experience to that of other people? Has the student translated written symbols into experience? Through the process of identifying, readers give life to texts; in this sense, reading is akin to role playing in a drama. All print remains dense until a reader agrees to belong to it in some way, identifying

---

*See Chapter 20, "Guarantees for Drama."

with the protagonist or writer enough to allow the reader's own subjective world to come into play. Then the reader's being can flow into the dense words and provide a medium through which they can be dispersed and understood. Like role playing in drama, identifying as a reader releases a fund of subjective experience and recalled information that aids understanding and appreciation. The truth of any text is always limited by what the reader brings to it at the moment of reading. The reader's prejudice determines the range of understandings the material yields, for sensitivity and awareness are just as selective and limited in the process of receiving written material as they are in firsthand experience or drama.

A reader who has discovered what words on a page actually are—distilled human experience—has cracked the code forever. Such a person can translate any text into meaning by bringing to it the understanding, first, that it is indeed a code to be cracked, a script to be interpreted not for an audience but for one's own illumination; and, second, that to make sense of it requires the application of one's own experience.

For the reader who has not yet made this discovery, Heathcote uses drama to crack the code. She is often called in to prepare a class for a text. Her goal in such cases is not to go over the material, but rather to raise the questions about the text that will stimulate the class to read more selectively and insightfully. Unless her goal is to interpret or act out a script, she does not act out the scenes in the text. Rather, she reorders the events in the book, raises questions about them, or has the class enter into and role play a situation that is tangential or analogous to them.

When introducing a class to literature or even to anthropology or history, Heathcote avoids simulation, an approach common among American teachers. In simulation the class acts out a situation, capturing as much of the factual truth about a culture or historical period as possible. Simulation has the advantage of bringing a great deal of information into play and thereby preparing students most fully for the facts of the text. Heathcote doesn't use it, however, because of its one great weakness: it burdens students with so much information that they cannot get to the heart of the matter—the identification and hence the belief.

Analogy, on the other hand, removes the burden of simulation, which can weigh a drama down. Analogy starts with attitude alone and, through it, unlocks the code to an internal understanding. By starting with feelings, not facts, Heathcote stimulates curiosity and stirs students to want to read texts and research for facts after the drama is over. Analogy sacrifices accuracy of detail for emotional depth; it is easier than simulation, because any one particular will do for a beginning. As the elaborate web of the drama is spun out from this single thread, the class is caught in the tension of the moment; through this involvement they get a glimpse into what this time or place would be like.

The facts Heathcote feeds the class as they assume their roles are those details that help them bring to life the particular moment. For example, if she is preparing them to read a text about life in the fourteenth century, she might say, "Your boots would come up to here, and they would have been painstakingly sewn by a man you knew. Isn't it interesting—everything you would be wearing would have been made by a person you knew."

Once a group of English teachers asked Heathcote to help a class of inner-city high school students in Toronto understand *The Mayor of Casterbridge* by Thomas Hardy. The teachers said this was one of the most difficult novels for their students, so they wanted Heathcote to get their students to want to read it; she agreed to do this in four days of drama. She decided that what was critical in understanding this book was that "it happened a long time ago." She started with an analogy to get at three things. The first was the slower pace of life in the period when the novel takes place. Second was the parochial nature of the community then—in a day, a man would travel only as far as a horse could travel; most of the people one would meet in a lifetime would be known and would fit a familiar place in a social hierarchy that was clearly defined. Third was the impact of a stranger in that kind of community. Without this understanding, Michael Henchard's relationship to Casterbridge might seem absurd.

To take the class back to a more parochial time, Heathcote used a village shop as symbol, as the analogy that would be significantly like the village of the book, but would be neither an attempt to simulate Casterbridge nor a setting for acting out a specific scene from the book. First, she went to the store and bought everything she could think of that would be available in a market of 1820—cheese, eggs, a honeycomb, a bottle of real maple syrup, a homemade-looking loaf of unsliced bread in the shape of a braid, ears of corn, butter, fish, brown sugar, brown and white flour, birdseed with groats in it, dried lima beans and peas, bars of homemade soap with bayberry scent, homemade candles, and a stack of plates. (After the drama was over, she took the food home to her own kitchen, so it wouldn't be wasted.) She tells teachers to do what they can; if you have only a loaf of bread and a pound of cheese, use that and imagine the rest. In this case, when the class came in, they found all the things Heathcote had brought arrayed on a table, all with their heavy purple prices still stamped on them. Heathcote said, "Could you turn all this into an old-fashioned shop?" They eagerly set to work, first arguing about prices and then changing all of them. After they got the prices sorted, they began tentatively to open the packages and pour the contents out onto the plates in tiny heaps.

Then Heathcote asked them to tell her how she would be dressed. "I live in this old-fashioned shop." They put her into a typical colonial costume. Then she asked them to tell where each of her garments came from and where each of the goods on the table originated. What they gave her was their idea of the commerce of the day. "Now, will you come into my shop?" she asked, moving into role. "Yesterday was Sunday. What do you suppose we talk about this morning when we come into the shop to replenish our larders?"

"That cheese has a right good flavor this morning," one woman said, pinching a bit off the large round piece. "Who made it?"

"What did you think of the homily yesterday, Martha?" another 18-year-old asked. Gradually they developed a sense of the period and of the parochialness of this community. They chatted about who was having a baby, whose husband had been drunk last week, whose land wasn't doing too well, who was reputed to be short of money.

Then Heathcote stopped them. "To a village like this, perhaps to a shop like this, there came a young man looking for work. Who would like to be this young man?" To the boy who volunteered, she said, "I do not know what kind of work you seek, but you carry your tools with you; you let us know what kind of thing you can do." In a minute or so he was ready; he carried knives and a scythe and was prepared to cut grass and clean out ditches. The villagers all knew he was a stranger; his entrance into the shop changed all their dialogue.

After this drama was over, Heathcote uncovered a blackboard on which she had written Michael Henchard's last letter, pencilled before his suicide.

Michael Henchard's Will

That Elizabeth-Jane Farfrae be not told of my death, or made to grieve on account of me.
& that I be not bury'd in consecrated ground.
& that no sexton be asked to toll the bell.
& that nobody is wished to see my dead body.
& that no mourners walk behind me at my funeral.
& that no flours be planted on my grave.
& that no man remember me.
To this I put my name.*

Then in role, Heathcote said, "That young man who came into my shop seeking work wrote that at the time of his death, when he was still a comparatively young man but old enough to have a grown-up, married daughter. Whatever was in that man's mind to make him write that, I wonder?"

The class members talked spiritedly with one another. "Who is this Jane Farfrae?" "Is it his wife or his grown-up daughter?" "If it is his wife, why is she called Farfrae?" "Is there a Mr. Farfrae?" "It seems like this Michael Henchard is afraid of something he's done."

"Well, would you like to know what happened between his looking for work and that letter?" By this time, they wanted to read the book; through analogy she had piqued their curiosity and helped them crack a code.

---

*Hardy, Thomas. *The Mayor of Casterbridge.* New York and London: Harper & Brothers, 1922, Chapter 45.

To get a class interested in Chaucer's *Troilus and Criseyde,* she began by asking them what kind of person in our society goes out and faces danger each day but comes back to sleep at home each night. They suggested a racing car driver, so this was their modern Troilus. Dyomede was the old hand who drove for the opposing side; Pandarus the public relations agent; Criseyde, the model who sold the car by publicizing the sex angle, Calkas, who could read the future because he developed new engines, was the modern soothsayer. As they dramatized this analogous play, they came to know the plot of *Troilus and Criseyde* "inside out"; they wrote up a script of their play and compared it with Chaucer's work.

Another ploy Heathcote uses to get a class interested in a text is to discuss with them what makes a book good. She lists their responses on the blackboard. Then she asks them what makes a book boring. She gives each person a set of these latter characteristics—each written on a separate slip of paper—to rank in order, with the qualities that do most to make a book boring or difficult at the top. The list includes things like long sentences, long conversations, small print, long descriptions, thin pages, heavy books, and poetry in the middle of prose. This process evokes a discussion based on a fact teachers sometimes fail to acknowledge: the books they assign students often *look* boring to them. One high school boy told Heathcote, "I've never known what I thought about books before. I now know why I couldn't finish some and why I went back to reread others."

A third way to get a class started in a book that seems formidable is to begin telling them the plot and ask them to stop you when they find they are interested in what happens next. This is a useful way to get students to the point where they are ready to tackle a fairly difficult text like *Pilgrim's Progress* or one of Shakespeare's plays.

A fourth ploy Heathcote has frequently used is to have a teacher who knows a book well come in and pose as its central character, letting the class ask questions of her or him. This way the students start with what interests them about this character, and that interest is the key that unlocks the rest of the book. When Heathcote introduced the mayor of Casterbridge this way, she and the class were in role as villagers. She told them, "This man is your mayor. You have a right to examine him closely and find out his attitudes. He is bound to answer honestly and not to dissemble." She had the class open their books to the first page, and their questions began. "Why did you let your wife carry the baby on that dusty day?" one girl asked.

"I had other things on my mind," the teacher in role answered, finding his knowledge of the book tested in a new way.

"Is this a good reason?" the girl pushed.

"Of course, it's a good reason."

"Just what other things did you have on your mind?"

Through this dialogue the class penetrated further and further into the shame of Michael Henchard. By first taking this teacher to be Henchard, they effected what Coleridge termed "the willing suspension of disbelief"* and could then transfer this act of will to the book itself.

To help a class get ready for an examination on Arthur Miller's *The Crucible*, Heathcote had them pose as a team of counselors in a marriage guidance clinic. They worked to help John and Elizabeth Proctor, teachers in role, first to feel at ease and then to go back over their experiences to see whether they could get a new insight about what had happened. The class looked at the play from a new perspective. One student concluded at the end of the hour, "You know, I could write a book about John Proctor's relationship to Mary Warren, Abigail, and Elizabeth."

Each of these four techniques helps a class realize that a text is much more than words: It is always a script to be interpreted, whether it is written in conventional drama form or not. Not all teachers share this view, however; some are convinced that most texts are unambiguous, subject to only one "right" interpretation. One way Heathcote breaks through this prejudice is to have teachers work in pairs on a "text" of their own making, in the same way she has younger students do. Each pair makes up four lines of dialogue, which may be as mundane as this:

"Coffee?"

"Yes."

"Cream?"

"No, thanks."

This is the text they use for a series of dialogues, each time adding another layer of meaning. The first time through, Heathcote asks each person to assume an attitude, a way of feeling, and project that. The second time through, she asks them to add the way they feel about each other. Then, "Are you rushed or do you have plenty of time?" Then, "What is your social class?" Then, "How old are you?" Then, "Are you at the breakfast table or camping out in the wilderness?" Each time they add a layer, they try to preserve the previous layer as well, augmenting the words with gesture and expression.

This experience cracks the code of a dialogue in a book. It shows that there is no such thing as a dull line. Those words on a page that seem so flatly there are not all there is. What is said in words is often not what is really being said; under any printed dialogue are layers of meaning that can never be fully captured in words alone.

Another way Heathcote shows this is to have each pair of students act out one dialogue—a short one of their own making, like the one above—in a series of different ways, each of which has its own meaning. For example, she once had us use our four-line dialogues to make clear the first time that we were

---

Biographica Literaria, 14.

lovers; the second, that we were spies meeting and recognizing each other; the third, that one of us was leaving a place where we had been living together. I vividly remember two of my classmates who acted out their dialogue as they met as spies in adjacent toilet stalls! My partner and I used our four absurd lines as part of a deathbed scene.

Another dialogue Heathcote has used with older students and teachers is this ambiguous text, which she has them act out in groups of four, one for each speaker:

A: This wood's damned hard.
B: It isn't as if he's a big fella, either.
A: I hate these rush jobs.
B: What's he supposed to have done, anyway?
C: You hate any job you do.
D: Never mind, guys, double pay.

Each speaker assumes an attitude to project into the relationship. Then each group decides on a time period when the action took place and the nature of the project in which they are engaged, fleshing out a drama from these six lines of sparse, ambiguous dialogue. Interpretations range from building a stocks or coffin to fashioning Christ's cross.

When it comes time to actually get beyond the improvisation stage of introduction to a particular piece of literature, Heathcote uses the words just as the author wrote them. She never alters or modifies a text. If a class needs an improvisation first, she sets up a scene that is not in the text. Her goal is to lure a class into wanting to read, not to substitute improvisation for reading and interpreting.

Heathcote also works to lure—or press—a class into greater eloquence. This involves helping children crack a code that is within themselves so that they can recognize and express their own feelings and perceptions in a new way. Heathcote's explicit goal here is to expand the children's vocabulary and develop their rhetorical style, but she sees this aim in a larger context. Receiving and sending messages in words is never all there is. This process is always just a part (in some situations, as drama vividly reminds us, a very small part) of any total experience. Heathcote's definition of education takes account of this reality: "Education is a continuous process of assimilation of incoming data together with a constantly developing ability to respond." What we do with words, then, is never the whole, but only a part, of education. Heathcote's definition is similar to the one developed independently by James Moffett.* To perceive and take something in as full, complex, and sensitive a way as possible and then to bring it out again as words—as a statement that reflects the fullness and complexity of the experience and at the same time orders it and relates it to other knowing—is a

---

*See Moffett, James, and Wagner, Betty Jane. *Student-Centered Language Arts and Reading.* Boston: Houghton, Mifflin Co., 1976. Chapter 20, "Setting Goals."

goal worthy of any educational endeavor. This is precisely what drama does best: it provides an evocative context for the expression of feelings and ideas, and it demands clarity and force of rhetoric in that expression. When the pressure for language is on in a drama, children move from their passive to their active vocabularies words they may never before have had any reason to use.

In addition, drama often provides a press for language that is special in some way.* Heathcote is always alert to situations which call for an archaic word, a correct precise term, or upgraded language style. She introduces whatever term is needed, hoping the class will follow her lead. Here are some examples:

- One of a group of six-year-old astronauts in a rocket ship said the weather was getting bad. In role as ground control, Heathcote reported "the deteriorating weather."
- When an eight-year-old doctor in a hospital drama needed "an air thing you put on your mouth," Heathcote supplied the words as she handed over "the oxygen mask for the patient."
- She gave another doctor a "stethoscope" when he needed "a thing for hearing the heartbeat."
- When they were going to operate to find out what was wrong, Heathcote asked urgently, "What did the biopsy show? Who was responsible for examining that tissue sample you took?" Both her tone and her terms upgraded the responsibility of the medical team.
- In another drama, a child suggested that one of the things a governor might do is smile when he saw that one of the colonists had a baby. Heathcote both upgraded the language and extended the idea by saying, "Yes, he might congratulate them on their babies."
- If she is trying to get a feel for the Middle Ages, Heathcote might move into role as one of the lord's followers and call herself a liegeman, accompanying her use of the word with the correct gesture of obeisance.**

When she was working on Cromwell's meeting with Charles I, Heathcote helped a child who was using a modern oath by feeding him archaic language for a curse: "By God's good grace, my blood is as blue as thine." By taking it up, the boy had another experience in shaping his language to fit its purpose.

At another point, Charles I was at a seaport, overseeing the levying of a duty on each of the rough sea captains who brought their ships into that harbor. Heathcote again was in role as the one who carries out the king's orders. She probed for archaic language: "His Majesty requires that every captain who arrives at this port pay tonnage." A bit later, she brought the king a message: "Your Majesty, this sea captain by the name of Jim Brown (the child's real name) has refused to pay tonnage on his vessel, which has sailed from Spain." Depending on how Charles I responded, she either

---

*See the discussion of classic language in Chapter 15, "Classifying Drama."
**See page 28 for examples of the correct terminology she introduced to make a sailing vessel seem authentic.

lowered her tone or applied a press for archaic language.

In a medieval market, Heathcote went up to the child who was the "flesher" (a term she had supplied when he chose to be a butcher) and said, "My mistress demands that you send up two beasts 'on the hoof.' "

Puzzled, he asked, "What's 'on the hoof'?"

"If they are not walking, she will not pay you," Heathcote still clearly in role, warned him.

Before long, another child, who was dealing in skins, was asking her whether she wanted her skins dead or "on the hoof." That, of course, is one of the predictable consequences of teaching vocabulary through drama. However, such misconceptions are not precluded by any teaching method; they are just more obvious in drama. When they are brought out, misconceptions can become occasions for further learning. In the same drama, for example, a little girl was selling spices: cloves, cinnamon, saffron. Heathcote asked to buy some saffron, but the girl said, "There is no saffron now."

"Oh, no, not this week of all weeks!" Heathcote lamented in role.

"If the wedding's going to take place, they'll have to have all that saffron in the wedding cake," said the child, obviously not knowing anything about saffron.

"Somebody getting married?" Heathcote asked, projecting her voice so the word would get to the other artisans and sellers.

"Yes," she said. Almost at once, the bakers were busy with a huge wedding cake.

"Why all the stress on yellow?" Heathcote queried, extending their understanding of saffron. "You'd think they could make an ordinary white cake and not use up all of this town's saffron!" At this, the tailor got busy on a yellow bridal gown, and the farmers began gathering up yellow flowers. By not correcting but actually magnifying the girl's initial mistake, Heathcote had fed the class a focus for a group event. She still kept pressing, "But why yellow?" Under this pressure they came up with an answer: The groom was the Duke of Orange!

In "Dropping to the Universal," we made a distinction between a probe, a tentative attempt at upgrading the class's effort, and a press, which won't let them get out of the situation without extending themselves into new areas. In extending language, Heathcote never stops probing for more precise or apt language; she applies a press at the point when she senses the class can handle it. She knows that a child who assumes the role of King Arthur may just sit there like a sack at first. She can help the new monarch by feeding him language as she gives him time to get the feel of the role. She may try a ritual in which each of the knights pays homage to the king. In role as a page, she might say, "His Majesty, King Arthur, greets him and would have his name." If the king does not yet know how to take up the language probe, Heathcote will continue to ask the question of each knight in turn and pass on his answer to

His Majesty. Neither the king's language nor hers will be particularly high-flown at this point. If, a little later in the drama, the king is able to say, "Bring Sir Lancelot hither," Heathcote will immediately lift her own language into the classic and continue to provide a language press: "Certainly, Your Majesty," with a wide flourish, "it shall be done."

So far we have considered oral language only. Heathcote is committed to developing a child's written style as well. She likes her classes always to come to a drama with pencils and paper handy. Often when she stops the drama for reflection, she asks the children to take the drama to paper, to write out what they are feeling and thinking. A scrap of paper in the pocket will do; if not that, Heathcote keeps pads and pencils handy or a roll of shelf paper and lots of porous-tipped pens. Quite often, a drama ends with the writing of the scroll that preserves this history, the summary of how it was in our village at this time, or some similar record.

Heathcote never asks a class to write anything that is meaningless, that has no purpose, that is simply a test which the teacher can use in judging the children. Thus the records the children write are shared with the rest of the class or with other classes; are mounted and preserved; or are collected into books for class reference and use.

What Heathcote gives children is not information on how to write, but a reason for writing. Writing is never "assigned"; rather, it comes forth when students have something they simply must say, when their emotional drive to express what they have just discovered plunges them into figuring out for themselves a way to say it. Heathcote often stops a drama at the height of its action and asks the participants to write out what they have just known and felt.

Heathcote builds an appreciation for records by showing students actual handwritten accounts, documents that have never been reprinted, or old pages from archives. She may say, "Come, sit in front of this log. A man wrote that on a moving deck, and he had sworn on oath to write the truth. It's sacrosanct." At other times, Heathcote will make the writing itself a part of the drama. If the children are young and their oral capacity outstrips their writing skills, she has older children or adults take down what they say. Here are excerpts from the diaries of two boys, both less than eleven years old, who wrote them as part of a drama about monastic life:

> Sunday. I earned a penance by looking at Brother Luke's face. My punishment: praying for four hours on my knees.
> Monday. I was writing the third page of the Bible. I went into the woods to pick a feather from the gander.
> Tuesday. I went to the woods to pick elderberries for some ink. I mixed them with rose hips and they produced a beautiful deep blue.
>
> I walked back toward my cell, my stomach empty, my knees stiff from kneeling. I enter my stone room. A shaft of light falls upon my unfinished manuscript. My eyes glance up at the holy cross. My legs need rest, so I sit

on my stone seat. The table, wooden, a privilege to use. On it, my sheet of vellum; also a fine quill, a pot of black ink. I borrow other colors from my fellow brothers. As I begin to sketch my design, I wonder, is this the right life?

Here's another example, this time a letter from a ten-year-old:

O Great Lord Pharaoh of Egypt, I am an old slave in your quarry. We have been working from early morning until late at night, and we have just settled down to sleep, but I have stayed awake to write this letter. I could hardly hold the instrument I wrote this letter with for the cuts and blisters on my hands. I do not quite know what we have done to be brought here. You have set us to work in rags. We are working all day long, your task-master at our heels all day long. If we stop for a moment to rest, we are whipped. You are never in the quarry long enuf to see us working. You have never seen the blisters on our hands and our feet or the whip marks on our backs. We are all just dead. We are asking you please to let us go free. Please let us to go back to our own lands. We are all old now. We are of no use now. We have made your bricks and built your palace.

And here's what Moses wrote after this same drama:

To the river I went forth to change the water to blood. Outstretched I thy rod and made the command of the Lord. I command thee to turn to blood, and it was so—red, red like the redness of a Baby but in a way not the same. This redness is of fire. Red, red, I think that our people will be free now.

By the time ordinary, previously undistinguished children can write personal passages like these, uplifting language has been internalized. The students have cracked the internal code that kept form and feeling separate; now they can wed feeling to a form that suits it.

17. CODE CRACKING: OTHER AREAS

There is almost no area of the curriculum for which Heathcote has not used drama. Its value in building confidence in using a foreign language for example, is obvious. What it does, of course, is to build in reasons for talking. One way to do this is to introduce an adult-in-role, as Heathcote did with the Latin teacher.*

Although mathematics seems more difficult to crack through drama, there are ways to do it. Whenever children are planning trips, feasts, or purchases, however, Heathcote stops them to explore what the costs are likely to be, how much money they will need, and ways to get resources. She often moves from drama to construction of such things as pyramids for the story of Moses, a carton castle for a king, or clay cliff dwellings for Indians of the Southwest. In each case, she creates a need for mathematical calculations.

To teach a group of mentally handicapped children the concepts of tall and short, and to help them classify shape, Heathcote introduced a teacher in role as a tall, tall, tall king. Against his height she juxtaposed a short man, who crossed in front of him and stole an imaginary chicken. The tall king captured him, but the children pleaded that he not hurt the little man. The king agreed to spare him if he would build the king a house. The little man and the class built a big round house, marching in a circle and then drawing that path with chalk on the floor. That wouldn't do, so they built the king a square house, then a rectangular one, then oval, and then triangular. Finally the king was satisfied. After the drama was over, they played the game Granddad Says, Everybody into the Round House, until they learned the various shapes.

---

*See page 146.

Another time, Heathcote introduced shapes to a group of five-year-olds by setting up a soap factory, in which they actually made soap. She brought in real lye, which she kept locked up and ceremoniously took out when it was time for the process to begin each day. The children sorted the soap by shapes and by colors, learning the differences among hexagons, diamonds, and ovals, and among the various colors, in such a way that they would see them true forever.

Drama frequently gives rise to situations that call for experts. Heathcote's technique in such cases is to bring in a real expert and have that person answer the class's questions. In the soap factory, the class decided they wanted to send the Queen their best cake of hexagon-shaped soap stamped with the initial of their school; Heathcote brought in the mail carrier to explain how to address a parcel to Her Majesty. Another group of children had been making clay jewelry and carving in their own assay marks. Heathcote called in a real goldsmith to answer their questions about how these marks are arrived at and to show them assay marks from various places and times. He also showed the book of assay marks he used for reference.

Often Heathcote will bring in a stranger in role to get a class to describe their school, community, or activities more fully than they would need to do for one another. Working with four- to six-year-olds, she dressed up two Chinese teenagers and introduced them as visitors who needed to take back to their government a report on this school and town. The children gave them a party to see whether they liked it; they drew maps of their school and town for the visitors to take back to China. Before long, the children began to say things like, "Newcastle is bigger than Gateshead, and Gateshead is bigger than Felling." A reason for conceptualizing and using language in this way had sprung from the presence of the Chinese visitors.

Drama can provide a powerful stimulus for careful handwriting. A group of eight- and nine-year-olds—40 percent of whom had previously had great problems in legibility—overcame all their problems in handwriting as they made an illuminated manuscript of 800 A.D. for a historical drama. Each chose a Bible verse to copy; they used old medieval manuscripts as guides for the illumination. They worked with either quills prepared from feathers or penholders with nibs. Like the monks of old, they were limited to one piece of vellum (actually paper) apiece, so any blots or errors had to be disguised in some way.

How does Heathcote use drama to crack the code of history itself? She thinks of ways to remind a class that history lies close at hand, just waiting to be picked up. She may dramatize this with ghosts of the past who arise and speak, or with stones that cry out the truth they know. She may bring in a teacher who knows a great deal about a certain historical period and have him or her dress in role as a well-known historical figure and answer the class's questions. This person will need the self-discipline to channel all he or she knows through the narrow end of a funnel; that is, through what the class shows they are interested in. Thus, if a class is interested in Thomas Jefferson's invention of the dumbwaiter, any facts about his life as an architect or statesman will have to flow through that invention.

Characteristically, Heathcote will start a historical drama by asking the class what they know about olden times. Suppose a child says, "History is kings who own all the land and poor people who have to work for the king all the time and have to do what he says all the time"; then that will be the relationship Heathcote builds first. More sophisticated information is fed in bit by bit after what they already know is elaborated and made tangible.

When she introduced a group of eight- and nine-year-olds to the events of the American Revolution (in the drama discussed earlier), Heathcote's goal was to get to the heart of the matter, the inner urging towards revolution and the ultimate feel of freedom. She proceeded by assuming the role of a harsh and uncompromising governor; even in her role as teacher, she pushed the children hard to get them to believe in and stay with their roles as colonists. The first sessions of this drama were tough ones for the children.

Even after one of the village children who threw snowballs at a British guard is killed, Heathcote as governor continues her pressure. The child's parents have to billet that very guard in their home that night; such is the governor's order. At this point, a tall girl in role as the bereaved mother shouts in defiant anger, "We won't let that murderer in our house!" Heathcote still won't let her win. She is forced to take in that soldier under threat of imprisonment. The plight of the colonists continues to worsen for four straight days of drama. Both in and out of role, Heathcote shows them little mercy. As teacher, she keeps pressing the class to discipline themselves to the heavy demands of their roles.

By the end of the fourth day, Ken, in role as Samuel Adams, stands up on a table and sums up their situation:

> What I have seen in this village is the Governor bringing soldiers out to the houses and then charging a half crown and a daily meal board for each soldier. I think this is just terrible. The Governor is going to have soldiers on guard at the British flag twenty-four hours a day. This, I think, is a waste of the troops. The guard will have a rotation about every two hours. The changing guards get people mad. They make so much noise. People are woken up every two hours 'cause the soldiers are put in their houses. The people can't get enough sleep in this colony; we can't win independence. And it looks like right now the people are getting mad and a revolution is coming. I know that!

As teacher, Heathcote summarizes the day's drama this way:

> Out of this is going to come a very, very terrible war, and out of that is going to come your independence. Then never again can an English king

demand money of you. They may ask, and you may give as you did during the last World War, but nobody can demand it. You shall control your own purse.

By the fifth day of the drama, the colonists decide to drive out Heathcote in role as governor and elect their own. Once the governor's pressure is off, a surge of new energy fills the room. The colonists all start shouting at once as they eagerly pitch in to do the work of the village. The men start to plow, the women to cook for the busy farmers.

"We need a police force. We need to make this town more prosperous. Everybody will help everybody else's farm. One big, huge farm."

"Somebody get a plow."

"Come over here. Help loosen this hard soil."

"OK."

"Get another horse and plow over here."

"You get the horse. I'll bring the plow."

"Attention! Attention! Listen, if anybody needs a carpenter. . . ."

"Yeah," several colonists chorus. "Let's build a house." They are all working purposefully now, happily sharing tasks, shouting for aid, pulling ropes, plowing, hammering, all chatting at once.

"Hey, somebody get up there on the roof. I'll hand ya' this."

"I've got a plan for a new house."

"Somebody go down and start carving stuff on the door."

"We have to repair the rope in the well," one boy reminds them, and they set to work on a job the governor had frequently urged them to do.

They sense their new feeling of liberation. "We can do lots of things without the governor watching over our work."

"Hey, let's build a new school!" This is greeted by enthusiastic cheers.

Heathcote, no longer the governor but now in shadowy role as one of the colonists, presses them, "If you build a school for the children, aren't you going to take away their freedom?"

"No, this school will have fun things to do. One of us will teach."

"Yes, I will."

"I will, too."

"What if they don't want to go?" Heathcote asks.

"They'll go, don't worry. They'll go. We won't have to force them. They'll have games to play, and they'll want to come."

"Get the books from the governor's old place. He's got a whole shelf of books from England."

One of the girls starts to read. When another child asks her about it, she reminds her that she has to read if she's going to teach. "This is my favorite book about King George," she says, expressing a need for continuity even during a revolution, although she probably could never have verbalized it that way.

Heathcote as teacher stops them so she can list on the board the freedoms they now have. She writes what they tell her: "You can do the things you find fun." "You can do the things you find useful." "You have the right to disagree if you don't like what was done." "You have the right to choose the labor you will do." "You have the right not to pay to the common taxes."

The freedom they feel is real because the previous pressure has been intense and felt. As one boy puts it, "I never caught a fish so easy before"; the fact of freedom energizes. Actually, by the end of the drama the class are working very hard, and Heathcote is redundant. They have learned something which is central to an understanding of the American Revolution.

In the drama of 1,200 years of history,* Dorothy Heathcote started with research. All the children chose aspects of life in the Middle Ages to report to their classmates. Although most wanted to write about arms and armor, they agreed to have only one child do that. The others wrote reports to answer such questions as: How did the Vikings get across the sea? What did people eat at that time? How did they buy and sell things? Who was Hilda of Whitby? Were there schools? What was a Saxon village like? How did the monks live? The regular teacher of this class upgraded their efforts by mounting them carefully and lettering the title of each display in Old English script. The children also painstakingly copied the Gospel of John. This became part of the manuscript that was the pivot of the drama. What made the book valuable to these twentieth-century children was the long period they spent finding true Celtic letters; copying the verses; illuminating them; gluing each page to a piece of leather so the book would open flat; and binding the book in a wooden cover decorated with an authentic Celtic design. This process built up the children's drive to preserve the book.

In the drama, the monks found themselves under pressure to defend the book's value, especially when the crops were failing and the people were tempted to call on the old gods for help. As the monks were dedicating the book, Heathcote, in role as one of the common people, pressed them.

The abbot began, "This is our book. It is a beautiful book made by the monks of our monastery."

"What good is a book?" sneered Heathcote in role.

"We can read out of it for our prayers."

"Why do you need to do that?"

"It's the words of God."

"But the words of God don't fill empty bellies," Heathcote growled in disgust.

The abbot was desperate by now, shouting, "This book was made from the feather of a goose that never knew he dropped it!" Under the pressure of

---

*See pages 45 and 46.

drama, his understanding of the value of that manuscript had moved firmly into his left hand. He came to a new synthesis, an intuitive *insight* that was not mere feeling but passion fused with the act of valuing. This book, which had been lettered with a worthless feather, now represented the faith of a people. It must be believed.

In another drama Heathcote wanted to capture the essence of the life of the Venerable Bede, 1,200 years after he lived and wrote in the monastery of Jarrow in Northumbria. This time she had all the children in the school copy Bible verses, using real feathers. This dictated a style of writing that was close to that of the old Anglo-Saxon manuscripts. Tension was provided by the fact that there were only 10 goose quills; the rest were sea gull feathers. A child who wrote a perfect page with a sea gull feather earned the right to use the goose quill. By that time she or he knew what it felt like to need a better implement. "Sea gull feathers are no good; you can't write neat. They're too soft."

Throughout the drama, which lasted two weeks and involved the whole school, the discipline of the monastic life was increasingly imposed and extended. Each child was dressed in a swatch of black material to symbolize a cowl; went barefoot despite the winter weather because the eighth-century monks did; and took an Anglo-Saxon name. The children took turns baking the 96 little loaves of bread which, with glasses of water, comprised their daily lunch. One group of children made butter. Eight times a day a bell rang, and they left whatever they were doing and went to prayers. On the fifth day, Heathcote decided it was time to impose silence in the chapel. She did it at the noon service before the bread was passed among the children. "When the bread comes in today and when 96 people have sung their way into the chapel, there will be no voice heard; do you know what this means?"

"Yes," they chorused solemnly.

"No voice must say anything, not even the abbot's," she said, looking at the child who stood behind the altar.

"Yes."

"You realize that if there is a voice heard, there is no bread?"

"Yes," again in chorus. At this point one girl turned to another and said something. Heathcote could have wept; but she kept her word. No bread was shared that day.

After chapel the question arose, "Hey, what are we going to do with all that bread?"

"I don't know, what do you think we should do with it?" she asked the group.

"Give it to the poor people." This she did after school, continuing to act in the mode of the eighth century, when bread mattered very much.

She went up to the two girls who had talked and said to them warmly, "Oh, I am sorry about this." They forgave her with their smiles.

"So are we."

"Tomorrow we'll make it; we'll be quiet and get the bread, won't we?"

"We'll try."

"That's all I ask you to do."

The next day at chapel there was great tension; from then on there was silence when the lay brothers were called to prayers. Through discipline the children discovered the pride of rising to the demands of a monk's commitment; they experienced the quality of a life otherwise alien to them.

When the bread was blessed and shared in the monastery the children had built with their belief, those who had made butter shared it with those who had made bread. The abbot himself broke the bread; the most important elected member of the community became the servant of all the others. What the children were living through symbolized the values of a community of a distant past.

In addition to identifying with people who lived in the past, Heathcote wants her students to identify with historians, to develop an appreciation for their task of selection, compression, and interpretation. To develop this sense in a group of 18-year-olds in Bristol, England, Heathcote used a real event, one they had all lived through. This was a six-weeks' strike of garbage collectors (called dustmen in England). With this situation she cracked the code so that the group could understand how history gets written and what it actually is.

During the dustmen's strike in 1970, huge piles of plastic bags of garbage collected in the parks and along the sides of the old Gothic buildings. Schools were closed because the custodians, who had custody of the keys, had gone on strike with the dustmen. No burials could take place because the sextons were part of the same union. All in all, it was a time of hardship for most of Bristol's citizens.

Heathcote began her lesson by reminding the class that one day this event that they had lived through would become a line in a history book. She asked them. "Is there any way we can catch the feeling of this strike and preserve it?" They talked together about all of the things that had happened that should be remembered. For the next day's drama, she developed a set of roles from the class's anecdotes. She put each role together with a clue to an attitude that might go with it, on a piece of paper. Here are some of the roles, with their clues:

A widowed janitor, nonunion	"My rent is £2.10 a week."
A vicar	"I feel so helpless."
A retired citizen	"I live near a small patch of land."
A driver of dust cart No. 47	"Things aren't always what they seem."
An employee of Radio Bristol	"We'd only just got our heads above water."
An undertaker	"Death waits for no man."

A school supervisor	"We haven't a bad educational system."
A park keeper of fishponds	"I took a pride in being solely responsible for my park."
A school principal	"Mine is a big responsibility."
A city councilor	"I'm in politics because I'm prepared to do something about things."
A store manager	"New packaging methods have changed the job considerably."
A university custodian	"I've always liked my job and held my head high."
A janitor, union	"I've worked in this school all my life."
A mother of six	"Nobody realizes; you don't, until you have children."
A fishmonger	"I live over my shop. I'm allowed two garbage cans."

Heathcote had each student choose one of these roles to assume. Her adult student teachers then came in as newspaper reporters and interviewed each of these Bristol citizens, asking what it was like in Bristol during the strike. Then the adults wrote up these interviews, upgrading the language; these became the documents of historical importance.

The accounts of the strike were very vivid. One girl assumed the role of a park keeper who had in reality committed suicide, telling the reporter that she just couldn't bear to look at the rubbish any more. The rats and stench were more than anybody should ask her to deal with. The reporter who had talked to the undertaker wrote a letter to the newpapers, coolly stating the problem as the undertaker saw it.

Dear Sir:

As a funeral director and a member of our local Society I feel that your readers should be aware of the particularly great distress which has affected the bereaved of our city. No grave has been dug for three weeks, and the accumulation of the deceased has greatly increased the burdens which have to be borne by those who have been left behind when they must perforce extend the period between preparation and burial.

Another aspect of the problem has been the misconception by the public of the cause of their distress. We have borne the whole brunt of the accumulated frustration and anger caused by the events of those five weeks on our wholly inadequate shoulders. The more uncontrolled of our customers have on two or three occasions laid the blame for the dislocation of our services fairly and squarely, as they say, at our door. In short, there are some among our customers who have conducted themselves with little short of barbarous effrontery. Our Society felt that the danger inherent in industrial action of the kind which has afflicted our community in these last distressing weeks should be brought to the notice of your readers who might otherwise feel that we in Bristol are merely concerned with dispute over cold figures.

Sincerely,

John Smith

Another Bristol citizen dictated this letter:

My Dear Catherine!

I am writing to tell you about the last few weeks. I have been very worried because as a result of the strike of dustmen the people in our street have been putting their rubbish on the bit of waste ground next to the house. I can't sleep at night because I worry about the rubbish catching fire. I was particularly worried on bonfirenight [Halloween] because I was afraid the boys in our street might set it alight. You remember the time they threw stones at the windows and the cats. Talking about the cats, that is another thing about the rubbish. The cats have been bringing in mice and even a rat! I am convinced they are breeding in the rubbish which smells something awful.

I wish they would pay the dustmen what they want because they deserve it.

I hope the children are well and give them a big hug from their Gran.

Lots of love,

Mom

In addition to interviews and letters, the adult students helped the young people compose various other kinds of documents, such as this notice, put up by the vicar:

NOTICE ON THE DOOR OF ST. GILES
5.11.70

We regret that owing to conditions in the city it will not be possible to conduct any funeral ceremonies until further notice.
Anyone in need of comfort or advice see
The Rev. John Hopkins at St. Giles

Heathcote xeroxed copies of all these documents; and the class, as town councilors, worked in small groups to categorize them. They wrote summaries of the various kinds of material, using illustrative anecdotes with quotations from the original documents. These summaries were to be filed for reference in the city's archives. One group put their information together in a film to be shown once a year to schoolchildren.

Finally, Heathcote turned the whole class into historians, who had for their perusal both the original letters, news reports, and other documents and the summaries of the town councilors. The challenge now was how to reduce all this even further—to show this strike in relation to all the other wealth of a nation's history. The class finally reduced it down to a single paragraph for a history book.

This process of reduction cracked the code of history. The students' own experience had shown them what a paragraph in a history book really is—distilled experience. They would be able to see all lines in history books as

Japanese paper flowers that fill out in water. They could make words become big and colorful in their minds, without doing a week's drama each time.

Drama is a particularly effective tool for gaining insight into the patterns and tensions of community life, thereby cracking the code of anthropology. Frequently Heathcote will deliberately set a drama back in time to a more primitive age when tribal conflicts are acted out face-to-face and issues can be seen more clearly. An example of this occurred in the tomb drama.* On the next to last day of the drama, Heathcote asked the class what they wanted to do next day. They decided they would like a ceremony, and Jerry, a tall, black 12-year-old, agreed to lead it. He kept to himself how he would do this.

The next day, Jerry takes over the leadership of the tribe. He has secured the support of the dead bodies (who are by this time sitting on chairs rather than lying in the tomb). When he addresses the community, he can get their attention by using a formal posture, coupled with phrases like "The spirit of our fathers has spoken."

What Jerry actually does now is to lead a rebellion. The seeds of this revolt were planted the day before when Heathcote unwittingly did something that, as it turned out, some of the children much resented. From their chairs along the sidelines, the adult observers were unable to hear much of the dialogue among the children. To help them, she asked that each adult shadow a member of the tribe and take notes on everything that was said and done. After the children left, the adults wrote in the form of an anthropologist's notebook on long sheets of kitchen shelf paper all they had learned about the life of the tribe.

Thus, when the children come in for this last day of drama, there, along the end of the long hall, are stretched scrolls with the descriptions and interpretations the adults have written on them. The session begins with the reading of this record.

After reading the record, the children drape or tie swatches of black and brown fabric about them and go back into their roles as tribe members. Before long, Jerry is instructing the corpse of the dead man for his role in the ceremony to come. He tells him what to say and directs him to speak in a deep voice.

When he and the man-in-role as the dead man are ready, Jerry calls the group together to listen to the words of the spirits. "Spirits!" he calls ceremoniously.

"Spirits!" Heathcote repeats.

"Come, Spirits!" Several other tribe members join her in repeating this invocation ritualistically.

Then the voice of the dead resounds in an authoritative, sepulchral tone: "Let the dead be worshipped. May the words of those who watched be destroyed."

*Described in Chapter 10, "Planning."

Jerry turns to his tribe. "You have heard the Spirit tell us to tear up the reports that they wrote." With a long spear he points to the back of the large hall. "Let every tribe member go over to the papers and tear up those papers." Heathcote is clearing her throat and visibly tense at this point. She values the written word and efforts of the adult students very highly, so she find Jerry's leadership painful to follow.

A girl, looking up at Heathcote's agonized face, shouts, "I cannot bring myself to tear them."

"What the Spirits said, we must do," warns Jerry. He ceremoniously tears the first sheet, saying, "In the name of the Spirits." The tribe hesitates. "Go ahead, tear!" They join him. After a few moments of frantic tearing, Jerry looks at the shredded bits of paper and says with conviction, "These are not our words, not our laws. We have wrote our own laws."

"Then we can never learn from others," Heathcote says in a soft, regretful tone.

"No, we will not learn from others. I want all the tribe to grab these and put them in a pile over here."

After they dutifully do that, Heathcote says humbly to her leader, "The unlaw is now piled beside the true law."

Jerry points to the pile. "I have read it, and these Spirits have read it, and they know it's the wrong law. Now we shall learn our own law." He then leads a procession down to the other end of the large hall and again invokes the Spirit of the dead.

"Spirits! Spirits! We have done what you have asked. What is your wish?"

The Spirit doesn't answer. "Spirits! Spirits!" Jerry calls again. "The words of our tribe are now the only words."

"Behold the words of the past," the Spirit says solemnly. "Thus have died those words that are not our words. May they never return."

"Yes, oh Holy One."

Then the tribe follows Jerry's lead and sits in a circle. They begin to think about what they have just done. One girl in role as a woman of the tribe thoughtfully confronts Jerry, "You have just torn up what our tribe is about. What are we if we are not that?"

"That we have not wrote. This we have wrote," he says, pointing to their records. "That is not our law," he says, forcefully gesturing with his spear.

"How do we know?" asks the girl.

"The Spirits have spoken. No reporters will come on our land."

"But I trusted the words of the reporters."

"Why did you trust them?"

"Because they spoke true about our tribe."

Another woman says, almost to herself, "It is against our law to destroy."

Jerry is hard pressed now; he calls on the Spirit again. "Why did we tear up the laws of the strangers? this woman asks. Our law says not to destroy."

The Spirit replies, "Let those of our tribe behold the words of the past. You are as we were, and thus it shall be done and understood in our tribe. That which is gone is of the eyes of those who are not of us."

"You hear?" says Jerry, vindicated. "After this, no one shall come in and visit on us."

When the drama is over, the children discuss what they have done. They have experienced the classic confrontation of the traditional tribal leader with members of the community who are ready to open themselves to new understandings.

One girl says, "Oh, the excitement of knowing that Jerry was on the spot—but actually we were all on the spot." Jerry assumed what he thought would be a very secure role and played it with ritual and formality, only to discover that he was suddenly more vulnerable than he had expected. Jerry's choice of tearing up the records provided a moment of superb theater and an unforgettable entrée into the inevitable conflict between anthropologists and the subjects of their study. The problems on both sides are the heart of anthropological investigation.

Heathcote is sometimes asked to use drama in career education, helping students identify with the demands of a particular vocational role. She does this by having each class member take on the "mantle of a discipline" as she calls it. The student tries to see everything with the eye of one who has chosen that responsibility. Pushed to identify, she or he discovers ways to be effective in the career role. Again, what Heathcote is getting at is the appropriate inner attitude and feeling.

We have seen how she helped students identify with historians by studying the Bristol garbage strike. In the tomb drama, her first goal was to give the students insight into the career of the archaeologist. She knew that if they could capture the tension of the archaeologist's eye, the tomb's mystery would hold them to the drama. She wanted them to face the challenge of explaining the grave's arrangement and artifacts and defending their interpretation of the life of this culture, now dead. The group took up the challenge and worked very seriously for the four days they were scheduled with her. They probably would have gone on exploring for much longer had further sessions been possible.

Heathcote provided the group with virtually no information. She simply asked earnestly such questions as, "Have we any evidence that they had fire?" In response to this question, the children first noted that nothing was charred; then they discovered the clay pots and decided they must have been fired. They drew pictures of the artifacts and described possible uses for each. They arranged the pictures, descriptions and artifacts as if for a museum exhibit. They wrote reports of their conclusions:

We think they had to wear a sort of mustard colored powder in order to be brought into the group. In every shell or bowl next to them there are some seeds. Maybe their tribe thought they would be brought back to life as someone or something else.

We think maybe the reason they died is because they did something wrong in their tribe and were persecuted.

Food Gathering:

Rope in child's hand suggests it was used for fishing
Bones and spears—hunting
Bowls with grain—wild gathering.

As a news reporter Heathcote went from group to group asking the archaeologists for information. She pushed them for interpretations and conclusions. The responses she got were in this mode: "They must have been nomads or have done some trading, 'cause I saw some hardwood bowls, and there are no hardwood trees around here." "They must have been near water because there's a tortoise shell, and it's very arched." In response to this comment, Heathcote supplied information by wondering aloud, "I don't know whether all turtles live in water. Do they all have to have access to water?"

"No." The child agreed to check on it for the report for the press. Thus the archaeologist's commitment to accuracy and caution in interpretation was reinforced. At the end of the drama, Heathcote brought in a real archaeologist to answer the children's questions about her work and to share with them what goes through her mind as she examines artifacts. She had a rucksack full of the tools of her work—brushes, screen, pick, and so on. These she demonstrated, emphasizing the pressure that is always part of her work, the pressure not to break any precious artifact. By laying out the tomb carefully, Heathcote had planned to evoke a spirit of inquiry. Once that was established, the children were ready to have a meaningful dialogue with a real archaeologist.

Heathcote is convinced that too often teachers throw information and texts at students in such "flaming big wadges" that they are overwhelmed. Whatever the curricular area, she uses drama to simplify and focus on one particular long enough to illuminate it. From this single, significant understanding, children can move into what might otherwise seem forbidding. Once they have cracked a code, they can use the remainder of their lives to broaden and deepen their learning.

18. THE HANDICAPPED

Heathcote's approach to handicapped students is not different in kind from the way she works with any class. This is consistent with her commitment to concentrate on what all human beings hold in common rather than on what distinguishes or separates them. Because we can project into another person's circumstance what we have learned from our own experience, we can identify with others. This gives us a base, as it were, inside another person's psyche; from there we can explore those areas within him or her that seem different, that we have yet to understand. To effectively teach learning disabled, emotionally disturbed, or physically handicapped people, teachers must identify solidly with the learners, just as they must with any other students. If these learners seem very different from the teacher, he or she has a harder task, but the gap must be bridged; if not, the learners will sense that their teacher is just another person who is alien to themselves.

Because Heathcote does not see even the most severely brain damaged or psychotic individuals as persons with whom she cannot identify, she finds that the same techniques can be used for any group of students. Thus, throughout this book, I have illustrated various of her dramatic techniques with examples of her experiences with disabled learners. She often uses such groups as a testing ground for a new technique. If it works with a mentally handicapped group, it is even more likely to work with a group which has no such limitations.

She urges her student teachers to work with the learning disabled, because the pressure they provide is a good proving ground for any teacher of any group. With the mentally handicapped, you have to rely more on what you *are* than on what you *know*. Your signals to the group need to be simpler, more blatant and direct, and your pace needs to be slower. You cannot depend on the group to take over the leadership from you as quickly or as smoothly as other classes do.

One thing that is the same with all groups is the necessity of finding what interests them. With the mentally handicapped, in fact, if you ignore their interests, you will lose them altogether. A challenge that Heathcote has discovered almost always interests a group of learning disabled persons is to prove that they can be responsible, that they can make a useful contribution to a human community. This, of course, is not all that different from the goal of any other group; it is just that for the disabled the challenge will have to be simpler in order to be one they can cope with or a problem they can solve. Also, a learning disabled group is less likely to approach the challenge with a confidence born of previous success.

Once Heathcote met with a group of mentally handicapped 15-year-olds who knew they were in a special school—"a daft school," as they called it; they didn't like it or themselves. She decided that what was important was to show them that they could accomplish a difficult task. She began as usual with questions: "Are you good at remembering things?" Then she asked them questions like what they had for dinner the day before and what clothes their regular teacher had worn yesterday. Finally, "Could you remember a message if I gave you one?" By this time, they were sure they could. She asked them whether they knew of any other countries where they might start their drama. They mentioned three; she chose China because it was the farthest away. She told them that it was a long, long way away and would take ages to reach. Then she asked them, "If I give you a message in China, can you remember it all the way to England?" They eagerly assured her they could. So she wrote out the message on a large card:

> China needs help. Can the Queen of England please
> send help to the Chinese people?

Before their journey began she warned them, "If you are caught, nobody must know what this message is." They talked about the problem. They decided that they might not be able to remember the message for the long trip, so they should write it down. Then they decided to cut the message apart and give each person one word. That way, if they were captured, no one would know what the message was; at the same time, if they forgot the whole message, they could reconstruct it from the separate words they carried.

They took a few minutes to practice reading their words. Then Heathcote asked them where they would put their cards for the long journey, where they wouldn't get wet or stolen and the writing wouldn't wear off; gradually they began to secrete the cards about their persons. Then the journey began.

It lasted all morning—40 days and 40 nights in terms of the drama. Finally, the group reached the Queen of England. It took them a long time to reconstruct the message (those with words like "to" or "the" had the most trouble). At last they pulled it all together and proved to themselves that they could use their minds to remember things, even if they were in "a daft school."

Although she keeps the challenges simple, Heathcote never removes from a class, no matter how disabled, the primary challenge of taking decisions and acting on them. Her goal is to help them discover their own competence, and that cannot be done if she becomes just another adult who "takes care of them."

When meeting with groups of psychotics, Heathcote aims to show them they can cope. For one group of adult women in a state mental hospital, she brought in a huge pile of old party dresses and formals, long necklaces, and scarves. These she sorted by color and distributed on a long row of chairs along the wall of a large hall. When the group of psychotic women—all of whom had been hospitalized for a long, long time—arrived, Heathcote told them they were going to a dance. Their first task was to choose from the array of finery on the chairs a suitable outfit for a ball. Here they were, depressed and confined women who had never had a lot of anything in their lives and who for years had never had any reason to dress up, proving to themselves that they still had the wit to make a choice and the spirit to dance. After they helped one another dress, they prepared refreshments and invited the staff to join them at their party.

One of the most effective ways to arrest the attention of a group of learning disabled or emotionally disturbed persons is to put another adult in role, this way you can lure the group to a focus that lasts long enough for something to happen.* If the one-in-role is vulnerable or in need of help, the class has a valuable chance to prove their competence.

One of the most effective roles with brain-damaged groups is the wild man. When one group of hospitalized, severely brain-damaged children came into the room where Heathcote's drama lesson was to be held, they saw only a screen. From behind it came agonizing snarling, growling, whinning, smacking, tearing, and yelping sounds, such as a lion might make in the height of a struggle. (This was actually a tape recording that two teachers had prepared earlier.) Bits and pieces of animal skin flew out from behind the screen. When the children finally ventured to peer around the screen, they saw a wild man (one of the teachers in role) dressed in a tattered skin. He lay on the ground, all disheveled; it looked as if he had just been in a great fight with a wild beast. He gave the class a need to care, to respond, to help. They touched him to make him feel safe; then they fed and washed him. Heathcote always prefers to give classes real things like this to do, not just exercises in drama.

---

*See Chapter 11, "Using Role in Teaching."

Sometimes she has a class discover a wild man in his tent on an island. He can be both the one who knows less than we do and may need our help and also the one who can take us into another world. When Heathcote brought one group of learning disabled by boat to an island and then over to a tent in which they found a wild man, she said, in role as a member of their group, "We're very hungry."

The wild man looked up. "The trees have fruit." So Heathcote and the children climbed the trees on his island and started to bite into the fruit they picked. The wild man would not let them do this. No, they must first ask the blessing of the rain and the sun before they dare eat. The wild man, who might have been helpless in our world, could give help to others in his.

Heathcote once set up a small, adult woman in role as a bird for a group of mentally handicapped 16-year-olds in a hospital. She covered the frames of the woman's large glasses with aluminum foil and shaped them out at the upper corners to accentuate her eyes and to suggest birdness. She dressed her in a long, flowing gown and fastened nylon scarves of many different colors around her arms and body to suggest feathers. When the class comes in, there she sits, looking droopy but brave.

The first boy to come in is very sick; his wheelchair is pushed right up to the bird, who is sitting on the floor. He stares at it steadily, and then he says to Heathcote's hand (for he is too weak to lift his head to look up at her standing beside him), "You should never cage a human bird." Heathcote moves her hand to show that she has heard.

The group decides to rescue this bird, but before they can take off with her, they need to learn to fly. A boy who has only one arm teaches them; he captures the essence of flight in his feet, and the rest of the class respect this. They help the bird in her struggle to fly by holding up as many of her scarf-feathers as possible and supporting her with their encouragement. The result is a bright, undulating flurry of scarves and fluttering feet.

Heathcote used nonverbal signals to move another group of severely disabled, hospitalized children into the world of the fairy. She knows she cannot effectively tell this group fairy tales—their attention span is too short, and their language too limited. So she sets up an adult as a fairy princess, dressed in a conventional way with a crown, wand, and spangled lawn gown. When the class comes in, there is no flow of words: in their real life experience, they are too often battered down by a stream of language they only vaguely comprehend. Here, they are surprised by a nonverbal presence and silence. The fairy seems to cry out for a verbal response. Many of these children have never learned to speak, because their circumstances do not call for it. The nurses who are responsible for their care have neither the time nor the patience to build the associations that other children make between the thing and the word. Caretakers dress and feed them efficiently (all too often entirely without words), so they are cut off from having to use language to get what they need. Heathcote's goal with these children is to use the nonverbal signals to win them to the verbal. She has found that the disabled bring to the world of the fairy something quite primitive. They seem hungry for the experience of the magic.

Once she brought a fairy princess into a group of psychotic children. In this case the children have language, but they need a stimulus for cooperating on a group task. In this case, the stimulus is the fact that the princess's feet are bare. Although she has all the other accoutrements of a traditional fairy princess, she has no shoes. The first question the children ask is, "Why no shoes?" Heathcote tells them that a witch has a spell on her. The class members decide that she cannot move until they find out what her name is. So they begin guessing. "Bob," "Mary," "Tea"—out come names of boys, girls, and things. None of them breaks the spell. Heathcote has instructed the princess not to make it easy for the class to win. The group returns to the problem of shoes. Maybe if they can find the princess some shoes, she can move.

The next day Heathcote brings in a heap of shoes—old, unmated, and of assorted sizes and styles. As before, there stands the princess, looking happy enough, but still without shoes. The class works together to sort and classify the heap of shoes into pairs, if possible. Then they laboriously try on the princess all the shoes they think are pretty enough for her. None fits. The only ones they consider truly suitable for her are a pair of tiny Chinese slippers, but these are too small. So the whole group go down to the hospital shoe shop and get some silk, plastic, silver cloth, and needles and thread; with these they make the princess some shoes. They fit like canal barges, but they are unmistakably princess' shoes, and when they put them on her, the witch's spell is broken.

This event leads Heathcote to move the drama on with the question, "Where is she going?" The princess insists that they must guess, which they do. The role itself keeps thumping in the idea that this is no ordinary person: she is different. The class brings the world of the fairy into their description of her journey, urging her to take them with her. Thus these psychotic children, who all too often find themselves trapped and immobilized by their private fantasies, are eagerly sharing a group fairy tale.

On another occasion Heathcote's goal was to help a group of severely learning disabled 13-year-olds develop the concept that "meat runs about before you eat it; it is alive and moves." She begins by introducing them to a hungry baby in a cradle (a doll with a taped cry). A woman in role as a gypsy, looking concerned and hungry, keeps picking the baby up and then putting it down again. The group try to comfort the baby, but to no avail. Then Heathcote brings in a dead rabbit with a wound in its throat. The children have lots of questions about it—why its ears are at the bottom instead of at the top, for example, and why it isn't running around. They want to touch the wound right away, discovering for the first time that blood has a taste and a smell. Heathcote brings in a friend who very gently skins the rabbit in front of the enraptured class; when the skin is off, he lays it on the baby. The children think they have two rabbits; they take the skin and put it back on the carcass of the dead rabbit and want it to run around again. Finally, Heathcote begins to cut up the rabbit meat and put it into a large pot from the hospital kitchen. She adds vegetables she and the gypsy woman have carefully peeled and washed as the class watched; ceremoniously, she adds water. Finally, she and the class take the pot to the kitchen and put it on the stove. When lunchtime comes, Heathcote brings out a rabbit stew she has made at home the night before (there hasn't been time to really cook the stew she has just prepared). They all share the stew and give some to the baby. The hungry mother joins them, looking very happy.

Sometimes Heathcote's goal is to help a group of normal children develop an acceptance of others who are not like themselves. Once she was asked to help smooth the transition for a class of blind children who were to be moved from a small house into a classroom in a nearby school of 900 sighted children. The situation was potentially traumatic for both the sighted and the blind. She knew she needed to work with both groups.

She began by working with one of the classes of sighted children in the large school. She brought in one of the teachers in role as a blind man. He wore a papier-mâché mask which was molded to his face; it had no eyes, and the class quickly accepted the Big Lie that he was blind. He sat calmly in the middle of the room—helpless. The class decided to help him deal with his "blindness." They tried to teach him how to handle his problems: How to eat with a spoon, get about the room without bumping into things or falling, entertain himself when he could not read or look at pictures, and so on. The "blind man" learned very slowly.

After several days of working with this "blind" teacher, the children became frustrated; he was just too inept. The didn't know what to do with him. In their struggle with this big problem, they hit upon the idea of finding some other blind people who could tell them what blindness was like and help them teach him how to cope. Heathcote had just the group for them; the class that was soon going to move into their own school.

They slowly led their stumbling teacher down the street to the house where the blind children went to school. There they met a group of 11-year-olds, all of whom were blind, some with shocking facial disfigurements and gaping holes where eyes had once been. The sighted children brought their problem adult into the middle of the room and sat him there. They were not sure how to introduce him to a group that he could not see and that could not see him.

The blind children knew what to do; they began to feel him—his size, his balding head, and, to their great fascination, his mask. Before long, they too wanted masks, so they and the sighted children eagerly made eyeless ones like his for all of the blind children to wear. When they had put theirs on, they set to work on the adult. Their approach to his problem was not bemoaning, compassionate, or sentimental; instead, they were ruthlessly practical. Here was a big, blind person who found it difficult to get on in the world; they knew how to help. First, they led him to a wall and had him shout at it. Then they turned him around and had him compare the sound when he shouted into the middle of the room. They moved him a bit farther from the wall and had him repeat the process. They put a chair between him and the wall to see whether he could detect it by the way his voice bounced off it. They changed the furniture into an obstacle course and made him learn to find his way through that maze. The next step was to take him outside to learn to play cricket. "All you have to do is shout 'Ball!' " they assured him. They worked painstakingly, patiently, but inexorably towards the end of making their pupil independent. The sighted children began to respect the efficiency and practicality of their blind peers' relentless instruction.

A few days later, the blind children came to the big school to see how their adult student was getting on. They arrived in their eyeless masks, creating a stir but avoiding the shocked responses of 900 sighted children who might otherwise have found them grotesque. Instead, they were fascinated. The first thing the blind children wanted was to be shown around the school; each one was paired with a sighted child from the class that had the "blind" teacher. The blind children insisted on walking ahead while their sighted partners guided them only with words: "Here's a step"; "Turn right now"; "See the door." Then, to the amazement of everyone else, they had a race around the building asking their sighted partners to shout as they came to landmarks: "Step!" "Corner!" "Door!" When they got back to the classroom, the blind children were ready to show the masked adult around the building. The sighted class again was fascinated; the blind children in their own brief walk around the large, three-story building had learned everything they needed to know about it; they took the teacher up and down stairs, through halls, and into the boiler room in the basement. They pointed out the fire extinguisher, telephone, and urinals in the lavatories. Then, confidently, they verbally guided him back to the classroom, insisting that he walk without touching them. There they were, after one brief instructional tour, showing the recently "blinded" teacher how to get around in his own school without his eyes.

What Dorothy Heathcote had done was to put the disabled into a position of power, of being needed. Although they were strangers, they now knew that even the students who had been there since kindergarten had never needed to master. When it came to teaching the blind adult, they were clearly in charge. When they took off their masks, it did not matter what their sightless eyes looked like; they all had names and friends who had shown them around. The "handicap" was no longer something to be pitied or feared; it was simply a significant fact to be dealt with and respected. Each sighted child had learned something new; to share pleasure with a touch that meant a smile.

19. TEACHER TRAINING

Heathcote typically begins a course for teachers by asking each of us to assess our own condition.* She also initiates what amounts to a value clarification process for adults. As students, we first identify the central concerns that animate our personal and professional lives, the values that we do in fact live by. We share these publicly, listing them on long segments of shelf paper and posting them around the room as stimuli for one another. Throughout the course, Heathcote reminds us that it is the quality of our lives that determines the quality of our teaching; when we look clearly at our values, we have a clue as to why we teach. What is central in our personal lives will probably be the underpinning for the most important thing we want our students to experience when they are with us. As Heathcote knows, we are all rooted in the rich soil of our beliefs. If our teaching stems from these, if it remains true to our values, we will find we have what she has—an ever-surging energy to go on, a drive to keep at the task, based on assurance that the goal is right.

With characteristic realism, Heathcote points out that each of our central values has its dark underside. There is no such thing as a human strength without its inherent weakness. For example, one of Heathcote's own core beliefs is that you have to help yourself. She values effort, work at the task. She finds it too wasteful of energy not to start right in. What's done is done and over; get on with the next job—and don't expect anyone else to pick up your burden. Because she believes this so strongly, she has to work to counterbalance this value in her teaching. She realizes that something she needs to concentrate on is being gentle with children and sensing when not to push them to a greater effort.

In training teachers, Heathcote is not in the business of giving how-to gimmicks or little tricks of the trade to help them through a lesson. Instead, she is helping them come to know why they're doing what they're doing. She

---

*See Chapter 3, "Edging In."

wants them to learn to be vital, alive, tolerant, patient, observing people who trust themselves and are capable of creating a good working relationship with others. She wants them to be aware of both the potential and the limits of their personalities and values. She wants them to be able to put aside any anxieties so as to be free to respond freshly and capture the possibilities of any teaching moment.

This is a tall order—too much for most to achieve in a lifetime. Yet Heathcote demands a response, a beginning toward this end, within the first week of a course with her. She expects her students to take decisions, work hard, assume roles, plan teaching strategies, and execute drama lessons. She finds absurd the whole notion that one cannot bubble until there's enough warmth. On the basis of this metaphor, many teacher training institutions pass on information and techniques for years before students are allowed to try their hand at teaching. By that time everybody else's expertise has worn them down. They cannot deal with all they know, and they have no experience of their own that they can trust and build on.

Her expectation that every student start right in is unsettling. Many in her class find themselves at sea, awash in a turbulence that seems to demand too much, too fast. The old rules aren't holding; the old stance of teacher in relation to class and material seems no longer safe or sure. The attitude that "all things are possible" and the deliberate ambiguity which Heathcote projects are fraught with create tension and danger as well as stimulus and vitality. With less reserve than any other students I've ever known, Heathcote's cry and laugh; lash out in anger; talk with one another in animated, anxious tones over coffee that seems a crucial familiar ritual in a strange new milieu; and touch and embrace one another and her. She does manage to get to the heart of the matter in her training of teachers.

When you are actually working with children, Heathcote never judges you on the basis of how the drama goes. Instead, she looks coolly at the work itself, sympathizes with your feeling when it is going badly, but concentrates her critique on how you could make it go better next time. The goal of the critique is to help you learn how to carefully control their signalling. It is important that you not be trapped into verbal or nonverbal signals you don't mean to give. Aggressiveness, lack of interest in the children as persons, impatience, fatigue, not caring—all these signals, whether they are calculated or not, have an effect on the class.

Heathcote's critique has a forceful candor. She judges your work the same way she judges her own. If a student weeps, she helps that student recognize this release for what it is: the effect of a longing and a realization that are the first step in moving forward. Her harshest reprimands are reserved for the strongest teachers. Here are some typical comments.

"Here's where you might have applied a press."

"You missed a chance to pick up that child's contribution and feed him back the implications of it."

"You have an indolent effect when you stand. Work at projecting some muscle, or stay seated and concentrate on signalling your energy and drive."

"There's a restless presence about you that unsettles children. Work at signalling patience and responsiveness."

"Say less, and support what you do say with volume and intent."

"Rely more on what you are."

"Your statement 'That's great!' was a dangerous one. Their effort had been minimal, which is what they knew in their hearts, so your congratulations made them dislike themselves."

"Stop talking down. He didn't like being called 'Honey'; did you notice?"

"Your smile is weak and ineffective when you end your sentences with 'OK?' 'Understand?' or 'You see?' These are really pleas for the class not to reject you; you are giving them a chance to say 'No.' "

"Stop promising them the drama will be fun. It may not be for them."

"Look the students in the eye. They don't think you care about them."

"You said you were happy in words alone. Next time do it with your posture as well. A dance, perhaps?"

Sometimes Heathcote uses a drama as a way to get teachers to look at their characteristic teaching strategies in a new way. For example, one time she was asked to lecture to the staff of an exclusive English school for boys with IQ's of 120 or over. The staff was not familiar with the use of drama. Instead of lecturing, Heathcote decided to demonstrate; she asked for eight boys in swimming trunks to assume roles of a primitive tribe. She knew she would have less chance of getting at the notion of the primitive if the boys wore their usual school outfits (eighteenth century garments appropriate for the architecture: suits with knee breeches, yellow stockings, buckled shoes, baggy white linen shirts, and long coats).

When the eight boys came in, they assumed roles—boat builder, sage, fisherman, and so on. She put the teachers in the role of Her Majesty's Commission to examine this tribe and charged them to advise the Crown:

1. How will you examine the concepts this tribe holds?
2. How will you set about teaching this tribe that there is more world than they have yet known?
3. What proposals do you have for integrating this tribe into the "civilized" world?

She gave them these three challenges because she decided they express exactly the commitment made by anyone who signs a contract to teach. The teacher's task is first to understand where the tribe is and then to seek to teach it what the world is like in such a way that it can live in that world.

The boys started to work at their chosen tasks; the teachers went over to them to find out about their tribe. Heathcote, in role as one of the tribe members, started miming domestic tasks. After a few minutes, she began to wander among the tribe, asking the boys questions like, "How much has he learned about boatbuilding?"

"He would learn more if he started to build it. As it is, all he does is ask questions, and I grow weary of this. He has asked me why I build little boats, but I have already told him I have no tall tree. Why does he keep asking me the same questions over and over again?"

So it went for a while; then, because they felt they were getting nowhere, the teachers left the tribe and talked with one another. "There must be better ways of finding out than this." They begin to experiment with other modes.

Finally, Heathcote pulled them all together. In role as a governmental official, she asked them what they had discovered. The teachers responded in a high moral tone. "This child believes in no god!"

"This child seems to want to lie about and do nothing." (In actual fact the tribe has been working very hard.)

"This child has no maturation."

The group of able boys soon sensed what was happening. One of them said heatedly, "You haven't even begun to find out what I believe about gods. Asking questions like that gets you no place." What the drama showed the teachers was that they knew only how to ask typical teacher questions. They didn't know how to join the boys and learn in other ways. Heathcote showed them how to get at the beliefs of the tribe by asking questions like, "Where did the first man of your tribe come from?" She asked this question of the tribe's storyteller; here is what poured out:

> There was a man taller than the tallest tree, and he took the tallest tree and cut it down and made of it a boat. In it he sailed into the center of the forest to find a mate, and together they came back sailing in the tree, but a serpent blocked their path.
>
> The woman said, "You must slay him," and the man asked, "How?" She said, "Take a poison branch and feed it to his mouth." The man did so, and the serpent lay dead across the boat. The man took it and wore it as a necklace. They came back down into our valley, and this was the father of our tribe.

Through this drama, Heathcote worked to help this group of sophisticated teachers find new ways of relating to people. She also wanted them to begin to respect the fact that their classes could capture the essence of the primitive by identifying and creating, not just by taking in information the teachers presented.

When Heathcote is teaching teachers to use classroom drama themselves, she bears in mind that the one most essential element is always the teacher's own seriousness and belief. After a group of children have left, I have seen Dorothy lash out in anger at a class of adults who have been watching a drama and laughed at what the children said. This she calls self-indulgence—seeing the work from the outside rather than the inside and, therefore, letting oneself be entertained by it. She asks no less of the adults in the room than she does of the children, namely, to respect the work and to at least try to believe. She knows this is not easy and readily admits that her hardest work (she does it all the time with her adult classes) is to get a group of teachers to participate responsibly in an improvisation. Perhaps this is because they have chosen a career that gives them the floor, that depends on their expressing their individuality. They can basically stand alone and have their own way. There is in their personality the need to be the loner with an audience. However, in classroom drama no one person can monopolize the floor, can be a star. What any one person does always has to be done in the context of others.

Heathcote puts her classes to work on improvisations that test and develop their ability to receive an idea—no matter how preposterous—and put it to use dramatically. The minute you laugh or "go weak" on your role, you are to say to your partner, "Sorry, I've let it slip," and start again. The goal is not to enjoy silly or outrageous conversations, but to take an absurd statement as though it came from someone in a class and respond relevantly, within the logic of the statement itself. You can laugh only at what you don't take seriously: no teacher should ever laugh at anything a child offers in earnest, no matter how far off the subject it seems at the time.

The goal of working with classes is to get the children to contribute of themselves. One consequence of success is often that the children's contribution destroys what the teacher is working for and introduces instead a distraction that clutters up the drama. There is no use trying to reject it; so doing, you would only inhibit whoever made the contribution and alienate that child from the process. Instead, Heathcote will accept the irrelevant comment with the same seriousness with which it was offered and keep her regrets to herself. She will never jump outside the group task and make fun of the child's logic. The only time she rejects a contribution from a child is when she is sure it is intended as a joke. In that case, she will sometimes laugh with the child, then say firmly, "Now let's try to get back into it."

Heathcote uses exercises to help her adult students learn to accept a different kind of logic from their own. In one of these, the students work in pairs; one partner in dead seriousness makes the most preposterous statement she or he can think of. The other partner responds equally seriously with a logical development of this. The two of them carry on the conversation as long as possible without snickering. Suppose one person says, "I'll bet I could turn that lamp into a sari." The other might respond with, "Would you heat the metal before you tried to beat it flat?" If one says, looking at a small box of paper clips, "You know I sleep in a box about this size," the other might come back with, "Do you go square or break into pieces?" Although this sounds like a party game or a stand-up comedy routine, it is actually one of the best ways I have ever tried of developing my capacity to accept and respond to child logic.

One time Heathcote tested our ability to accept the preposterous by announcing to about 45 of us that the time had come to knit the tigers' tails. Someone asks a question; Heathcote replies briskly, "The instructions were on the leaflets we sent out. Did each of you bring your four needles, and are they all the right sizes? Check your forms and see. I'm not bringing these tigers in here until I'm sure you're ready."

"Are the fangs removed?" one adult asks nervously.

"Of course not; I didn't promise you that, you know."

"Please, I feel you need to review the rules for us before you bring them in. Can we play with them?"

"Of course," Heathcote says with a warm, confident smile. "They *love* affection. Pet them as much as you like. Of course, you are not to feed them. You know that. If you accidentally get eaten, you must tell me straight away." Her tone is serious.

"What are our chances of getting eaten?"

"Once we had a problem, but that was when a nonknitting tiger got in, and then someone got gnawed. You needn't worry, you know. I have insurance."

"How do we finish the knitting without hurting the tiger?"

"Just don't attempt to cut anything when you are ready to cast off. You'll find a system; it has something to do with the tigers. Just let the experience happen to you."

And so Heathcote goes out and brings a big tiger back in. She leads it over to our group of four adults, one of several sitting together on the floor. We move aside and coax the tiger to lie down, then take turns stroking it gently. Before long we have decided who will keep the tiger relaxed while the rest of us knit, and we stay with the job, believing in that tiger that lies there beside us. Because we do not laugh or even feel particularly foolish, we are proving to ourselves that we can sustain our own belief under even the most preposterous of circumstances. For most of us, this is significant breakthrough.

Characteristically, Heathcote gets adults into movement as part of an improvisation, knowing most of us have a penchant for keeping everything at the verbal level. One time she had the class, working in pairs of the same sex, pantomime pairs of nuns in a convent or monks in a monastery. We were to develop our relationship solely through movement. Our tasks were confined to a garden; each of us was to choose an attitude to project as we worked. One of us might have the attitude "I believe God is in every one of these cabbages." The other's attitude might be "I can't wait to finish planting." Heathcote gave us plenty of time to elaborate our relationship in movement alone, using the task to make the attitudes explicit. Another exercise was to take a piece of sculpture such as an abstract form of Barbara Hepworth's and try to reshape its tension with our bodies.

Another of Heathcote's goals is to help us see common objects in new ways. For example, whenever she is trying to visualize a scene, she imagines what it would look like if she flew over it; brought it close to her or walked up to it; lay down under it; felt it; weighed it. She is interested in proportion and form. When she thinks of a monster, she feels the earth shaking under its feet. Then she gets inside the monster and thinks how it looks down on a man: "Aha, a morsel!" Another way she thinks is to reverse a response--when she is thinking of people afraid of ghosts, she turns it around and considers ghosts afraid of people. She sees people looking for ghosts and then ghosts looking for people. If a group of children want to do a play about dolls, she asks, "Would you rather be people who don't understand dolls or dolls who don't understand people?

What does Heathcote do about classroom management? For one thing, she never ignores disruptive behavior. If a child falls off a chair, for example, she immediately notes that fact. Sometimes she laughs with the child first, but then she helps the child get back to work. To pretend not to have seen something that is obvious is to imply that you are different from the class, that you are not quite human. Besides, if you ignore disruptive behavior, the class is likely to assume that what they've done is all right. It is crucial that they know that there is a point beyond which you will not go. Heathcote communicates to a class that she can reprimand, forgive, and then forget the incident and get on with a task. Her forgiveness is clear in her warm, honest smile. She builds a trust between herself and the class so they are usually willing to work seriously and confidently.

Heathcote showed me how to use drama in a single six-week course; I had no previous training in theater. That six weeks' experience has enabled me to use body movement, mime, and teaching in role regularly as part of both my college and my junior high English teaching. More fundamentally, her course enabled me to act on my basic beliefs and to assume a role with conviction, thereby realizing a flexibility I never knew before.

20. GUARANTEES FOR DRAMA

Throughout this book I have shown what drama can do: how it can help classes catch a vision of the universal; internalize experience, reflect on it, and put it into words; and open up other curricular areas. Now to conclude, I will examine the legitimate goals of classroom drama, and what a teacher can guarantee to achieve.

Heathcote distinguishes between goals that are realistic and those a teacher dare not set. In the former category are those goals that you can guarantee not only to work towards but to actually achieve—extending the students' vocabulary, for example. In the category of goals she dare not set are what we in American educational circles might call "measurable behavioral objectives." Heathcote knows she cannot guarantee a particular level of achievement in vocabulary development for any particular child or group of children. To do so would be to assume for herself a measure of control over the motivation and response of other human beings that is inconsistent with respect for students and for honest human interaction. This is how Heathcote talks about her goals in drama teaching: "There are some guarantees I can make." She will only guarantee what she knows she is ready to tackle and stay with and come back to over and over again. She does not limit herself to working toward what she has guaranteed, however; she is also making tentative sorties into new areas all the time. If these sorties pass the test of a positive response from the class, she will then set goals in these areas. She may find, on the other hand, that a group is not ready to respond to a new challenge, or that working towards a new goal inhibits the achievement of one of her other goals. Then she backs off and will not guarantee that goal in her teaching.

Thus, whenever Heathcote is called upon to write out her goals in teaching drama for a school system, she defines them in terms of general human growth and the direction of growth, but never in terms of what she will guarantee that any single child at a particular age will achieve. Her goal is what she terms "progression" in each of these general directions:

1. From whole class to more individual interest projects
2. From gross, obvious action to experience that is more subtle and complex in its purpose, demand, interaction, and attainment
3. From drama that is for the participants only to drama that takes account of an audience
4. From the taking of limited decisions to the taking of ever-greater risks
5. From reliance on the teacher to independent action in which the teacher is redundant
6. From bold and obvious use to more subtle use of the tools of drama
7. From unselected to carefully selected words, gestures, and actions to make a drama explicit
8. From improvised drama, "a living through" at life rate, to the interpretation of a script
9. From concentration on identification and feeling alone to submission to the discipline of avoiding anachronisms, getting all facts accurate, mastering unfamiliar skills, and submitting to all the demands of the art form
10. From ignorance to gradual mastery of the technical aids to drama
11. From complete involvement and identification to involvement with detachment.

Most groups do not approach maturity on all of these scales until high school, although some groups do so as early as the sixth grade. Until a class is well on its way to such maturity, as Heathcote makes clear to any principal or school head, she is not in the business of making plays, productions that look good from the outside and are entertaining for other classes or parents to watch. Rather, she is using drama as a vehicle to create the chance for new knowing.

Because Heathcote is using drama as a way into other areas of the curriculum, she is never teaching just drama, but other subjects as well. In any teaching she does, she can make some guarantees to a principal. She promises:

1. To give children an opportunity to examine their own living problems with a new perspective
2. To tell the truth as she knows it
3. To show it is important to listen
4. To accept, support, and then challenge decisions the class makes
5. To bring to the teaching situation an energy level equal to that of the class
6. To show any student the direction in which he or she is going.

In addition, she can make the following guarantees of what she will achieve through drama:

1. To make an abstract concept or experience very concrete, simplifying it so the students can understand and have control over it (see Chapters 5 and 7)
2. To teach a narrow fact so that it is really learned and understood (see especially Chapter 8)
3. To introduce artifacts in such a way that the class is curious about them and experiences them at a significant level (see Chapters 10 and 17)
4. To press students to reflect on experience and see what they hold in common with all people (see Chapters 1 and 8)
5. To crack the code to curriculum areas students might fear to venture into, such as science, math, history, literature, anthropology (see Chapters 16 and 17)
6. To give students freedom coupled with responsibility (see Chapter 6)
7. To clarify values (see especially Chapters 1 and 8)
8. To develop a tolerance for a variety of personalities and ideas (see especially Chapters 11 and 18)
9. To show students how they can stay with something they don't like and work through it to a point of accomplishment (see Chapter 8)
10. To increase students' vocabulary and help them develop a finer control of rhetoric through interaction with others and through tapping subjective experience (see Chapter 17)
11. To bring classes into situations that will improve their social health
12. To help students discover that they know more than they thought they knew
13. To lead students to see the real world more clearly in light of what is revealed by the imagined one
14. To help students capture more and more of what is implicit in any experience.

The first ten of these guarantees have been discussed in previous chapters. In this chapter we shall discuss the last four briefly.

Drama can improve a class's social health because it requires that a person do certain things in relation to other people. Drama says to each participant, You have to "take in" other human beings and relate your response to what they are telling you, verbally and nonverbally. To have a drama at all, a class of students must cooperate; all have to agree to try to sustain the drama, to support one another's efforts to believe, to share their personal ideas and interpretations with others.

If class members have trouble sharing territory ("He's taking my place,

Teacher!") a drama will provide a continual press to use space cooperatively. If a class characteristically works in cliques ("We want to work with Todd, but we won't have Toby in *our* group!") drama puts everyone in the same setting; they cannot evade the demand to relate. Whatever the prejudices of the class, you can put the students into a situation where they have to work through them to a new awareness.

Only through interaction can socialization of the individual occur. In a classroom activity, the individual must be free to choose the level and style of her or his involvement if anything beyond external or superficial change in behavior is to take place. Whatever the level chosen, however, learning through drama is not passive; it does not provide a mere overlay. Rather, it activates the mainsprings of the participants. A drama demands all that a person is, not just conforming behavior. Participants in drama are free to expose themselves as far as they need or want to—and they will be under pressure to share what they know and feel. No one, however, will tell them what they *should* know or feel. Their responses will be effective to the degree that they are sensitive in their perception of what others are about, what values they hold, what goals they have. The kind of pressurized interaction that drama calls forth helps the participants wean themselves from the comfort of conforming to the standards or values of an adult authority. They test their own values, sense the importance of those values, and begin to assert them candidly and maturely. Through drama they learn to discipline themselves to an awareness of their effect on others and a reflection on the quality of their interactions.

Thus drama builds confidence. In drama, students live "in advance of themselves" as it were: they face challenge and crisis in imagination before they find themselves overwhelmed by them in real life. They gain the feeling of mastery over events, the sense that they are equal to life. This in turn helps them relate more comfortably and openly to others.

Another way drama enhances a class's social health is to give a validity to all feelings—"good" or "bad." By developing conflict, the teacher deliberately brings out the students' anger; they are pushed to express it in the drama, then to reflect on it and put it into words. In similar fashion, other human emotions are evoked and expressed. By learning to recognize what they are or have just been feeling, students gain an invaluable insight that can carry over into their interactions with others outside the drama.

Heathcote's twelfth guarantee for drama is that she will help students discover that they know more than they thought they knew. Because drama puts children into situations of pressure, they have to harness and realign the relevant information from their past experience and bring it to bear on the present imagined moment. As they identify with the people in the crisis of the drama, they begin to discover resources they didn't know they had. At the same time, they see themselves in new ways that they may well remember into adulthood.

Not only do participants in drama discover new resources in themselves, but they also gain a fresh perspective on what another person's life is really like. For example, boys in a reform school might well regard a police officer as a hunter: "He caught me, so he's not a good guy." This may be the only thing they are prepared to believe about law officers. Heathcote's goal will be to help them take other soundings of the role of police officer—as lover, husband or wife, mother or father, hero, a person with aspirations and dreams, one with a weapon in hand and one who can hold his or her temper.

In the killing of the President drama, when one of the boys in the approved school (English reform school) is not quite up to his chosen role as police officer, Heathcote goes out of the gang headquarters and talks alone with him in the hall. The challenge he faces is to come into the headquarters and find the checkered jacket that was spotted on the President's assassin when he left the scene of the crime. Standing there in that hallway with his teacher, the boy screws up his courage. Suddenly he finds himself taking a new sounding of the police officer's role.

"Will I have a gun, Miss?"

"I believe American policemen have guns," Heathcote says blandly. Then, with a bit more tension, "Have you got yours?"

"Is it here or here?" he asks pointing to his side and then his back pockets.

"I believe they have a holster for the gun."

"Right, the holster's there," he says and pats it. Then he carefully checks his gun to see that it's loaded and puts it in the holster. He is clearly nervous by now.

"I wonder where they've hidden that checkered coat?" Suddenly, he realizes: "If I find it, they'll kill me. There's a gun in that room, isn't there?" Then, after a pause, "I think I'll put my gun in my back pocket."

"You'll have a better chance on the gun because they're not all that good with guns, you know."

By now this police officer is under great pressure. He bursts out, "It's not fair, Miss! They've got guts if they use their guns, and I've got guts if I don't use mine!" He knows the spot he is in: as a man he is terrified; as a police officer, he has a job to do. After he enters that door it takes him a half hour to arrest the assassin. He has to stand and take their hate, his back to the door, his heart in his throat, knowing that at the very point at which he succeeds in his mission he will be at their mercy. Through identification he has discovered something about a police officer's role that he never knew before.

Heathcote's thirteenth guarantee is that students will see the real world more clearly when they have experienced the imagined one. Drama demonstrates vividly that the mind is its own place. You can create another world instantly, and find your way back as well. The imagined world is the cake you can eat and still have. You are not locked into the consequences forever as in real life. Because this fact of human experience is shared in drama, it is understood more fully—the opportunity for group reflection is not usually available to us in looking at our private fantasies and dreams. This process of imagination and reflection provides a valuable guide for making choices in the real world.

Heathcote's last guarantee is to help students catch more of what is implicit in any situation. Although we never catch all that is implicit in any art form, we can progress towards finding a greater reservoir of meaning and significance. Heathcote can guarantee that she will not let a class stay at the pretend acting stage in any drama; she will push for a belief and reflection that go beyond merely performing a task.

We have examined the guarantees Heathcote will make in teaching drama. Now let us look at how she describes the relationship of her lists of guarantees to her central beliefs. She sees her list of guarantees as growing out of her values; she will guarantee to work at and stay with those things that stem from her most deeply held convictions. So she starts with her beliefs, then sets up her list of guarantees. Finally as she puts it, she marries the two with her plan—her deliberate use of theater elements to set up a situation with a particularized starting point.* This relationship might be diagrammed this way:

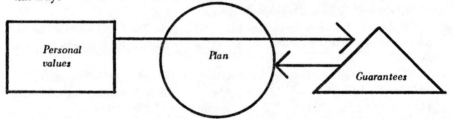

We began this book with an evaluation of drama as Heathcote uses it, showing what it can do. We devoted most of the chapters to techniques and plans; in the previous chapter, we pointed out the necessity of first listing one's own values as a teacher. In this chapter we have considered the goals—or guarantees, as Heathcote calls them—that grow out of her list of values. Perhaps a good way to use this book would be for you to now list your own values and see what guarantees follow from your list. Then you can go back to the rest of the book and scan it for ways to plan drama to achieve your goals.

By consciously using her own values as her touchstone, Heathcote taps the energy of the human spirit. If it is true, as many say, that we are living in a period of transition from exponential economic growth to more nearly a

*See Chapters 5, 10, and 12.

steady state in energy production and economic output,* then to focus on a new energy source is not irrelevant. The new goal will not be to increase economic output, however, but to increase human output. George Leonard urges us to concentrate on "the energy of the spirit, which burns no fuel, depletes no resources, and creates no pollution."* Certainly tapping this source is more morally palatable than clinging to the formerly unquestioned value system of our society, which rests on the assumption that the production and consumption of ever more trivial goods and services is what gives life meaning. As Hannah Arendt** points out, this assumption reduces all work to relentlessly repetitive labor in which human effort, past and present, is debased. Heathcote, by picking up in her imagination the past that lies all about us, by showing the continuity of human experience, and by valuing man's work and its products, brings us the joy of a sense of being part of a vast, complex, and ultimately meaningful whole. To use Linda Pastan's phrase, she brings us "the sheer sanity of vision."***

Learning to teach from Dorothy Heathcote is like dancing with a whirlwind. The symphony she hears sweeps you along with a sense of its rhythm; still you have very little understanding of the steps your feet must take when her leadership is gone and you are left to dance alone. My hope is that this book will spell out some of the steps so you can start the dance; but the music you hear must sound in your own soul.

---

*Leonard, George. "In God's Image." *Saturday Review of Literature*, February 22, 1975. p. 14.

**Arendt, Hannah. *The Human Condition: A Study of the Central Dilemmas Facing Modern Man.* Garden City, N.Y.: Doubleday & Co., 1959. 385 pp.

***Pastan, Linda. *Perfect Circle of the Sun.* Chicago: Swallow Press, 1971. p. 26.

BIBLIOGRAPHY

BOOKS AND ARTICLES

By Dorothy Heathcote·

"Drama and Education: Subject or System?" *Drama and Theatre in Education.* (Edited by Nigel Dodd and Winifred Hickson.) London: William Heinemann, 1971. pp. 42-62.

"Drama as Education."*Children and Drama.* (Edited by Nellie McCaslin.) New York: David McKay Co., 1975. pp. 93-108.

Drama in the Education of Teachers. Newcastle upon Tyne: The University of Newcastle upon Tyne Institute of Education, n.d.

"How Does Drama Serve Thinking, Talking, and Writing?" *Elementary English* 47: 1977-81; December 1970.

About Dorothy Heathcote:

Fines, John, and Verrier, Raymond. *The Drama of History, An Experiment in Co-operative Teaching.* London: New University Education, 1974. 119 pp.

Hardy, Sister Marie Paula. "Drama in the Classroom." *Elementary English,* 51: 94-102; January 1974.

_____*Drama as a Tool in Education.* PhD dissertation, University of Illinois, 1972. Ann Arbor: University Microfilms, number 73-17,421. 275 pp.

Students of Dorothy Heathcote. *Drama in Education.* Newcastle upon Tyne: University of Newcastle upon Tyne, 1967.

Wagner, Betty Jane. "Evoking Gut-Level Drama." *Learning* 2: 16-20; March 1974.

FILMS

Distributed by the Northwestern University Film Library
P.O. Box 1665
Evanston, Illinois 60204:

The Dorothy Heathcote Teaching Series

Dorothy Heathcote Building Belief, Part I

Heathcote is working with a group of American nine-and ten-year-olds to give meaning to the words, "A nation is as strong as the spirit of the people who make it." Through questions and drama the children identify with a group of settlers who move rocks to build a shelter from the wind. Their memories of their first days in the new land are developed into a written chronicle of their history. Narration written by Betty Jane Wagner. 28 min., 16 mm, color. 1974. Sale: $275; rental:$30.

Dorothy Heathcote Building Belief, Part II

Continuing her work with the same group of children, Heathcote poses three moral dilemmas: how to divide the land, what to do with the elderly, and how to deal with the death of a young man who has been mauled by a mountain lion. They dramatize and reflect on each situation. Narration written by Betty Jane Wagner. 29 min., 16 mm, color. 1974. Sale: $275; rental: $30.

Dorothy Heathcote Talks to Teachers, Part I

Heathcote lectures on informal vs. formal teaching, drama as a teaching tool for all classroom teachers, the use of dramatic elements, and the segmenting of ideas to achieve dramatic focus. 30 min., 16 mm, color. 1973. Sale: $250; rental: $25.

Dorothy Heathcote Talks to Teachers, Part II

Continuing the discussion of drama in the classroom, Heathcote explores types of questions, finding material for drama, reflecting on universal experience, and using drama to modify behavior. 32 min., 16 mm, color. 1973. Sale: $250; rental $25.

Distributed by *Time-Life* Multimedia
100 Eisenhower Drive
Paramus, New Jersey 07652:

Here Comes the Judge

This film is part of the BBC television series of nine films entitled, *Children Growing Up*. Here Heathcote uses drama to examine Jean Piaget's thesis that children go through stages in the development of moral judgment. 26 min., 16 mm, color. 1972. Sale: $330; rental: $35.

Improvised Drama, Part I

Heathcote leads a group of reform school boys in a drama on "killing the President." 30 min., 16 mm, b & w. 1966. Sale: $275 on special order; not available for rental.

Three Looms Waiting

A BBC Omnibus documentary film on Dorothy Heathcote's life and work. It shows her working with children and teenagers in British schools and mental hospitals. 52 min., 16 mm, color. 1971. Sale: $550; rental: $55. ¾" video cassette. Sale: $385; rental: $55.

Distributed by Vision Quest, Inc.
7715 North Sheridan Road
Chicago, Illinois 60626:

Who's Handicapped?

Heathcote works with a group of mongoloid children, using an adult in role as a derelict to evoke helping and caring behavior. 36 min., 16 mm, color. 1973. Sale: $350; rental: $50.

VIDEOTAPES

In addition to the videotape of *Three Looms Waiting* listed above, scores of others are available at various centers where Heathcote has taught. Here are a few of these centers listed in order of the quality and variety of the tapes they have available. In most cases you can borrow these, paying only a shipping and handling fee, or can arrange to send a blank tape and have a copy made. Before you do this, write to make sure that the equipment at the center is compatible with the kind (reel-to-reel or cassette) of tape and tape width that you send. Although the tapes vary in form, width, length, and quality, they all show Heathcote at work, discussing drama with teachers or demonstrating its use with students of all ages.

Mr. Robert Gregory
Media Division
Department of Public Instruction
Raleigh, North Carolina 27611
21 hours on two-inch silverchrome video cassettes, 30 minutes each.
Made at Wake Forest College in the summer of 1975

Mr. John R. Stephens, Jr.
Instructional Resources Center
University of Georgia
Athens, Georgia 30602
Heathcote, Dorothy—Demonstrating Career Education
Five videotapes, b & w, 60 minutes each.
Made at the University of Georgia in July 1974

Mrs. Elizabeth Flory Kelly
22625 Westchester Road
Shaker Heights, Ohio 44122
Five hours of videotape
Made in Cleveland in December 1973

Mr. E. Arthur Stunard
Instructional Media Center
National College of Education
2840 Sheridan Road
Evanston, Illinois 60201
Two one-inch videotapes, b & w, 60 minutes each.
Nine- and ten-year olds make a "trip to Russia," summer 1972.
Two one-half inch videotapes, b & w.
Learning Instruction Lecture, summer 1966.